# Qualitative data analysis

Learning how to analyse qualitative data by computer can be fun. That is one assumption underpinning this new introduction to qualitative analysis, which takes full account of how computing techniques have enhanced and transformed the field. The book provides a practical and unpretentious discussion of the main procedures for analysing qualitative data by computer, with most of its examples taken from humour or everyday life. It examines ways in which computers can contribute to greater rigour and creativity, as well as greater efficiency in analysis. The author discusses some of the pitfalls and paradoxes as well as the practicalities of computer-based qualitative analysis.

The perspective of *Qualitative Data Analysis* is pragmatic rather than prescriptive, introducing different possibilities without advocating one particular approach. The result is a stimulating, accessible and largely discipline-neutral text, which should appeal to a wide audience, most especially to arts and social science students and first-time qualitative analysts.

**Ian Dey** is a Senior Lecturer in the Department of Social Policy and Social Work at the University of Edinburgh, where he regularly teaches research methods to undergraduates. He has extensive experience of computer-based qualitative analysis and is a developer of Hypersoft, a software package for analysing qualitative data.

# Qualitative data analysis

## A user-friendly guide for social scientists

Ian Dey

## Routledge
Taylor & Francis Group

**LONDON AND NEW YORK**

First published 1993
by Routledge
2 Park Square, Milton Park, Abingdon, Oxon, OX14 4RN

Simultaneously published in the USA and Canada
by Routledge
270 Madison Ave, New York NY 10016

Reprinted 1993, 1995, 1996, 1998

Transferred to Digital Printing 2005

*Routledge is an imprint of the Taylor & Francis Group*

© 1993 Ian Dey

Typeset in Times by Solidus (Bristol) Ltd, Bristol

*British Library Cataloguing in Publication Data*
A catalogue record for this book is available from the British Library

*Library of Congress Cataloging in Publication Data*
A catalog record for this book is available from the Library of Congress

ISBN 0-415-05851-1 (hbk)
ISBN 0-415-05852-X (pbk)

# Contents

# Figures, illustrations and tables

## FIGURES

## ILLUSTRATIONS

## TABLES

# Preface

A new book on qualitative data analysis needs no apology. By comparison with the numerous texts on statistical analysis, qualitative data analysis has been ill-served. There is some irony in this situation: even a single text might suffice for the standardized procedures of statistical analysis; but for qualitative analysis, oft-noted for the diffuse and varied character of its procedures, we might reasonably expect a multiplicity of texts, not just a few. Teaching a course on methods makes one especially aware of this gap. This book is my contribution to filling it, and I hope it will encourage – or provoke – others to do the same.

A contemporary text on qualitative data analysis has to take account of the computer. The days of scissors and paste are over. While those steeped in traditional techniques may still harbour suspicions of the computer, a new generation of undergraduates and postgraduates expects to handle qualitative data using the new technology. For better or worse, these students will not give qualitative analysis the same attention and commitment as quantitative analysis, if only the latter is computer-based. This book is written primarily for them. I hope it may also be of some interest to other researchers new to qualitative analysis and to those using computers for this purpose for the first time.

Although the methods presented here assume the use of specialist software to support qualitative analysis, those seeking an introduction to individual software packages must look elsewhere (for example, Tesch 1990). My intention is to indicate the variety of ways in which computers can be utilized in qualitative analysis, without describing individual software applications in detail. No one application – including my own package, Hypersoft – will support the whole range of procedures which can be employed in analysing qualitative data. The researcher will have to choose an application to support a particular configuration of procedures, and one of my aims is to permit a more informed choice by identifying the range of analytic tasks which can be accomplished using one software package or another.

The challenge of developing a software package to analyse qualitative data has been a useful stimulus to clarifying and systematizing the procedures involved in qualitative analysis. It has also allowed me to write a text informed by what we can do with the computer. In my view, the advent of the computer not only enhances, but in some respects transforms traditional modes of analysis.

The book is based on my experiences as a researcher and teacher as well as a software developer. My research has involved a variety of qualitative methods, including observation, in-depth interviewing and documentary analysis; and through it I have learnt some of the procedures and paradoxes of qualitative analysis. As a teacher, I have become convinced of the merits of 'learning by doing', a perspective which has informed the skills-based methods course I have taught over the last few years with my colleague, Fran Wasoff. For those interested in skills acquisition, a text which provides a variety of task-related exercises and small-scale projects for students would be an invaluable asset. But this is not my aim in this book. Experience of teaching qualitative methods has also persuaded me of the value of a clear and uncomplicated introduction providing essential background knowledge and helping to structure the learning experience. This is what I hope this book will do.

A text introducing computer-based qualitative data analysis may need no apology, but my decision to illustrate analytic procedures using everyday material – mostly humorous – probably does deserve some explanation. The shortest explanation is that it works. Methods courses are notoriously dull. Pedagogical devices which work well enough for substantive issues can fail to engage students sufficiently in a course on methods. Students quickly tire of reading about methods, when what they want is to acquire and practise skills. In recent years I have been involved in teaching a methods course which aims to stimulate student interest and maintain motivation. One lesson I have learnt in teaching this course is that the problems students work on should be interesting and entertaining as well as instructive: that methods can be fun. We have used everyday material and humorous examples in our methods course, and it never fails to stimulate students' interest and engage their attention. I think this is a question of Mohammed coming to the mountain, rather than the mountain coming to Mohammed. It is better to introduce qualitative analysis on students' terms, rather than one's own. Students unfamiliar with research find familiar examples reassuring. They can relate to the material without effort. Because they can relax and even enjoy the substantive material, they can concentrate better on procedures and process. If students can easily grasp research objectives, and quickly become familiar with the data being analysed, they are more likely to find qualitative analysis a manageable and rewarding challenge.

In this book, I have mainly used humour as the medium through which to discuss the methodological problems of qualitative data analysis. Apart from offering light relief, humour is a subject we can all relate to. Whereas substantive issues are likely to be of minority interest, humorous exemplars are accessible to all. We can analyse humour from any number of perspectives – anthropological, linguistic, psychological, sociological and so on. This is a significant advantage in a text which is addressing methodological issues germane to a number of subjects and disciplines. Humour might be thought distracting, but in fact I want to reduce the distractions which can derive from using substantive topics and issues as exemplars. By using humour as the subject of analysis, I want to ensure that attention remains focused on how to analyse data, and not on what is being analysed. Needless to say, the examples used are not intended to be taken too seriously. My main examples, from Victoria Wood and Woody Allen, are chosen for their entertainment value rather than any academic import.

Two other advantages accrue from using humour as a subject for analysis. Humour often turns on ambiguities in meaning, and therefore raises some of the central problems in analysing qualitative data. In particular, it precludes a merely mechanical approach to analysing data. Humour is also an experience which suffers from dissection: analysis kills humour, just as surely as vivisection kills the frog. This underlines the limits (and limitations) of analysis, which can describe, interpret and explain, but cannot hope to reproduce the full richness of the original data.

Familiarity with the data is also important because it is a prerequisite of qualitative analysis. This presents a problem in teaching qualitative analysis, which typically deals with large volumes of data. My 'solution' is to teach analytic procedures through very limited sets of data, with which students can become thoroughly familiar. Although this has drawbacks, I think it gives more feel for what qualitative analysis is about. It avoids students being overwhelmed by a mass of material, and gives them more confidence that they can analyse data effectively. It also helps to focus on method, and counter the almost fetishistic concern with the sheer volume of material produced by qualitative methods. Using limited data in this way may seem like dancing on the head of a pin; but, after all, it is learning the dance that matters, and not the pin.

# Acknowledgements

My thanks are due to Elisabeth Tribe of Routledge for her support, to my colleagues for their encouragement and assistance, and to the members of my family for their forbearance while I was writing this book.

The author gratefully acknowledges permission to reproduce the following copyright extracts:

Allen, Woody (1978) 'If the Impressionists had been Dentists' *Without Feathers*, London: Sphere. © Woody Allen 1972. Reprinted by permission of Random House, Inc. and Hamish Hamilton.

Extracts from: Wood, Victoria (1985) *Up to You, Porky: The Victoria Wood Sketch Book*, London: Methuen; and Wood, Victoria (1990) *Mens Sana in Thingummy Doodah*, London: Methuen. © Victoria Wood. Reprinted by permission of the author.

Illustration 1.1 on p. 2, from Tesch (1990: 58), is reprinted by permission of the author.

# Chapter 1

# Introduction

Q. What colour is snow?
A. White.

To most of us, the answer 'white' may seem satisfactory, but to an Eskimo it would seem a joke: Eskimos distinguish between a wide variety of 'whites' because they need to differentiate between different conditions of ice and snow. So it is with qualitative data analysis: in a recent review of the field, Tesch (1990) distinguishes over forty types of qualitative research (Illustration 1.1). Just as the Eskimos distinguish varieties of white, so researchers distinguish varieties of qualitative analysis. There is no one kind of qualitative data analysis, but rather a variety of approaches, related to the different perspectives and purposes of researchers. To distinguish and assess these different perspectives fully would be a formidable and perhaps rather fruitless task, particularly as the boundaries between different approaches and their relation to what researchers actually do when analysing data is far from clear. But is there a basic core to qualitative research, as there is a basic colour 'white', from which these different varieties are derivative?

Different researchers do have different purposes, and to achieve these may pursue different types of analysis. Take a study of the classroom, for example. An ethnographer might want to describe the social and cultural aspects of classroom behaviour; a policy analyst might want to evaluate the impact of new teaching methods; a sociologist might be most interested in explaining differences in classroom discipline or pupil achievement – and so on. Different preoccupations may lead to emphasis on different aspects of analysis. Our ethnographer may be more interested in describing social processes, our policy analyst in evaluating results, our sociologist in explaining them. This plurality of perspectives is perfectly reasonable, remembering that social science is a social and collaborative process (even at its most competitive), in which (for example) descriptive work in one project may inspire interpretive or explanatory work in another (and vice versa).

*Illustration 1.1* Different approaches to qualitative research

| | | |
|---|---|---|
| action research | ethnographic content | interpretive interactionism |
| case study |    analysis | interpretive human studies |
| clinical research | ethnography | life history study |
| cognitive anthropology | ethnography of | naturalistic inquiry |
| collaborative enquiry |    communication | oral history |
| content analysis | ethnomethodology | panel research |
| dialogical research | ethnoscience | participant observation |
| conversation analysis | experiential psychology | participative research |
| Delphi study | field study | phenomenography |
| descriptive research | focus group research | phenomenology |
| direct research | grounded theory | qualitative evaluation |
| discourse analysis | hermeneutics | structural ethnography |
| document study | heuristic research | symbolic interactionism |
| ecological psychology | holistic enthnography | transcendental realism |
| educational connoisseurship | imaginal psychology | transformative research |
|    and criticism | intensive evaluation | |
| educational ethnography | | |

*Source:* Tesch 1990: 58

Given the multiplicity of qualitative research traditions, one might reasonably wonder whether there is sufficient common ground between the wide range of research traditions to permit the identification of anything like a common core to analysing qualitative data. On the other hand, the very notion of 'qualitative' data analysis implies, if not uniformity, then at least some kind of family kinship across a range of different methods. Is it possible to identify a range of procedures characteristic of qualitative analysis and capable of satisfying a variety of research purposes, whether ethnographic description, explanation or policy evaluation is the order of the day? The relevance and applicability of any particular procedure will, of course, depend entirely on the data to be analysed and the particular purposes and predilections of the individual researcher.

Having identified a multiplicity of perspectives, Tesch manages to reduce these to three basic orientations (1991: 17–25). First, she identifies 'language-oriented' approaches, interested in the use of language and the meaning of words – in how people communicate and make sense of their interactions. Second, she identifies 'descriptive/interpretive' approaches, which are oriented to providing thorough descriptions and interpretations of social phenomena, including its meaning to those who experience it. Lastly, there are 'theory-building' approaches which are orientated to identifying connections between social phenomena – for example, how events are structured or influenced by how actors define situations. These distinctions are not water-tight, as Tesch herself acknowledges, and her classification is certainly contestable. No one likes to be pigeon-holed (by some one else), and nothing is more likely to irritate a social scientist than to be described as atheoretical! However, Tesch does suggest a strong family resemblance between these different research orientations, in their emphasis on the meaningful character of social phenomena, and the need to take this into account in describing, interpreting or explaining communication, cultures or social action.

Thus encouraged, we can look for a basic core of qualitative data analysis, though not in some consensus about research perspectives and purposes, but rather in the type of data we produce and the way that we analyse it. Is there something about qualitative data which distinguishes it from quantitative data? And if qualitative data does have distinctive characteristics, does this also imply distinctive methods of analysis? My answer to both these questions is a qualified 'yes'. In Chapter 2 I distinguish between qualitative and quantitative data in terms of the difference between meanings and numbers. Qualitative data deals with meanings, whereas quantitative data deals with numbers. This does have implications for analysis, for the way we analyse meanings is through conceptualization, whereas the way we analyse numbers is through statistics and mathematics. In Chapter 3, I look at how we conceptualize qualitative data, including both the articulation of concepts through description and classification, and the analysis of relationships through the connections we can establish between them.

I said my answers were qualified, for though we can distinguish qualitative from quantitative data, and qualitative from quantitative analysis, these distinctions are not the whole story. We can learn as much from how meanings and numbers relate as we can from distinguishing them. In social science, number depends on meaning, and meaning is informed by number. Enumeration depends upon adequate conceptualization, and adequate conceptualization cannot ignore enumeration. These are points I take up in Chapters 2 and 3. My aim is to introduce the objects and methods of qualitative analysis, as a basis for the subsequent discussion of procedures and practice.

It is easy to exaggerate the differences between qualitative and quantitative analysis, and indeed to counterpose one against the other. This stems in part from the evolution of social science, most notably in its efforts to emulate the success of the natural sciences through the adoption of quantitative techniques. The fascination with number has sometimes been at the expense of meaning, through uncritical conceptualizations of the objects of study. Nowhere is this more apparent than in the concepts-indicators approach, where specifying the meaning of concepts is reduced to identifying a set of indicators which allow observation and measurement to take place – as though observations and measurement were not themselves 'concept-laden' (Sayer 1992). The growing sophistication of social science in terms of statistical and mathematical manipulation has not been matched by comparable growth in the clarity and consistency of its conceptualizations.

Action breeds reaction. In response to the perceived predominance of quantitative methods, a strong undercurrent of qualitative research has emerged to challenge the establishment orthodoxy. In place of the strong stress on survey techniques characteristic of quantitative methods, qualitative researchers have employed a range of techniques including discourse analysis, documentary analysis, oral and life histories, ethnography, and participant observation. Nevertheless, qualitative research is often cast in the role of the junior partner in the research enterprise, and many of its exponents feel it should have more clout and more credit. This encourages a posture which tends to be at once defensive of qualitative methods and dismissive of the role of the supposedly senior partner, quantitative research.

Beneath these rivalries, there is growing recognition that research requires a partnership and there is much to be gained from collaboration rather than competition between the different partners (cf. Fielding and Fielding 1986). In practice, it is difficult to draw as sharp a division between qualitative and quantitative methods as that which sometimes seems to exist between qualitative and quantitative researchers. In my view, these methods complement each other, and there is no reason to exclude quantitative methods, such as enumeration and statistical analysis, from the qualitative toolkit.

Reconciliation between qualitative and quantitative methods will undoubtedly be encouraged by the growing role of computers in qualitative analysis. The technical emphasis in software innovation has also encouraged a more flexible and pragmatic approach to developing and applying qualitative methods, relatively free from some of the more ideological and epistemological preoccupations and predilictions dominating earlier discussions. The development of software packages for analysing qualitative data has also stimulated reflection on the processes involved, and how these can be reproduced, enhanced or transformed using the computer. The development of computing therefore provides an opportune moment to consider some of the main principles and procedures involved in qualitative analysis. I outline the general contribution of the computer to qualitative analysis in Chapter 4. In doing so, I take account of how computers can enhance or transform qualitative methods. This is a topic I address explicitly in Chapter 4, but it also forms a recurrent theme throughout the discussion of analytic procedures in the rest of the book.

On the other hand, software development has also provoked concerns about the potentially damaging implications of new technological forms for traditional methods of analysis. Some developers have emphasized the potential danger of the software they themselves have produced in facilitating more mechanical approaches to analysing qualitative data, displacing traditional analytic skills. This concern has highlighted the need to teach computing techniques within a pedagogic framework informed by documented analytic principles and procedures. Paradoxically, however, existing accounts of qualitative methodology and research are notoriously deficient in precisely this area. Burgess (1982), for example, in his review of field research, complains that there are relatively few accounts from practitioners of the actual process of data analysis or from methodologists on how data analysis can be done. The literature is littered with such complaints about the lack of clear accounts of analytic principles and procedures and how these have been applied in social research. Perhaps part of the problem has been that analytic procedures seem deceptively simple. The conceptual aspects of analysis seem frustratingly elusive, while the mechanical aspects seem embarrassingly obvious. Thus Jones suggests that qualitative data analysis involves processes of interpretation and creativity that are difficult to make explicit; on the other hand, 'a great deal of qualitative data analysis is rather less mysterious than hard, sometimes, tedious, slog' (Jones 1985: 56).

The low status and marginality of qualitative research generally have fostered defensive posturing which emphasizes (and perhaps exaggerates) the subtleties and complexities involved in qualitative analysis. It has also led to a heavy emphasis on rigorous analysis. The resulting analytic requirements can seem quite intimidating, even to the experienced practitioner. There has also been a tendency to dress methodological issues in ideological guise, stressing the supposedly distinctive virtues and requirements of qualitative analysis, by contrast with quantitative methods, for example in apprehending meaning or in generating theory. At its worst, this aspires to a form of methodological imperialism which claims that qualitative analysis can only proceed down one particular road. As Bryman (1988) argues, more heat than light has been generated by the promulgation of epistemological canons that bear only a tenuous relation to what practitioners actually do. To borrow an apt analogy, we need to focus on what makes the car run, rather than the design and performance of particular models (Richards and Richards 1991).

This lacuna has been made good to some extent in recent years (e.g. Patton 1980, Bliss et al. 1983, Miles and Huberman 1984, Strauss 1987, Strauss and Corbin 1990), though not always in ways accessible to the first-time practitioner. This book is one more attempt to help plug the pedagogical gap referred to above. The focus is on the engine rather than on any particular model. My assumption is that the practical problems of conceptualizing meanings are common to a range of different perspectives. For example, the interpretive approach of Patton (1980) emphasizes the role of patterns, categories and basic descriptive units; the network approach of Bliss and her colleagues (1983) focuses on categorization; the quasi-statistical approach of Miles and Huberman (1984) emphasizes a procedure they call 'pattern coding'; and the 'grounded theory' approach of Strauss and Corbin (1990) centres on a variety of different strategies for 'coding' data. Despite the differences in approach and language, the common emphasis is on how to categorize data and make connections between categories. These tasks constitute the core of qualitative analysis.

Perhaps more than in most other methodological fields, the acquisition of qualitative analytic skills has been perceived and presented as requiring a form of 'learning by doing' (Fielding and Lee 1991: 6). As most methods courses remain wedded to formal pedagogies, this perspective may explain some of the difficulties experienced in teaching qualitative methods. However, my own experience suggests that even a course stressing skills acquisition through research experience and problem solving requires some sort of framework indicating the variety of skills and techniques to be acquired. With qualitative data analysis, even this is deficient. Practitioners have been reluctant to codify or even identify their analytic procedures, and in a field which stresses the subjective sensibilities and creativity of the researcher, have generally been suspicious of a 'recipe' approach to teaching qualitative methods.

Of course 'recipe' knowledge is devalued in our society – at least amongst academic circles. Even so, recipes, by indicating which ingredients to use, and what procedures to follow, can provide an important foundation for acquiring or developing skills. No one would pretend, of course, that learning a recipe is the same thing as acquiring a skill. Baking provides a relevant analogy, for it requires a knack which only experience can impart, as anyone who bakes bread will know; like qualitative analysis, baking also permits creativity and the development of idiosyncratic styles. But though the skilled analyst, like the experienced chef, may eventually dispense with the recipe book, it remains nevertheless a useful pedagogical device for the newcomer to the art.

A recipe book provides a guide to practice rather than a rule book. Although I have tried to write this book in a constructive rather than didactic manner, it is all too easy to slip from the language of 'can do' to that of 'should do.' It is not my intention to lay down 'rules', so much as show what can be done with qualitative data. Nevertheless, my own values and inclinations no doubt intrude, and I shall try to make these explicit at the outset.

First of all, I take a rather eclectic view of the sources of qualitative data. The association of qualitative data with unstructured methods is one which I challenge in the following chapter. Problems of conceptualization are as important in surveys as in any other research methods, and problems of interpretation and classification are as important to survey data as in any other context (Marsh 1982).

Secondly, I take a similarly eclectic view of qualitative analysis. Analysis aimed at describing situations or informing policy seems to me no less legitimate and worthwhile than analysis geared to generating theory. I also assume that we may be as interested in identifying and describing 'singularities', in the sense of unique events or cases, as in identifying and explaining regularities and variations in our data. Throughout the book, I assume that qualitative analysis requires a dialectic between ideas and data. We cannot analyse the data without ideas, but our ideas must be shaped and tested by the data we are analysing. In my view this dialectic informs qualitative analysis from the outset, making debates about whether to base analysis primarily on ideas (through deduction) or on the data (through induction) rather sterile (Chapter 5). This dialectic may be less disciplined than in the natural sciences, where experiment and quantitative measurement provide a firmer basis for examining evidence; but the search for corroborating evidence is nevertheless a crucial feature of qualitative analysis (Chapter 14). It is also a vital element in producing an adequate as well as an accessible account (Chapter 15).

Thirdly, I take a pragmatic view of analytic procedures (cf. Giarelli 1988). My main aim is to give a practical introduction to analytic procedures. The book describes a range of procedures we can follow for managing data (Chapter 6), reading and annotating (Chapter 7), categorizing (Chapters 8, 9 and 10), linking data (Chapter 11), connecting categories (Chapter 12) and using maps and matrices (Chapter 13). While these procedures are presented sequentially, in practice the mix and order of procedures adopted in qualitative analysis will vary. The choice of any particular permutation of procedures depends upon factors like the characteristics of the data, the objectives of the project, the predilections of the researchers, and the time and resources available to them.

If we consider qualitative data analysis (somewhat misleadingly) in terms of a logical succession of steps leading from our first encounters with the data through to the production of an account, then the various steps considered in this book can be depicted as in Figure 1.1. Because of its importance in conceptualizing data, three chapters are devoted to the tasks of categorizing, and a further two chapters to ways of making connections between categories. The intervening step (Chapter 11) is concerned with linking data, as an innovative technique for overcoming the fragmentation of data produced by categorization, and providing a firm basis for identifying conceptual connections between categories.

As my aim is to provide an accessible and practical guide to analytic procedures, I have avoided burdening the text with references to related work. With respect to existing literature, the three chapters on categorizing data and the preceding chapter on reading and annotating draw mostly on the work of Strauss (1987) and Strauss and Corbin (1990), though I have made no effort to remain within the restrictive confines of grounded theory. Patton (1980) and Becker and Geer (1982) also review the main analytic procedures involved. The discussion of associating categories and mapping data in Chapters 12 and 13 draws upon work by Bliss and her colleagues (1983) and by Miles and Huberman (1984). The related discussion of linking data derives mainly from my own work, although I am

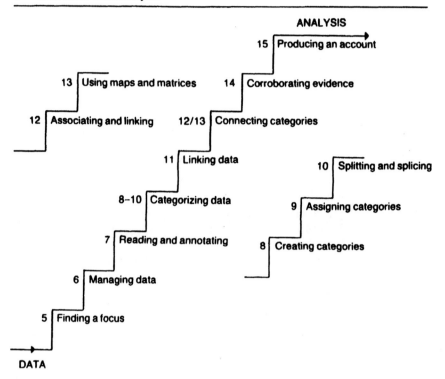

*Figure 1.1* The steps involved in data analysis – chapter by chapter

indebted to Sayer (1992) for an epistemological review of the relevant issues. The chapter on corroborating evidence draws on work by Becker and Geer (1982). None of these texts relates analytic procedures to computing techniques, and for further discussion the reader should refer to the works by Tesch (1990) and Fielding and Lee (1991).

Finally, a word on language. The proliferation of different research styles and software packages has led to marked inconsistencies in the terminology used by qualitative analysts. For example, when bits of data are demarcated in some way for the purposes of analysis, I call these bits of data 'databits', but in other texts they may be referred to as 'chunks', 'strips', 'segments', 'units of meaning' and so on. I call the process of classifying these databits 'categorizing' but in other texts it is variously described as 'tagging', 'labelling', 'coding' and so forth. In the absence of linguistic consensus, the best one can do is to choose terms which seem appropriate, and define these terms as clearly as possible. Accordingly, I have included a glossary of the key terms used in the text.

# Chapter 2

# What is qualitative data?

Compare the following reports of a game of soccer (Winter 1991).

| |
|---|
| Wimbledon 0 Liverpool 0 |

| |
|---|
| There was more excitement in the Selhurst car park than on the pitch ... |

Here we have both a quantitative result, and a qualitative assessment of the same game. Which do we care more about – the result, or the game? The points, or the passion? Which we find more important or illuminating will depend on what we are interested in. If we are team managers or fanatical fans, we may care more about the result than about how it was achieved. If we are neutral spectators, then we may care more about the quality of the game than about the result – in which case the match report confirms our worst fears of a no scoring draw! In social research as in everyday life, our assessment of quantitative and qualitative data is likely to reflect the interests we bring to it and the use we want to make of it.

We use quantitative data in a whole range of everyday activities, such as shopping, cooking, travelling, watching the time or assessing the Government's economic performance. How long? How often? How much? How many? We often ask and answer questions such as these using quantitative data.

Suppose I take 30 minutes to jog 5 miles to a shop and spend £5 on a litre of Chilean wine and 100 grams of Kenyan green beans. My behaviour may seem somewhat eccentric, but the terms in which it is expressed – minutes, miles, pounds, litres and grams – are entirely familiar. Each of these is a unit of measurement, in terms of which we can measure quantity. How do we measure quantities? We can count the coins or notes. We use a watch to tell the time. We weigh the beans on a weighing machine. We can use a milometer to check on distance and a measuring jug for volume. In each case, we have a measuring device which can express variations in quantity in terms of an established scale of standard units. But what is it that varies? We use minutes to measure time, miles to measure distance, pounds to measure expenditure, litres to measure volume and grams to measure weight. Time, distance, expenditure, volume and weight can be thought of as variables which can take on a range of different values. We don't always agree on how to measure our variables – we could have used kilometres, dollars, pints and ounces. But the important point is that for each of these variables we can confidently measure numerical differences in the values they can adopt. This is possible because we can establish a unit of measurement agreed upon as a common standard which is replicable, i.e. it can be applied again and again with the same results (Blalock 1960).

While 'quantities' permeate our everyday life, they are most likely to be used in a physical or physiological context, where measurement in terms of standard units is well established. We readily accept conventional measures of time, space and weight. Even in a physical context, though, we make qualitative as well as quantitative assessments. Is the bus dirty? Is the meal appetizing? Is the view breath-taking? These involve assessments for which we either cannot or do not use concepts which can be measured in quantitative terms. In a psychological or social context, we are much more likely to rely on qualitative assessment. Is this person sympathetic? Is this city exciting? Is this book interesting? These are areas where we tend to rely on qualitative assessment rather than on some quantitative measure.

By comparison with quantities, qualities seem elusive and ethereal. We often use 'quality' as a measure of relative worth, as when referring to a 'quality performance' or 'a person of quality', or asking whether something is of good or poor quality. Suppose I have just watched a film and I am asked what I thought of it. What was the film like? My evaluation will refer to the qualities of the film. Was it entertaining, or profound? Did it make me laugh or cry? Was the plot plausible? Were the characters convincing? Was the acting good? Was the script well crafted? These questions are all concerned with what I made of the film. But my evaluation of the film cannot be separated from how I understood and interpreted it. Quality is a measure of relative value, but based on an evaluation of the general character or intrinsic nature of what we are assessing. What was the story? What was the point of the film? What values did it express? Did the film achieve what it set out to do? In short, what did the film mean to me?

Whereas quantitative data deals with numbers, qualitative data deals with meanings. Meanings are mediated mainly through language and action. Language is not a matter of subjective opinion. Concepts are constructed in terms of an inter-subjective language which allows us to communicate intelligibly and interact effectively (cf. Sayer 1992: 32). Take the very idea of a film. The word derives from the Old English word 'filmen' meaning a membrane, and in modern usage has been extended to include a thin coating of light-sensitive emulsion, used in photography, and hence to the cinema where it refers rather to what is recorded on film. The meanings which constitute the concept 'film' are embodied in changing social practices such as the drive-in movie or the home video. What it may mean to make or see a film has changed considerably over the past twenty years. My somewhat dated dictionary defines films in terms of cinema-going and has not yet caught up with TV movies, never mind the video recorder. Because concepts are subject to such continual shifts in meaning, we have to treat them with caution.

Meaning is essentially a matter of making distinctions. When I describe a film as 'boring', for example, I am making one or more distinctions: this situation is 'boring' and not 'exciting' or 'stimulating' or 'interesting' or 'amusing'. Meaning is bound up with the contrast between what is asserted and what is implied not to be the case. To understand the assertion that a film is 'boring', I have to understand the distinction being drawn between what is and what might have been the case.

Meanings reside in social practice, and not just in the heads of individuals. Going to the movies expresses meaning, just as much as does reviewing them. The 'social construction' of a night out at the cinema is a complex accomplishment in terms of meaningful action. The cinema itself is not just a building, but one designed and constructed for a particular purpose. Showing a film in the cinema is the culmination of a complex sequence of meaningful actions, including the whole process of producing, making, distributing and advertising the film. My 'night out' at the cinema is a comparable accomplishment, predicated upon social practices in the form of transportation (I have to get to the cinema), economic exchange (I have to buy a ticket) and audience behaviour (silence please!).

Such social phenomena are, in Sayer's words, 'concept-dependent': unlike natural phenomena they are not impervious to the meanings we ascribe to them (1992: 30). The film industry, the entertainment business, the transport system and the 'night out' are social practices which can only be understood in terms of the meanings we invest in them. To vary a stock example, when one billiard ball 'kisses' another, the physical reaction that takes place is not affected by any meaningful behaviour on the part of the billiard balls. But when one person kisses another, the reaction can only be understood as meaningful behaviour. The natural scientist may worry about what it means when one billiard ball kisses another, but only about what it means to the scientist (e.g. in terms of force, inertia, momentum). The social scientist also has to worry about what the kiss means for the persons involved.

As my example of the film suggests, in dealing with meanings we by no means need to confine our attention to text. On the contrary, we should note the richness and diversity of qualitative data, since it encompasses virtually any kind of data: sounds, pictures, videos, music, songs, prose, poetry or whatever. Text is by no means the only, nor is it always the most effective, means of communicating qualitative information; in an electronic age, art and design have become powerful media tools. The importance of image as well as text is not merely an aspect of contemporary culture; the art historian Michael Baxandall (1974) comments that 'a painting is the deposit of a social relationship'. Qualitative data embraces an enormously rich spectrum of cultural and social artefacts.

What do these different kinds of data have in common? They all convey meaningful information in a form other than numbers. However, note that numbers too sometimes convey only meanings, as, for example, when we refer to the numbers on football jerseys, car number plates, or the box numbers in personal ads. It would be absurd to treat these numbers as numerical data, to be added, subtracted or otherwise subject to mathematical manipulation. But it is not always so easy to distinguish between the use of number as a descriptor of quality and its use as a measure of quantity. This is particularly true where, for convenience in manipulating data, we use numbers as names. It is then all too easy to forget that the numbers are only names, and proceed as if they 'meant' more than they do. Often, for example, response categories in an interview are coded by number. This may be convenient for the analysis. But if we forget that these numbers are really just names, we may analyse them as though they conveyed more information than they actually do. In distinguishing between quantitative and qualitative data in terms of numbers and meanings, we have to avoid the fallacy of treating numbers as numbers where they are used only to convey meaning.

By comparison with numbers, meanings may seem shifty and unreliable. But often they may also be more important, more illuminating and more fun. If I am a boringly meticulous jogger, I may use a pedometer to measure the distance I jog, a watch to measure my time, and the scales afterwards to measure my weight. For each concept – distance, time, weight – we can measure behaviour in terms of standard units – yards, minutes and pounds: 'I jog 3,476 yards every day, in 20 minutes on average, and I hope to lose 5lb after a month'. However, I happen to know that with jogging this obsession with quantitative measurement is counterproductive: it adds stress and reduces enjoyment. I also know that by replacing fat with muscle, I am liable to gain rather than lose weight! Therefore, I prefer to measure my jogging in qualitative terms: 'I jog until I am tired out. By the end of the month I hope I'll feel fitter.' Short of conducting some medical tests, there are no quantitative measures in terms of which to quantify my exhaustion, or my fitness. But I can describe my exhaustion, and I can compare how much fitter I feel now than before I began to jog. Although I could use quantitative measures (e.g. my pulse rate) as a way of assessing my fitness, these may not provide a very meaningful assessment of how fit I feel.

It would be wrong to assume that quantitative data must take precedence over qualitative data simply because it involves numbers. Take the ever topical question of weight watching. There are various ways we can weight watch. We might use the scales and measure how many kilos or pounds we weigh. This is a quantitative measure, but it doesn't tell us how the weight is distributed, nor how a particular point in the scale translates into overall appearance. We might prefer to rely on how we look, whether 'fat' or 'thin' or maybe 'just right'. These are qualitative judgements, but in a social context these may be the judgements that count. If we do not measure data in quantitative terms, it may be that (at least for the moment) we lack the tools necessary to do the job. Or it may be that we simply prefer qualitative assessments because they are more meaningful, if less precise, than any quantitative measures.

Take colour as an example. For most purposes we are content to use a fairly crude classification based on a very limited colour range. If we are buying (or selling) paint, though, we may want a more sophisticated classification. And if we are using colour in an industrial or scientific context, we may want more precision: a spectrophotometer measures the amount of light reflected or transmitted across the visible spectrum, allowing colours to be measured precisely in terms of their wavelengths. However, the mathematical specification of a colour does not reveal how it will look to different observers in variable light conditions; although measurement is more accurate, it is less useful for everyday purposes than cruder methods which rely on visual classification (Varley 1983: 134–5).

Because qualitative assessments are less standardized and less precise than quantitative measures, there are areas of social life where we do attempt to establish the latter. Money is the medium through which we measure equivalence in market transactions, though in contrast to physical measures, confidence in currencies can collapse completely. Qualifications are another medium used to measure educational achievement, though here also 'inflation' can undermine confidence in established standards. Attempts to measure educational performance, intelligence, health status, social adjustment, quality of life and so on in quantitative terms are dogged by suspicion that these do not capture the 'quality' of psychological or social aspects of life. For example, compare the following statements on educational achievement.

| | |
|---|---|
| 'Only 5% of British employees in commercial and clerical work have educational qualifications above A-level standard.' | 'Education is what survives when what has been learnt has been forgotten.' |

In reducing educational achievement to a quantitative measure, do we neglect or overlook altogether what is important about education – its quality?

This tension between quantitative measures and qualitative assessment is also apparent in social research. On the one hand, qualitative data is often presented as 'richer' and 'more valid' than quantitative data. On the other hand, it is often dismissed as 'too subjective' because assessments are not made in terms of established standards. In practice, this implies an unnecessary polarization between the different types of data. We have to consider the reliability and validity of whatever measures we choose. But as is often the case, the existence of a dichotomy has tended to polarize not only thinking but people (Galtung 1967: 23). Qualitative data has become narrowly associated with research approaches emphasizing unstructured methods of obtaining data.

Qualitative research has become a fashionable term to use for any method other than the survey: participant (and non-participant) observation, unstructured interviewing, group interviews, the collection of documentary materials and the like. Data produced from such sources may include fieldnotes, interview transcripts, documents, photographs, sketches, video or tape recordings, and so on. What these various forms of research often have in common is a rejection of the supposedly positivist 'sins' associated with survey methods of investigation, most particularly where data are elicited through closed questions using researcher-defined categories. A grudging exception may be allowed for open questions in a questionnaire survey, but in practice – for the sake of purity, perhaps – data from this source are often ignored. The hallmark of qualitative data from this perspective is that it should be a product of 'unstructured' methods of social research.

However, it is not very helpful to see qualitative data simply as the output of qualitative research. Distinctions between different methods are as hard to draw as distinctions between types of data! For example, we might contrast the survey as a method involving the collection and comparison of data across a range of cases, with the single case study approach more commonly associated with qualitative methods. However, in recent years there has been an upsurge of interest in 'multi-case' (or 'multi-site') fieldwork methods, eroding the force of the case study/survey distinction. Moreover, the survey itself can be used as a data collection instrument within the context of a case study; for example, we might survey teacher opinion as part of a case study of a particular school.

Another distinction sometimes drawn between qualitative and quantitative methods is that the former produce data which are freely defined by the subject rather than structured in advance by the researcher (Patton 1980). 'Pre-structured' data are taken to involve selection from a limited range of researcher-defined alternatives, for example in an observation schedule or multiple choice questionnaire. With subject-defined data, the length, detail, content and relevance of the data are not determined by the researcher, but recorded 'as spoken' or 'as it happens', usually in the form of notes or tape recordings.

However, it is difficult to draw such a sharp divide between these methods. Observations may be more or less 'structured' without falling clearly into one type or another. Similarly, between the 'structured' and 'unstructured' interview are a variety of interviewing forms which resist such ready classification. Take open and closed questions in interviewing as an obvious example. With the closed question, the respondent must choose from the options specified by the researcher. With an open question, respondents are free to respond as they like. But these alternatives are not really so clear-cut. For example, questions which indicate a range of response categories may still include the option: 'Other – please specify'. And even the most non-directive interviewer must implicitly 'direct' an interview to some extent if it is to cover certain topics within the time available. It would be naïve to discount the role played by the researcher as participant observer or unstructured interviewer in eliciting and shaping the data they obtain.

The point is that any 'data', regardless of method, are in fact 'produced' by the researcher. In this respect, the idea that we 'collect' data is a bit misleading. Data are not 'out there' waiting collection, like so many rubbish bags on the pavement. For a start, they have to be noticed by the researcher, and treated as data for the purposes of his or her research. 'Collecting' data always involves selecting data, and the techniques of data collection and transcription (through notes, tapes, recordings or whatever) will affect what finally constitutes 'data' for the purposes of research.

A method of data collection may in any case produce various types of data. The most obvious example is the questionnaire survey, where we can design a wide range of questions, more or less 'open' or 'closed', to elicit various types of data. The same holds true of fieldwork methods, such as document searches or observation; while the data produced through these methods may be predominantly qualitative in character, there is no reason to presume that it will be exclusively so. Sometimes of course we simply do not get the kind of data we expected.

| | |
|---|---|
| What's the main difference between students of 1960s and the 1990s?<br><br>Thirty years. | What result would you get if you laid a class of 30 students, average height 5'5", end to end?<br><br>They'd all fall asleep. |

In practice, research often involves a range of methods producing a variety of data. We would do better to focus on the data which has been produced, rather than implying rigid distinctions between styles of research and methods of data collection.

If qualitative research is equated with the use of unstructured methods, it follows that qualitative data is therefore seen as 'unstructured'. The difference between 'structured' and 'unstructured' data turns on whether or not the data has been classified. Take the example in Illustration 2.1 of structured and unstructured responses to a question about the use of closed questions in an interview.

*Illustration 2.1* Structured and unstructured responses to the question 'What are the main advantages and disadvantages of closed questions in an interview?'

| Structured response | Unstructured response |
|---|---|
| • Closed questions expedite the interview for both interviewer and respondent<br><br>• Closed questions expedite later processing of data<br><br>• Closed questions convey more exact meaning by defining the range of appropriate responses<br><br>• Closed questions improve reliability | Well, it can put people off, not being able to answer in their own words. But the important thing is that people may not be able to answer as they'd like. Answers to open questions are more likely to reflect a person's own thinking – to be more valid. It's much better to analyse the data afterwards, even if it's more time-consuming. Of course time is of the essence, especially when you've had the kind of medical problems I've had over the last year. I had that operation in January, etc. etc. |

The structured response has been classified, for the data is divided into separate statements denoting distinctive advantages of closed questions, relating to the conduct of the interview, the ease of data processing and the communication of meaning. By contrast, the unstructured response is descriptive but unclassified: the response covers a range of points – not all of them relevant – which are not organized and presented as distinctive elements.

Lack of structure is evident in the characteristic volume and complexity of much research data: in those apparently endless pages upon pages of fieldnotes; in the varied mass of documentary materials; in those lengthy and lavish interview transcripts. Such data may often lack structure, but this can be a problem as much as a virtue. The idea that qualitative data is mainly 'unstructured' is useful, if this is taken not as a definition but rather as an imperative for analysis. Although unstructured data may not be classified, it can be classified and indeed one of the main aims of qualitative analysis is often to do just that. While a lot of qualitative data may be unstructured, it is misleading to define qualitative data as 'unstructured' data. Is a response less 'qualitative' because I classify my observations? Suppose I am asked to describe the colour of my hair. Is my response less 'qualitative' if I (sadly but honestly) select 'grey' from a list of alternatives, than if I write 'grey' in the space provided?

Ironically, in defining qualitative data in terms of unstructured data or a particular family of research methods, qualitative analysts underestimate the significance of qualitative data across the whole research spectrum. They also underestimate the concern amongst other research traditions with problems of meaning and conceptualization (Fielding and Fielding 1986, Bryman 1988). Rather than counter-posing qualitative and quantitative data in this way, it makes more sense to consider how these can complement each other in social research (Giarelli 1988).

To do so, let us look in more detail at different levels of measurement in social research. Here I am taking measurement in its broadest sense, as the recognition of a limit or boundary. As Bohm (1983: 118) has argued, this is also its most ancient sense, as in the idea of a 'measured' action or response which acknowledges the proper limits to behaviour. Measurement referred to insight into the proper nature of the phenomenon; if behaviour went beyond its proper measure or limit, the result would be ill-health – or tragedy. Such limits can be recognized through qualitative assessment as well as specified more precisely through quantitative measures. Indeed, the specification of precise proportion was initially a subsidiary element of measurement, of secondary significance, though it has since supplanted the more general notion of recognizing the proper limit or boundary of some phenomenon.

When we look at different levels of measurement, we find that numbers and meanings are related at all levels. A concept is an idea which embraces a *number* of observations which have characteristics in common. When we bring observations together as having some significance in common, we *count* them as belonging to the concept. The word count derives from the Latin 'computare', with the roots 'com', meaning together, and 'putare' meaning to calculate or reckon. (The term computer derives from the Latin 'computare'). Counting therefore has a double meaning. We use it to refer to significance, as in the expression 'that observation doesn't count'; and we use it to refer to enumeration, as in the expression 'count the observations'. So conceptualization even at the most elementary level is informed by number. And even at the most elementary level of enumeration, counting depends on the meaning of what we 'reckon together'.

The first step in recognizing a limit or boundary is to give a description of something. When my daughter describes 'what happened at school this afternoon', she is telling a story about a unique sequence of events. Much of the qualitative data produced through fieldwork methods or open-ended interview questions may be of the same narrative form. We describe by focusing on the characteristics of something – perhaps a person, object, event or process. No explicit comparison need be intended: we can be interested in recognizing and denoting something as a 'singularity', in the sense of a unique bit of data. A singularity can also mean something unusual, rare, or even extraordinary – in other words, something which 'stands out' as worthy of attention. Think of how a figure stands out against the background of a painting. Perhaps more appropriately, think of a ripple

or eddy in a flowing stream (Bohm 1983: 10). In describing a singularity –
such as observing what happened today at school – we identify a ripple in
the stream of experience (Figure 2.1).

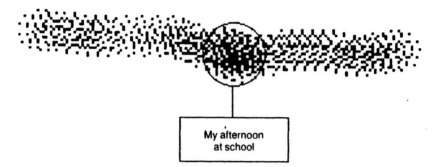

*Figure 2.1* Describing a bit of data as a ripple in the flow of experience

A singularity is a single constellation of observations which constitutes
the identity of a person or object, or the history of a unique event (or
sequence of events). But like the ripple in the stream, it cannot be
abstracted from the wider flow of experience in which it is implicated. The
figure depends upon the background; to recognize an exception, we have
to understand the rule. Description depends on recognizing patterns of
events. For example, what is this 'school' where this unique sequence of
events occurred? What is a 'teacher' and what does 'doing maths' mean?
We identify things – events, processes, even people – by attending to their
characteristics, and by recognizing the boundaries which separate these
'things' from the flow of experience in which they are implicated. For this
to be possible, these characteristics have to be stable over time. We have to
compare observations between different bits of data, and classify these
observations according to their distinctive characteristics.

For example, to recognize something as a 'school' we have to have some
measure of agreement on a set of characteristics which define the boundaries of what can or cannot count as a 'school'. We may think of it as a
building designed or used for a particular purpose; or as a social institution
with a characteristic set of social relations, and perhaps even a characteristic 'ethos'. In describing something as a 'school', we implicitly classify it as
belonging to a group of observations which we have named 'schools'. This
demarcates the concept 'school' from other kinds of observations, such as
'hospitals', 'banks' or 'swimming pools'. A concept is an idea which stands
for a class of objects or events. Where we fail to reach a measure of agreement on how to define these boundaries, conflicts may arise. This happens,
of course, when teachers 'define' school as a place to work but children
treat school as a place to play.

It follows that our observations are concept-laden abstractions from the flow of experience – and we should be wary of taking these products of our thinking as enjoying an existence independent of it. We have no independent access to reality apart from our conceptualizations of it. That does not mean that reality or experience is reducible to how we observe it – as though, if we were all to shut our eyes, the world would disappear. Experience is mediated but not determined by the concepts we use.

We can think of this conceptual process as 'categorizing' data. In Figure 2.2 two similar observations in the stream of experience are related in terms of a unifying category. Clearly categories can refer to a potentially unlimited series of similar observations.

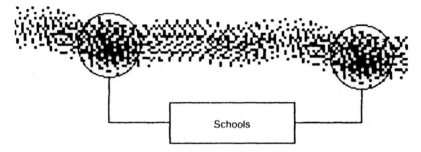

*Figure 2.2* Category relating two similar observations

Even at this level of measurement, where we are only defining the limits or boundaries of objects or events, we are implicitly using both qualitative and quantitative measures. To answer the question 'what counts as a school' we refer to our idea of what a school is, i.e. to the meaning of the concept. But these meanings are typically articulated in relation to a *number* of observations (or experiences) through which we define the boundaries of our concept. Concepts are ideas about classes of objects or events: we decide whether to 'count' an observation as belonging to a category, in terms of whether it fits with a number of similar observations. We compare this observation with similar examples. So we are already 'counting' in both senses of the word, if the meanings we ascribe to an object or event are stable over a range of experience.

When we categorize data in this way, we make a distinction between this observation and others. We want to know what makes this observation 'stand out' from others. Often this is through an implied contrast – e.g. this is school, not home; where we work, not play. For most purposes, we do not bother to make rigid and complete distinctions, so long as we can make some reasonably rough and ready decisions about what 'belongs' where. When Eve said 'here's an apple' to Adam, she wanted him to recognize it for what it is: an apple. She named the fruit an 'apple' to signify that it has certain characteristics: according to my dictionary it is a 'rounded firm edible juicy fruit of a tree of the genus *Malus*' or 'any of various similar fleshy many-celled fruits'. 'Edible and juicy' was probably enough for Adam. The category 'apple' signifies these characteristics, more or less vaguely defined. The categories we use may be vaguely defined, but we don't worry unduly so long as they 'work' for us. We want to know that the apple is juicy and edible, not dry and inedible.

Our categories can be 'fuzzy' and overlapping. For most purposes, we may think of schools as a set of purpose-built buildings. But a school can also double as a community centre, a sports facility, and during elections as a voting centre. For parents educating their children at home, part of the house may function as 'school' for part of the day. And there may be little agreement on what a school does. For some it may an institution for imparting skills and certifying achievement, for others it may be little more than a giant child-minding institution. A concept can convey very different connotations. So the distinctions we draw in describing something as a school may vary according to context.

Categorizing at this level therefore involves an implicit and loosely defined classification of observations. Categorizing brings together a number of observations which we consider similar in some respects, by implied contrast with other observations. But the boundaries are not tightly defined, and we are typically vague about the precise respects in which we differentiate our observations. This means that in assigning something to one category, we do not automatically exclude it from others. We discount other possibilities, rather than exclude them altogether. For example, in counting certain observations as 'schools', we discount other categories such as 'community centres', but we do not explicitly exclude them as possibilities. So counting how many schools there are tells us nothing about how many community centres there may be. In this sense, our categories are inclusive rather than exclusive. We focus on whether or not to include an observation within the category (e.g. to count it as a school) rather than whether in doing so we exclude the observation from other categories. In Figure 2.3, for example, our observations are related to two different categories, 'schools' and 'community centres'.

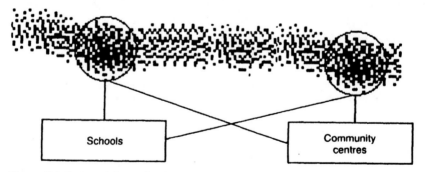

*Figure 2.3* Categorizing using inclusive categories

At a more sophisticated level of classification, we can differentiate more explicitly between observations. Typically, we can do this where we can identify some characteristics which observations have in common, the better to understand what distinguishes them. We may want to distinguish clearly between 'apples' and 'pears', for example, as different varieties of fruit. Here the concept 'fruit' becomes a variable, whose values are 'apples' and 'pears'. A variable is just a concept which varies in kind or amount. This type of variable is often called a 'nominal' variable because its values (or categories) are 'names' rather than numbers.

With nominal variables, the values we use must be mutually exclusive and exhaustive. 'Mutually exclusive' means no bit of data fits into more than one category. For example, suppose we classified a box of apples according to colour, and assumed that the apples are either red or green. 'Colour' is then our variable, with two values 'red' and 'green'. What if we encounter some apples which are red and green? Our values are no longer mutually exclusive. 'Exhaustive' means you can assign all your data to one category or another; there's nothing that won't fit somewhere into a given set of categories. Suppose we encounter some yellow apples lurking at the bottom of the box. Our categories no longer exhaust all possible values for the variable 'colour'. To make our values exhaustive and mutually exclusive, we would have to add new categories for the yellow and red/green apples.

Classifying in this way adds to our information about the data. For any bit of data which we assign one value, we can infer that we cannot assign the same bit of data to other values of the same variable. Our categories have become exclusive. For example, suppose our categories refer to 'primary' and 'secondary' schools. 'Schools' becomes our variable and 'primary' and 'secondary' its mutually exclusive values. The observations can no longer be assigned to either category (Figure 2.4). If we encountered another bit of data which fits our variable but not our values, such as a 'middle' school, then we would have to modify our classification to keep it exclusive and exhaustive.

At this level of measurement, we have adopted a more rigorous measure of both the qualitative and quantitative aspects of our data. At a conceptual level, our criteria for categorizing (or counting) a school as either primary or secondary have to be clear: they cannot be fuzzy and overlapping. As these categories are both values of the variable 'schools', we are also clear about what they have in common. In terms of counting numbers, if we add our observation to one category, we automatically exclude (or subtract) it from another. We can now consider the proportion of our observations which fall into any particular class. This advance in counting numerically is only possible, though, because of our advance in what counts conceptually as belonging to one class or another. We have defined our classes more comprehensively (so they are exhaustive) and more precisely (so they are exclusive).

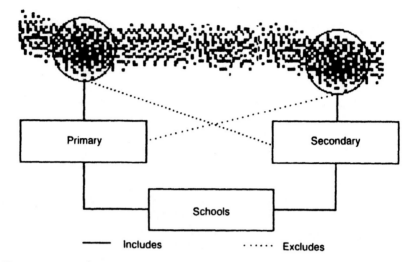

*Figure 2.4* Nominal variable with mutually exclusive and exhaustive values

Sometimes we can put values into a rank order. For example, we may distinguish schools in terms of some idea of educational progression, and rank primary schools as more elementary than secondary schools. If we can order values in this way, we can convert our nominal variable into an 'ordinal' variable, so-called because it specifies an order between all its values. A common example of ordinal variables in social research can be found in the ranking of preferences, or where we ask respondents to identify the strength of their feelings about various options. Ordinal variables give us still more numerical information about the data, because we can now indicate how one bit of data is higher or lower in the pecking order than another (Figure 2.5).

From a quantitative perspective, we can now rank these values along a continuum. If primary schools fall below middle schools on this continuum, we can infer that they also fall below upper secondaries. But for this ranking to be meaningful, it must also make sense from a qualitative perspective. In the case of schools, the idea of educational progression provides a conceptual rationale for distinguishing an order in terms of the degree of progression exhibited by different schools.

To progress to higher levels of measurement, we have to improve or refine our conceptualization of the data. What is a school? Can we classify schools into primaries and secondaries? Are primaries more elementary than secondaries? Each of these questions raises conceptual issues which must be satisfactorily resolved if we are use a higher level of measurement. The same applies to measurement in terms of standard units. A standard unit is one which defines fixed limits to the intervals between different possible values of a variable, which can be thought of as different points on

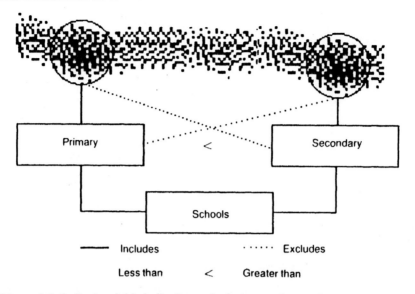

*Figure 2.5* Ordinal variable indicating order between observations

a scale. Concepts which can be measured in this way are called 'interval' variables. (If the scale happens to have a fixed point, such as zero, we call it a 'ratio' scale). For example, a ruler fixes intervals in terms of inches or centimetres, or some proportion thereof. Fixed intervals allow us to measure the 'distance' between different values, such as the difference between something 4 cms and something 10 cms wide. Once again this adds to the information about our data, this time specifying in numerical terms the distance between different values. For example, in Figure 2.6 our observations are measured in terms of variable 'age at entry to school.'

Measurement in terms of standard units is often presented as the core of scientific method. But note that quantities mean nothing in themselves – except perhaps to the pure mathematician. That is not to disparage the power of mathematics, which obviously has been a crucial tool in scientific development. What tends to be overlooked is the critical role of qualitative concepts in interpreting the mathematics. Although we take this type of measurement for granted in the physical world, it depends upon long-established conceptual conventions underpinned by sophisticated theoretical relationships between categories. For example, a metre was initially established by social convention but is now defined in terms of the distance travelled by light in 0.000000003335640952 seconds (Hawking 1988: 22). This measurement depends upon conceptual assumptions about the nature of light. Quantitative measurement applied to the world can only be achieved on the basis of qualitative assessment. With many everyday physical measures, such as of distance, time or temperature, we may have

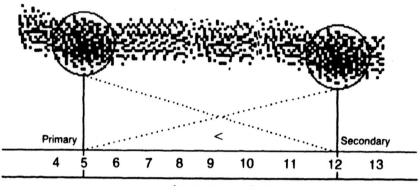

Age at entry to school

*Figure 2.6* Interval variable with fixed distance between values

only a vague (and perhaps erroneous) notion of the qualitative concepts upon which they are based: we take these measures for granted. In social research, with relatively few well-established measures, we cannot afford to do likewise.

We can rarely establish in social research comparable conventions fixing the distance between values (or categories), let alone specify this distance with accuracy. Measures in social research such as those of age and income are the exceptions rather than the rule. Social scientists do not have standard units in terms of which to measure things like poverty, health or quality of life. The prime reason is that we cannot agree in the first place about the meaning of what we are trying to measure. For example, the definition of poverty remains a bone of contention between a variety of rival political and academic perspectives. Many of the concepts used in social research are similarly contestable.

Qualitative assessments can easily become eclipsed by standard measures, which seem to offer simple but powerful tools for quantifying data. But despite their undoubted appeal, standard measures which ignore qualitative meaning can easily mislead. Let us consider a couple of simple examples, age and family size. These may easily but mistakenly be taken as quantitative variables whose meaning is self-evident. Take a mother who is forty years old and has three children. Surely here we have such clear-cut quantitative data that we can focus quite legitimately on the quantities and not the 'qualities' involved? Perhaps. But we are assuming that 'years' are of (sufficiently) equal length and therefore bear a consistent relation to the length of a life. If our mother was an ancient Roman, the number of years lived might bear no consistent relation to the length of her life. The Romans used a lunar rather than a solar calendar, and had to continually adjust the year by adding in extra days. The calendar was in such a mess by 47 BC that Caesar made the year 445 days long (Coveney and Highfield

1991: 43)! The variable 'years old' in fact expresses a quite sophisticated classification, one which is a cultural product reflecting the culmination (to date) of a long and complex political and scientific process. If this example seems obscure, then consider contemporary Japan, where years of age are reckoned prospectively rather than retrospectively – a Japanese baby during the first year is reckoned as a one-year-old. We can all tell (or lie about) how many years old we are, but only because (and insofar as) the calendar has become established as a standard measure of the passage of time.

What about the number of children? This too depends upon common, taken-for-granted assumptions about what it means to 'have children'. But with the growth of single parent families and 'step' relationships, and technological advances in the shape of artificial insemination and test tube babies, this has become problematic. In this changing cultural context, our common understanding of what 'having a child' means has become less definite. It may be necessary, for example, to distinguish clearly between biological and social relationships. For example, we might define 'having children' as 'giving birth to a child' (effectively excluding men from having children!). But in some circumstances, even this may not be sufficient. Redmond O'Hanlon (1988) recounts the story of a social scientist trying to establish for social security purposes the number of child dependents in an Amazonian village. The hapless researcher was confounded by two women claiming to have given birth to the same child! Before we can determine how many children a mother has, we have to achieve a common under-standing of what this means. If we intend to make quantitative compari-sons, we must first make certain we are comparing 'like with like' by achieving a consistent qualitative interpretation of what it means to 'have a child'.

We must therefore look behind the numbers, to what the information we have means and how it can be used. In other words, we must identify the appropriate level of measurement for the data. If we ignore the level of measurement, we can easily think we know more about the data than we actually do. For example, in the university where I work the grading and marking scale in Illustration 2.2 is in operation.

*Illustration 2.2* Example of a grading and marking scheme

| Grade | Mark |
|-------|------|
| A | 75–100 |
| B | 65–74 |
| C | 55–64 |
| D | 50–54 |
| E | 45–49 |
| F | 35–44 |
| G | 0–34 |

The different bands refer to qualitative differences in performance. For example, grade A means 'excellent'. But what do the marks mean? Note that the grades refer to bands of marks of unequal size (Illustration 2.3).

Although we have a numerical scale from one to one hundred, we do not have standard units. Compare two essays marked ten and thirty with another two essays marked fifty and seventy. The former are in the same grade – that is, have the same meaning, 'bad fail' – the latter are separated by two grades, and therefore have different meanings. As marks in some grades are given more weight than marks in others, it would be misleading to average marks to determine overall performance. Yet once performance is measured in terms of marks, the temptation to do just that may be overwhelming, even if the interpretation of such an average must be obscure!

*Illustration 2.3* Grades with different mark bands

| Grade | Mark band |
| --- | --- |
| G | 35 |
| A | 25 |
| B & C & F | 10 |
| D & E | 5 |

To interpret data in social research, it may be more important to use meaningful categories than to obtain precise measures. As a category 'forty years old' is not especially meaningful (except perhaps to forty-year-olds!) and age data organized into different categories by 'years' may be very hard to interpret. Therefore we may prefer to reclassify 'years' data in terms of age groups e.g. 'under twenty-fives' etc. which are more meaningful, even though we cannot then measure just how old those in each age group are.

Problems of interpretation are pervasive in any science, whether we are thinking of 'strange attractors' in physics, 'black holes' in astronomy or the 'nuclear family' in social science. Numbers are never enough: they have to refer to concepts established through qualitative analysis. While quantities are powerful precisely because of the complex mathematical operations they permit, they mean nothing in themselves unless they are based on meaningful conceptualizations. In other words, social science (and science for that matter) without qualitative data would not connect up with the world in which we live.

If it is folly to disregard the problems of meaning in science, it is also folly to discount the contribution of numbers in analysing qualitative data. When A.E. Maxwell, the Senior Lecturer in Statistics at the Institute of Psychiatry in the University of London, wrote about 'Analysing Qualitative Data' three decades ago, he explained to his readers that his book could have been called 'Chi-Square tests' (Maxwell 1961). At that time, it was taken for granted that qualitative analysis meant the statistical analysis of variables which were not amenable to more quantitative measurement. Now, we take for granted precisely the opposite: that no book on qualitative data analysis will be concerned with the statistical analysis. This shift in paradigm has had some virtue, for it has placed more emphasis on the meaning and interpretation of data through the processes of description and classification. However, this emphasis also exaggerates distinctions between alternative methods which ought more properly to be viewed as partners than as competitors.

It may indeed be difficult if not irrelevant to count examples, if our data is entirely descriptive and we are analysing singularities rather than looking for patterns within our data. However, as I suggested earlier, even 'singularities' are likely to be embedded in a language full of more or less implicit comparisons and classifications. My daughter cannot tell me what happened at school today without them. Classification is not just a product of structured interview schedules; it is the stuff of everyday thinking. One of the main aims of analysis may be to recognize and make explicit the classifications used by subjects. Another may be the development of the analyst's own classification of the data. But once data has been classified, it can be counted.

Enumeration is implicit in the idea of measurement as recognition of a limit or boundary. Once we recognize the boundaries to some phenomenon, we can recognize and therefore enumerate examples of that phenomenon. Once we know what a 'school' is, we can count schools. Indeed, it may be hard to describe and compare qualities entirely without enumerating them. To identify a boundary to our concept of a 'school', we may need to consider more than one example. If for many examples we can recognize some characteristics commonly associated with this concept, then we may have more confidence in assigning this category. The development of categories is rooted in repeated observations, and this entails enumeration of what data does or does not 'fit'. Therefore enumeration is not a luxury extra, but integral to how we classify data.

Statistics is just another form of counting. However, statistical procedures often require assumptions about the probability of obtaining responses which can only be satisfied when using random samples, typically through the survey method. Where we have satisfied these assumptions, there is no reason why we should not adopt the appropriate procedures, whether for testing for associations between variables or generalizing from a random sample to a larger population. Where we have not satisfied these assumptions, we can still use statistics to examine the quantitative aspects of our data, for example, to be more rigorous in recognizing or creating classification schemes. Some simple statistical procedures, for analysing frequencies and cross-tabulations, may prove useful in analysing even the most idiosyncratic and unstructured data. This use of 'quasi-statistics' (Becker and Geer 1982) can enhance the rigour and power of a qualitative analysis – providing always that we keep in mind just what the numbers mean.

It is more useful to define qualitative data in ways which encourage partnership rather than divorce between different research methods. In suggesting that quantitative data deals with numbers and qualitative data deals with meanings, I do not mean to set them in opposition. They are better thought of as mutually dependent. Number depends on meaning, but in a sense meaning also depends on number. Measurement at all levels embraces both a qualitative and a quantitative aspect. However, the nature of this relationship changes as we move up the measurement hierarchy. The more stable and fixed the meanings we can assign to data, the more we can use with confidence the elegance and power of mathematics. The more ambiguous and elastic our concepts, the less possible it is to quantify our data in a meaningful way. We can use a T'ai-chi T'u diagram (Figure 2.7) to symbolize this relationship, as this depicts a dynamic balance of apparently opposing forces (cf. Capra 1983: 119–120), in this case qualitative and quantitative.

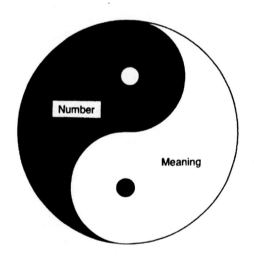

*Figure 2.7* Quantitative and qualitative data in dynamic balance

The diagram reflects the mutual dependence of both types of data. It indicates that meanings cannot be ignored when we are dealing with numbers, and numbers cannot be ignored when we are dealing with meanings. Each complements the other, though at lower levels of measurement questions of meaning are uppermost, while at higher levels of measurement, questions of number loom largest.

- Quantitative data deals with numbers
- Qualitative data deals with meanings
- This includes the meanings of those we are researching
- Meaning is expressed through actions as well as text (or images)
- Meanings are not a prerogative of unstructured methods or unstructured data
- Meanings and numbers are important at all levels of measurement
- Numbers must be based on meaningful conceptualizations
- Meaningful conceptualization is informed by numbers

# Chapter 3

# What is qualitative analysis?

You can't make an omelette without breaking eggs. And – to extend the aphorism – you can't make an omelette without beating the eggs together. 'Analysis' too involves breaking data down into bits, and then 'beating' the bits together. The word derives from the prefix 'ana' meaning 'above', and the Greek root 'lysis' meaning 'to break up or dissolve' (Bohm 1983: 125 and 156). It is a process of resolving data into its constituent components, to reveal its characteristic elements and structure. Without analysis, we would have to rely entirely on impressions and intuitions about the data as a whole. While our impressions and intuitions certainly have their place in analysing data, we can also benefit from the more rigorous and logical procedures of analysis.

Like the omelette, the result of this process of breaking down and beating together is something quite different from what we started with. But that is not surprising, since, after all, the aim of analysis is not just to describe our data. We want to describe the objects or events to which our data refers. Such description forms the bedrock of any science. And often we want to do more than describe: we want to interpret, to explain, to understand – perhaps even to predict. We want to know how, and why, as well as what. The way we do that is to analyse our data. In doing so, we go beyond our initial description; and we transform our data into something it was not.

Description lays the basis for analysis, but analysis also lays the basis for further description. Through analysis, we can obtain a fresh view of our data. We can progress from initial description, through the process of breaking data down into bits, and seeing how these bits interconnect, to a new account based on our reconceptualization of the data. We break down the data in order to classify it, and the concepts we create or employ in classifying the data, and the connections we make between these concepts, provide the basis of a fresh description (Figure 3.1).

The core of qualitative analysis lies in these related processes of describing phenomena, classifying it, and seeing how our concepts interconnect. Let us look at each of these processes in turn.

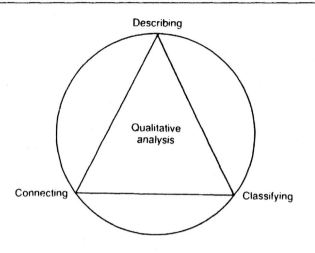

*Figure 3.1* Qualitative analysis as a circular process

## DESCRIPTION

To describe is 'to set forth in words', to 'recite the characteristics' of a person, object or event. Description has a low status in social science. Descriptive studies can be contrasted unfavourably with more analytic and theoretically oriented research, as though description is a 'low level' activity hardly worth attention. This is somewhat ironic, since description permeates scientific theory and without it theories could have neither meaning and nor application. Ironically, the physicists, who spend much of their time absorbed in efforts to 'describe' the origins and evolution of the universe or the characteristics of the 'subatomic' world, seem to have no such aversion to description; indeed, they seem to approach the task with relish.

The first step in qualitative analysis is to develop thorough and comprehensive descriptions of the phenomenon under study. This has become known as 'thick' description (Geerz 1973, Denzin 1978). In contrast to 'thin' description which merely states 'facts', Denzin suggests that a 'thick' description includes information about the context of an act, the intentions and meanings that organize action, and its subsequent evolution (Denzin 1978: 33). Thus description encompasses the context of action, the intentions of the actor, and the process in which action is embedded. Qualitative analysis often aims to provide 'thorough' descriptions (to adopt a more apt adjective than 'thick') in each of these areas. Thinking of observation as an abstraction from the flow of experience, these various aspects of description can be depicted as in Figure 3.2.

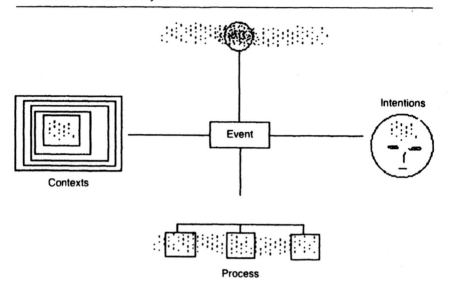

*Figure 3.2* Three aspects of description in qualitative analysis

## CONTEXTS

The need to take account of contexts is a recurrent theme in qualitative analysis. Contexts are important as a means of situating action, and of grasping its wider social and historical import. This can require detailed descriptions of the social setting within which action occurs; the relevant social contexts may be a group, organization, institution, culture or society; the time frame within which action takes place; the spatial context; the network of social relationships, and so on.

Suppose we want to understand the role of personal ads in dating behaviour. We may want to describe the relevant social contexts, including the normal patterns of dating behaviour, the advertising medium, how personal ads are submitted, and so on. These patterns of interaction may be specific to particular spatial contexts – compare urban and rural settings, or New York and the Isle of Skye. They may also vary over time, for example, reflecting changing social mores about marriage and promiscuity. To understand the role of personal ads in dating behaviour, we may therefore include much complex detail about apparently ordinary and perhaps even seemingly superficial aspects of social settings.

In a more literal way, contexts can also be seen as a key to meaning, since meaning can be conveyed 'correctly' only if context is also understood. This is most obviously true of pronouns where the meaning depends entirely on information already given or known from the context – such as the meaning of the word 'this' at the start of this sentence. But communication in general involves inferring meaning from the context in which it occurs (Sperber and Wilson 1986). When I say 'coffee?' to my wife at 11 a.m., she may infer that I am asking her to make, or that I am offering to make, or that I have just made her, a cup of coffee. The meaning of my question may be clear from the context in which it is asked – whether I am empty-handed, headed for the kitchen, or have a cup of coffee to hand.

Mostly we take context as given. Communication errors can occur when a 'wrong' context is assumed, sometimes with humorous results. Take the exhortation: 'leave your clothes here and spend the afternoon having a good time' – which appeared on a sign in a laundry in Rome. Without knowledge of the context, we might mistakenly infer that we are being exhorted to strip off and 'have a good time'. However, knowing the context obliges us to infer a rather more pedestrian meaning!

Although it is convenient to write about taking account of 'the' context of communication, this may be misleading. There is not just one context, but many. Take that cup of coffee, for example. In the cultural context of tea and coffee breaks, my offer fits a normal and taken for granted pattern of behaviour. Imagine I had offered a whisky instead! Or take the social context. My wife's inference only makes sense if we are at home. If we were out shopping, she would take my statement as an offer to buy a coffee, not to make it. And is the coffee to be a gift, or subject to some sort of economic exchange?

The meaning of a communication often depends, therefore, on knowing the relevant context(s) in which it is made. Note that we communicate through action as well as words. If I take the coffee to my wife and leave it with her, and take mine into my study, I communicate a quite different meaning than if I put both coffees on the coffee table and sit down on the sofa obviously expecting a chat. Despite the old aphorism that 'actions speak louder than words', social scientists sometimes write as though the world were inhabited by creatures who only speak or write. They don't smile, scowl, spit, slam doors or communicate meaning in the many other ways which we experience in our daily lives. Communication through action is no less interesting, effective or bizarre than communication through language. (Anyone who has watched how soccer players communicate with each other after one of their team mates has scored a goal will know what I mean.)

Since meaning can vary with context, communication can convey more than one meaning. Take the story of Jack and the Beanstalk, for example. In a literary context, this can be understood as a straightforward children's tale of Jack's adventures with the giant at the top of the beanstalk. In a psychoanalytic context, the story can acquire a deeper meaning, in which Jack's adventures convey some key stages or tasks in the development of the child's psyche (Bettelheim 1991: 183–193). Thus the exchange of the cow for magic beans symbolizes the end of oral dependency and expulsion from an infantile paradise; and the phallic beanstalk symbolizes social and sexual development, which when used to resolve oedipal conflicts with the father (the giant in the story), leads finally to development as a mature and independent human being. Considered as a symbolic representation of the problems a child must solve on the road to maturity, each detail of the story acquires another meaning. Jack steals successively a bag of gold, a hen that lays golden eggs, and a golden harp. Each represents a higher stage in development – the harp for example symbolizing progress from material to aesthetic concerns. (I hesitate to suggest a symbolic meaning for the climax of the story, when Jack cuts down the beanstalk.)

Such meanings need not – indeed, Bettelheim argues, must not – be explicit for the child to absorb the underlying message of this and other fairy-tales. Advertising is another medium in which the symbolic character of communication may be more significant than the explicit content of the message. In this case, the 'hidden' message may be intentional: the advertiser deliberately plays upon our identification with certain characters, or the positive associations invoked by particular images. Here, contexts are consciously designed to evoke multiple meanings. But in general, communication occurs in a variety of indeterminate contexts, and multiple meanings remain implicit rather than explicit. Feminism has made us acutely aware, for example, of the meanings implicit in communication considered in the context of gender. Apparently 'innocent' language – such as the preferential use of the masculine pronoun 'he' – conveys a meaning which only becomes evident when the context of gender is rendered explicit through criticism.

This situation may seem unsatisfactory, since it makes meaning contingent on how we choose to observe it. By shifting contexts, we can undermine or alter the original or intended import of a communication. For example, take the following sign at the entrance to a Bangkok temple: 'It is forbidden to enter a woman even a foreigner if dressed as a man.' Despite the lack of grammar, it is obvious that this means that women – even if they are foreigners and dressed as men – are forbidden to enter the temple. If we shift from a religious to a sexual context, however, we can introduce a new and more humorous interpretation, in which it is women rather than temples we are forbidden to enter. Is this new interpretation a misinterpretation? Yes – if we were foolish enough attribute this meaning to the sign-writer. No – if we attribute it to the reader. This new interpretation is not 'wrong' even though it does not coincide with the meaning intended by the sign-writer. It is a perfectly reasonable and legitimate interpretation; and indeed, we may imagine a (male) traveller, oblivious of the religious context, understanding (if not acting upon) the sign in just this way!

Communication of meaning is an action which requires – at a minimum – both an initiator and a receiver, and neither has a monopoly on the meaning of what passes between them. The contexts of initiator and receiver are both relevant to understanding, and meaning is therefore not a fixed 'thing' but always subject to negotiation between observers.

It is comforting to realize that the situation I am describing has its parallel in modern physics, where the 'reality' that is observed cannot be separated from the context of the observation and the action of the observer. Space and time have become conditional on the speed and position of the observer in relation to the events being observed. This does not preclude or deny a reality separate from our observations of it. But reality in physics is no longer a realm about which we can obtain information independently of the observer. If you find this hard to believe, imagine an astronaut watching a colleague playing darts while orbiting earth. To the astronaut, the dart travels a few metres, while to the observer on earth it travels several miles; and since the speed of light is constant, and light takes longer to reach the earth observer than the astronaut, not only does the dart's flight occur at a different time, but also the time it takes seems shorter to the astronaut than to the observer on earth.

However, this does not mean that observations are arbitrary. Although observations of the same event by different observers may no longer agree, observations are related in the sense that once an observer's speed and position are known in relation to the event, we can establish how that event will be seen by the observer (Hawking 1988: 22). In other words, interpretation depends on context, but this does not preclude an objective appraisal of how events are interpreted.

Now imagine a game of darts (on earth this time) being played in the local pub, in a TV quiz show, or in a professional darts tournament. The significance of a throw may vary dramatically according to the contexts in which it is made. For the amateurs in the pub, it may be no more than a bit of fun. For the contestants, it may be an opportunity to enjoy the limelight. For the professionals, it may be humdrum routine, or perhaps a critical turning point in their career. Although the meaning varies according to context, if we knew the relevant contexts we could provide an objective description of the game.

In qualitative analysis, our position and procedures parallel those of physics even if our measurements lack a similar precision. Meaning depends on context, and has to be related to the positions and perspectives of different observers. We can make mistakes in attributing particular meanings to particular observers, but the biggest mistake would be to imagine that meaning can somehow be understood independently of the contexts in which it is observed.

## INTENTIONS

Ambiguity of meaning is a pervasive characteristic of communication, most dramatically demonstrated in the language of humour. Parody, puns, *double-entendre,* irony – humour often works by conveying an implicit message. If this message doesn't register with its recipient, then the humorist fails to communicate his or her meaning successfully. We don't get the joke. (This is different from seeing the joke, but not finding it funny.) In humour, there is no recovery from this disaster, and the joke falls flat. But in social research, we can always ask humorists to explain themselves.

In qualitative analysis there is a strong emphasis on describing the world as it is perceived by different observers. For some, this is the hallmark of the qualitative approach, distinguishing it from supposedly 'positivist' social science. Setting aside this ideological debate about 'legitimate' methods, we can certainly acknowledge that qualitative analysis is usually concerned with how actors define situations, and explain the motives which govern their actions. Though as researchers we may develop our own concepts for analysing these actions, we want to ensure that this relates to intentions of the actors involved.

If we were studying dating and mating through the personal ads, then it would obviously be useful to describe the intentions of the advertisers in submitting ads and of respondents in replying to them. The intentions and perceptions of subjects often enjoy a privileged position in qualitative research, because of the access they can give us to the meaning of action for particular observers. But this does not entail that meaning is reduced to a personal matter. For example, the meanings of our personal ads can be examined through a variety of contexts, including the 'rules of the game', its cultural significance, its social organization and its psychological or economic rewards as well as its personal meaning for participants or audience. Often our description of these various facets may depend on what the subjects of our research can tell us about them. But there are also other sources which – through observation and experience – may give access to the meanings invested in social action.

There is another sense, too, in which meaning cannot be reduced to a personal matter. If meaning is inherently ambivalent and context-dependent, we cannot rely on our subjects' intentions as an unequivocal guide to interpretation. Our subjects perceive and define situations, including their own intentions, according to their understanding of their own motivations, and of the contexts in which they act. Neither motivations nor contexts are self-evident, and we have to allow for the usual mix of ignorance and self-deception, delusions and lies. We may sometimes behave as rational actors whose actions are governed by knowledge, but we also sometimes behave as social actors whose actions are dictated by drives, impulses, appetites, instincts and intuitions. Alongside the conscious intellect we must recognize the subconscious will. The Freudian division between id, ego and superego emphasizes the inconsistencies and contradictions which characterize the human personality and shape human action. Perhaps nowhere is this more evident than in the potential for misunderstandings, confusion and conflict associated with dating and mating.

We also know that strong social forces – obsequiousness towards power, pressures for conformity, fears of embarrassment or conflict – can distort behaviour and disguise individual motivations. On a more positive note, deception and denial can also derive from more generous qualities – such as politeness, civility, and the desire to protect others. Perhaps a mixture of these motives explains why those who exercise power rarely receive an undisguised reaction from those on its receiving end.

Thus we cannot rely on subjects to give a rational account of their intentions, nor can we infer intentions unequivocally from their behaviour. Neither in action nor in intention can we find an unequivocal guide to interpreting behaviour, and such interpretations are therefore inherently contestable. The communication of meaning is always negotiable.

## PROCESS

Since meaning is negotiable, it can also evolve and change over time. An orientation to process is the third characteristic we noted of qualitative description. Qualitative research often seeks to illuminate the ways individuals interact to sustain or change social situations. Qualitative data may sometimes be produced through snapshot methods, such as a one-off survey; but more typically they are a product of data collection over a period, such as the material produced through participant observation or successive interviewing. Unlike the snapshot survey, these methods produce data which can illuminate more directly the interactions and interconnections between action and consequence. The data is descriptive of social relationships and interchanges which unfold in the succession of actions and events in which the actors are engaged.

The significance of process in qualitative analysis is also exemplified in interactive methods through which qualitative data is often produced. Data collection can itself be conceived as an interactive process through which the researcher struggles to elicit meaningful interpretations of social action. Analysis often proceeds in tandem with data collection, rather than commencing on its completion. The resulting analysis is contingent in character, since it in turn stimulates and is modified by the collection and investigation of further data. The researcher meanwhile becomes a participant in his or her own research project, for their own interpretations and actions become a legitimate object of subsequent analysis. Information on the researcher's own behaviour and thinking, in the form of fieldnotes, memos, diary or whatever, can become a vital source of data for the analysis.

The idea of process is bound up with the idea of change, and the circumstances, conditions, actions and mechanisms through which change comes about. Let us return to the example of dating and mating through the personal ads. We may be able to identify a number of stages in the process, from first thinking of putting in an ad, through submitting the ad, receiving a reply and making initial contact, to subsequent rejection – or romance. Or we can identify and examine the evolution of events in terms of key incidents, such as the first quarrel or first kiss. We can focus on the complex interplay of factors which produce a particular result. By describing this process, we can obtain a sense of how events originate and evolve, and their shifting significance for those involved. Process refers to movement and change over time. In place of a static description, we can develop a more dynamic account of events.

The temptation to divide process into different stages or phases is a strong one, but not always appropriate (cf. Strauss and Corbin 1990: 156). Phasing tends to imply a product or end-point as the culmination of process: for, example, either rejection or romance. However, process need not imply progress towards a conclusion, but simply a significant change in the pattern of events.

I suggested earlier that action is a medium for communicating meaning. But it would be wrong to reduce action to the meanings which it may import. This would imply that we live in the world entirely through our minds, whereas the reality is that we live predominantly through our bodies. We have a physical presence in the world, which commits us to action independently of what that action means or how it may be interpreted. If I fall asleep during a seminar, it may mean by accident or design, an embarrassment or an insult. Or it may be that I am just tired. To survive, we have to eat, sleep and attend to a variety of bodily functions, such as keeping warm. We may or may not invest these activities with a variety of meanings, but act we must.

Indeed, we are condemned to act throughout life, if only in opting between a series of limited choices, the character of which may be beyond our control. We may act on impulse, or through force of habit. We should not assume that all behaviour is purposeful, especially when we know how difficult it can be to establish any clear sense of purpose. This point is often made in a political context, where policy-making is often perceived as a process of 'muddling through' rather than rational action. It is easier to agree on what to do than why to do it, and many policies attract consensus because people can agree over means despite confusion or conflict over ends.

The other side of this coin is the familiar problem of 'unintended consequences.' Pregnancy is a classic example where the result may not have been anticipated or intended in the original act. Like true love, the paths of life rarely run smoothly. Promises are broken, ambitions unfulfilled, dreams shattered. We find opportunities and rewards where we least expect them. Even if our purposes are clear, it does not follow that we can anticipate all the consequences of our action, nor that our actions will secure the intended consequences. Thus President Gorbachev initiated policies in the Soviet Union which culminated in its demise, a result which was far from his original intentions.

In focusing on process, ther we shift attention from context and intention to action and consequence. In doing so, we need to take account of the material as well as social conditions and consequences of behaviour (Sayer 1992: 33). The evolution of the Soviet Union into a Commonwealth of Independent States is affected by material conditions, such as the abundance of nuclear weapons and the shortage of food, as well as by nationalist ideologies and ethnic rivalries. Such material factors are not independent of how society produces and perceives them, but neither are they reducible to their social significance. If I die of hunger, I die.

---

- Meanings are context-dependent
- Meanings are always negotiable between different observers
- In social science we can ask subjects what they mean
- Subjects' intentions are not always a reliable guide to interpretation
- Process involves analysing changes over time
- Change can be analysed through phases, key incidents or the complex interplay of factors
- Material as well as social factors affect change

---

Qualitative description is likely to encompass all these elements in its effort to provide an adequate basis for interpretation and explanation of social action. One distinctive feature of description is its integrative function. By summarizing data, for example, we strip away unnecessary detail and delineate more clearly the more central characteristics of the data. Moreover, it is in pulling together and relating these central charac-teristics through a reasoned account that description acquires its unity and force. The terms of a description may have little meaning except as integral aspects of the story as a whole. We 'tell a story' about the data, and use a range of techniques – such as summarizing events, focusing on key episodes, delineating roles and characters, setting out chronological sequence – to construct an illuminating narrative.

## CLASSIFICATION

Interpretation and explanation are the responsibility of the analyst, and it is his or her task to develop a meaningful and adequate account; the data merely provide a basis for the analysis, they do not dictate it (Burgess 1982). This requires the development of a conceptual framework through which the actions or events we are researching can be rendered intelligible. To interpret is to make action meaningful to others, not just or even necessarily within the terms used by the actors themselves. To explain is to account for action, not just or necessarily through reference to the actors' intentions. It requires the development of conceptual tools through which to apprehend the significance of social action and how actions interrelate.

We can grasp the nature of this task more readily if we imagine it is like the completion of a jigsaw puzzle. (A more apt analogy might be a three-dimensional puzzle, such as one of those wooden blocks which come apart with deceptive ease and fit together with frustrating difficulty, since we can represent time and process through the third dimension.) The only point of taking the puzzle apart, of course, is to find a way of putting it together again. The finished puzzle represents the results of our research, and through it we can identify different facets of social action and their mutual connection. Qualitative analysis involves more than fitting the bits together, however. Our data start as a seamless sequence, from which we ourselves must first of all cut out all the bits of the puzzle. We must cut them out in ways which correspond to the separate facets of the social reality we are investigating, but which also allow us to put them together again to produce an overall picture.

How do we do jigsaws? There are some pieces of puzzle which are so unique that we can see straight away their place in the picture. These exceptions apart, classification is the key to the process. Before I can fit a piece into the puzzle, I have to assess its characteristics and assign it to some category or another. This bit is a corner, that's an edge, this blue bit is sky, that brown bit is earth, and so on. The categories we use are organizing tools which allow us to sort out the heap of bits according to relevant characteristics. Gradually, all the blue bits together may make the sky, the brown bits the earth, the green bits a forest, and so on until we have built up a complete picture. The categories through which I initially organize the bits – flat-edged, blue, brown and green – lead on towards a new classification – sky, earth, forest – in terms of which I can finally describe the picture.

Without classifying the data, we have no way of knowing what it is that we are analysing. Nor can we make meaningful comparisons between different bits of data. It would be wrong to say that before we can analyse data, we must classify it, for classifying the data is an integral part of the analysis: it lays the conceptual foundations upon which interpretation and explanation are based. This process is not unfamiliar, for classification is part and parcel of the processes of practical reasoning in everyday life, though (hopefully) social scientists may bring a more rigorous and systematic approach to it. For example, when I take the bus into town to buy slippers in a shoe shop, my action is based on a whole series of (implicit) classifications (Table 3.1). These (implicit) classifications allow us to make sense of our experience and communicate intelligibly about it.

Since I suggested classification can be seen as a form of practical reasoning,

Table 3.1 Implicit classifications in everyday life

| Designated class | Other classes |
|---|---|
| Bus | Other forms of transport |
| Town | Other forms of settlement |
| To buy | Other forms of acquisition/exchange |
| Slippers | Other types of footwear |
| Shoe shop | Other kinds of shop |

let us take a practical problem as an example. Suppose we want to find a prospective partner, and decide to use the 'Lonely Hearts' column in our local newspaper. In Illustration 3.1, I have taken some examples from a current edition of my local newspaper, replacing the original box numbers with fictional names. How can we choose a likely prospect?. We might rely on impression and intuition, and make a selection on this basis. But being social scientists, let us opt for a more systematic approach.

Illustration 3.1 Personal ads

| | |
|---|---|
| GOOD-LOOKING professional male, 44, into most sports, theatre, eating out and flying, wishes to meet sincere, caring, mature lady, 30–50, for friendship, possible romance. [Alex] | PUSSYCAT seeks tomcat for exchanging pedigrees. Must be well groomed, tame and handsome, aged between 18–27. Would like nights out, friendship and cosy nights in. No scrooges please! [Alice] |
| GORGEOUS GEMINI seeks sexy Sagittarian, for fun nights out; no expense spared for £2.00; who could resist; hope I'm still 26 before you answer; photo appreciated. [Pat] | LONELY TALL dark male, 24, seeks fun loving, non-smoking female of similar age who enjoys cinema, music, sports, nights out and in, for possible romance. Photo appreciated. [Neil] |
| GORGEOUS (immodest or deluded?) single professional female, 22, seeks single, professional, handsome hunk to restore my faith in human nature; photograph preferred but not essential. [Morag] | LIFE BEGINS at 40. Are you fit? Glamorous granny seeks grandad to go out and show them how to jive or stay in and babysit and find romance. [Leslie] |
| SLIM 34 year old female, 5'8" tall, reasonably nice looking, seeks tall handsome gent who likes eating out and socialising. Must have good sense of humour and like children. [Fiona] | SCORPIO MALE tall, slim, handsome and fun loving, seeks good looking professional female for nights out, wild times, romance and fun. Photo please. [Alistair] |

Even in this small selection of ads there are some surprises. For example, Morag tells us she's single; we can presume that not many of those advertising in the personal columns would tell us otherwise! On the other hand, Pat doesn't tell us whether s/he is male or female. Someone may be in for a shock. Perhaps gender doesn't matter to Pat, though most of the other advertisers seem to think it does!

Most of the information supplied by these erstwhile suppliants is qualitative; some, such as age, is quantitative. Incidentally, this balance of information offered in the personal columns mirrors that available in most other areas of social life. The qualitative data gives us information about a whole range of 'qualities', such as whether the individual is 'sincere', 'sexy', 'fun-loving' and so on. Much of this information is straightforwardly descriptive: it allows us to form an idea of the individual's character and interests.

The personal ads are literally 'unclassified'; but in order to choose a mate we can sort the data according to relevant characteristics, i.e. we can classify it. The first thing we might do is assign individuals to various categories, according to character, interests or the like; for example, this one is 'lonely', that one 'likes eating out'; this one is 'glamorous', that one 'likes nights out'. By sorting the information into different categories, we can make comparisons between cases much more effectively. If we want someone interested in sports, for example, we can identify all those who like sports, and then compare them. Or we may want to discount all those who fall within a particular category, for example, such as those who suggest a photo would be appreciated. We may be interested in all those who belong to a particular category or combination of categories, such as those who express interest in 'possible romance'. There is no obvious limit to the number of categories, and no reason why they shouldn't overlap. You can enjoy as many hobbies as you like, and if you like 'fun nights out' or 'cosy nights in' that certainly doesn't preclude any other activities (only hinted at) of which politeness prohibits mention. Few advertisers frankly admit to an interest in sex!

We can picture categorization as a process of funnelling the data into relevant categories for analysis (Figure 3.3). The data loses its original shape, but we gain by organizing it in ways which are more useful for our analysis.

I have chosen a straightforward example, but categories may have to be more sensitive to capture the subtleties of the data. For example, the style of the ad may be as revealing as the content. How can this be categorized? What do different styles convey? And are there oblique messages which the advertisers are trying to convey? Just asking these questions is sufficient to underline that categorization is a conceptual process. It involves ideas and it requires thought, sometimes a great deal of it.

Once the data has been organized into categories, we can retrieve it in a variety of ways. We may want to find someone who has a number of characteristics we find desirable in a prospective mate. We may want to exclude anyone with a characteristic or combination of characteristics we dislike. We want to restrict our search to those individuals who share a particular set of characteristics. From a practical point of view, categorizing the data allows us to make comparisons more effectively and hence locate individuals who seem most likely to fit the bill. From a research point of

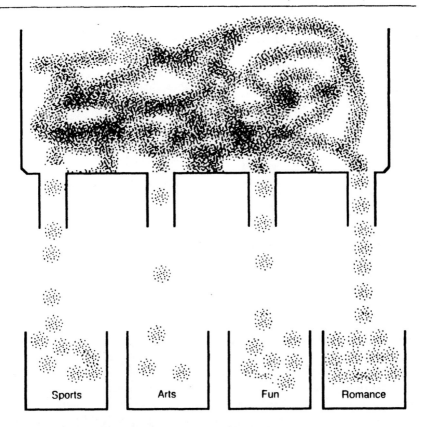

*Figure 3.3* Categorizing as a method of funnelling data

view, we are more likely to be interested in the overall picture which emerges of the dating and mating game. As we shall see, classifying the data therefore lays the basis for making new connections between different bits of data.

So far we have used inclusive categories: we have created categories to include all those who are sporting, fun-loving or whatever. For some data we may want to develop a higher level of classification. Suppose we are particularly interested in how our advertisers describe their personal appearance. We might begin by using categories based on these descriptions, such as 'tall' or 'glamorous'. Although these are both aspects of appearance, they relate to different dimensions: physical and aesthetic. We can group all the other adjectives which 'belong' to these dimensions: 'short' is a physical description, 'gorgeous' an aesthetic one; and so on. Within each dimension, we may begin to sort the categories into groups: for example, 'gorgeous' and 'glamorous' may be taken as indicators of 'good looks', while 'not bad looking' may suggest something rather less becoming, perhaps 'plain'. We may also define the boundaries between categories more precisely, identifying clearer guidelines for allocating data to one category or another. Additional data may oblige us to make further refinements to our categories: for example, 'fairly attractive', may not fit any existing category and require a new one. Logically, I might also identify a category 'ugly', though regardless of their physical appearance few advertisers are likely to present such a personal description! While we would certainly be rash to take an advertiser's description at face value, by classifying the data in this way we can begin to distinguish effectively amongst their subjective aesthetic assessments.

Eventually, through a more rigorous process of conceptualization, we may be able to classify some of the data at the nominal or ordinal levels. Such variables allow us to classify data in a more coherent and systematic way, since classification tells us not only what falls within categories but also something about the boundaries between them.

Starting with two inclusive categories, the clarification and definition of related concepts can result in the identification of nominal variables with exclusive and exhaustive values. As Figure 3.4 suggests, this process is one of distinguishing and grouping categories. To define the limits of categories more precisely, we must first conceptualize the relationship between them more clearly. Distinctions between categories can only be drawn by relating the categories in terms of some underlying concept. Moving through these different levels of measurement requires increasing conceptual rigour.

Some data we can immediately classify at a nominal level: gender is an obvious example. We can treat gender as a nominal variable with the mutually exclusive and exhaustive values; unless you are hermaphrodite, you cannot be both 'male' and 'female', at least in a biological if not in a social or psychological sense. Nor can you be anything else. Notice, though, that we can treat gender as a nominal variable only within a given conceptual context.

We may even construct an ordinal variable, distinguishing for example those for whom a photo is 'essential', those for whom it is 'preferred but not essential' and those who do not want one at all. In other words, we can rank the individuals according to the degree of interest they profess in receiving a photograph; Alistair expresses more interest than the others in our example. This classification gives us information about what falls within categories, the boundaries between them, and how the categories are ordered in relation to each other.

Classification is a conceptual process. When we classify, we do two things. We don't just break the data up into bits, we also assign these bits to categories or classes which bring these bits together again, if in a novel way. Thus all the bits that 'belong' to a particular category are brought together; and in the process, we begin to discriminate more clearly between the criteria for allocating data to one category or another. Then some cate-

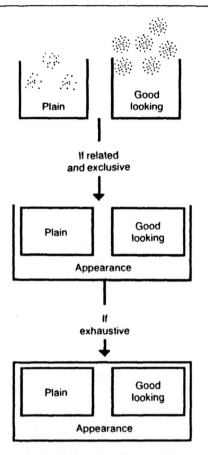

*Figure 3.4* Derivation of nominal variables with exclusive and exhaustive values

gories may be subdivided, and others subsumed under more abstract categories. The boundaries between these categories may be defined more precisely. Logic may require the addition of new categories, not present in the data, to produce a comprehensive classification. Thus the process of classifying the data is already creating a conceptual framework through which the bits of data can be brought together again in an analytically useful way.

Self-satisfaction apart, there is no point in re-inventing the wheel. If I could bring an existing classification scheme to bear on this data, for example one based on a culturally and psychologically rooted theory of beauty, then I would do so. Conjuring up concepts is challenging work, and there is little point in adding to the burden by refusing to sharpen existing tools. Naturally, such tools must be appropriate, or adapted, to the task in hand.

Note that classification cannot be neutral; it is always classification for a purpose. In classifying this data, I am guided by the practical purpose of finding a prospective partner. I want to make comparisons which will allow me to select the most promising amongst these advertisers. As a social scientist, I will be guided by my research objectives. Since I can only achieve these objectives through analysing the data, this is (or should be) an interactive process, in which my research objectives are in turn guided by conceptual clarification I achieve through classifying the data.

Graphic forms of representation can provide an appropriate set of tools for constructing classification schema, such as those depicting logical relations of hierarchy and subordination between concepts. Returning to our personal ads, we can show in this way some of the concepts used in analysing how advertisers present themselves (Figure 3.5).

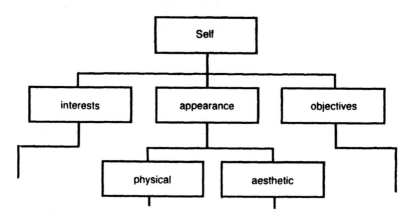

*Figure 3.5* Formal connections between concepts

The connections between the concepts are 'formal' in the sense that they refer to logical relations of similarity and difference, or inclusion and exclusion, rather than any 'substantive' connections between them. The latter refers to connections such as causality and can connect things which are formally quite unrelated, such as the relationship between a dog and a lamppost. To consider the latter, we have to turn to the ways we can analyse substantive connections like causality.

---

- Classifying involves breaking up data and bringing it together again
- Classifying the data lays the conceptual foundations for analysis
- Classification is a familiar process of practical reasoning
- Categorizing and retrieving data provides a basis for comparison
- Redefining categories can produce more rigorous conceptualization
- Classifying should always be guided by research objectives

## MAKING CONNECTIONS

According to Alvin Toffler, we are so good at dissecting data that we often forget how to put the pieces back together again (Coveney and Highfield 1991: 296). This problem only arises, however, if we forget that description and classification are not ends in themselves but must serve an overriding purpose, namely to produce an account of our analysis. Concepts are the building blocks of our analysis. In qualitative analysis, the first task is to make these building blocks. But building requires more than blocks. The blocks must be brought together. Connecting concepts is the analytic equivalent of putting mortar between the building blocks. Classification lays the foundation for identifying substantive connections. But now we are no longer concerned about similarities and differences between the blocks. It doesn't matter whether one block looks like another or not, what counts is how (or whether) the blocks interact to produce a building (Figure 3.6).

How can we identify substantive connections? One common method is through identifying associations between different variables. Once the data is classified, we can examine regularities, variations and singularities in the data. In studying the personal ads, we may find that those who describe themselves as good-looking tend also to express particular interests, such as an interest in forming romantic attachments. If so, we have identified a 'pattern' within the data. By studying such correlations between different categories we can build up a picture of our data which is both clearer and more complex than our initial impressions. We can begin to fit the different parts of the jigsaw together. For example, we may find that the sports-lovers are looking for company, the arts-lovers are looking for companionship, the fun-lovers are looking for romance and the home-lovers are looking for partners. By looking for such patterns, we can find fresh perspectives on the data.

Where we find regularities, we can also find variations and exceptions. Perhaps some of our sports-lovers just want company, but others are looking for something more serious. We can compare them, and perhaps identify some common factors which could 'explain' this variation. For example, perhaps all the sports-lovers are men, and that may explain why they are reluctant to suggest (or admit) they want a more serious relationship? By examining the association between different variables, we can begin to identify connections between them.

*Figure 3.6* Formal and substantive connections between building blocks

Perhaps only one of our sports-lovers wants a partner. We can study this exception to the rule. We have already considered the search for singularities, in our hunt for that paragon of all virtues who fulfils our wildest dreams of a potential mate. In social research as in life, there are key moments, individuals, and episodes, whether because they epitomize a theme or stand out as exceptions to it. We may have noticed these at first glance, but once the data is classified, we can examine more precisely the connections between 'key' episodes and the patterns they exemplify or contradict. What exactly are the characteristics of our ideal mate? And how many of these characteristics does s/he share with other individuals in our sample? Just how typical or exceptional is our singularity?

Gradually our data acquire a new complexion, as we build up a clearer picture of the main characteristics, good and bad, of the advertisers in our sample, and the associations between them. We can enhance our identification of patterns in the data by analysing the frequencies with which characteristics occur, and even by cross-tabulating different characteristics. Once data have been categorized they can be counted, and data which can be enumerated can be analysed statistically, if only at a simple level. This provides one means of identifying or confirming regularities and variations within the data. We can infer connections between concepts by examining how categories combine. Are fun-lovers also art-lovers? Do more men than women like sport? Can we differentiate between different types, in terms of clusters of characteristics? And do these different types attract similar types, or are they looking for opposites? Through this kind of analysis, we can 'interrogate' our data (Richards and Richards 1991) and explore the connections between our categories.

This approach to connecting concepts is powerful enough in its way, but it examines relationships as though they were external and contingent. We may or may not find that art-lovers are also fun-lovers. And if they are, we are no nearer to understanding why this connection apparently exists between them. I say 'apparently' because, of course, we have to allow for the possibility of spurious correlations and intervening variables. The association of one variable with another is not sufficient ground for inferring a causal or any other connection between them. In effect, we have to interpret numbers in terms of meanings. Only if we can identify an intelligible meaning does the numerical correlation between different variables acquire significance.

In qualitative analysis, we can at least return to the data to see whether such a connection can reasonably be inferred. For example, suppose we observe that most male advertisers receive replies from women, while most women advertisers receive replies from men. In other words, there is a high correlation between the gender of the advertiser and the gender of the respondent. Now, following the approach outlined above, we could check whether there is any evidence in our data explaining why these events (the advert and the reply) should be correlated in this way. And of course, we are likely to find such evidence in the expressed sexual preferences of advertisers and respondents. But in any case, we would have no difficulty in accepting this correlation as evidence of a significant connection between the events of advertising and receiving a reply. The reason for our lack of difficulty or doubt is that we can readily supply a very plausible explanation of the nature of this connection. This explanation refers to the power of the sex drive and the force of attraction between the opposite sexes. We could throw in some cultural factors too, such as the repression of homosexuality or the powerful influence of prevailing social expectations encouraging heterosexual relationships. These factors can account for the pattern in our data, and give us confidence that we are inferring a genuine connection between events.

What kind of explanations are these? If they also depend on recognizing some regular conjunction of events, then we face an infinite regress, where correlations between variables must be perpetually re-analysed in terms of correlations between other variables. For example, we could cite the regularity with which men and women live together as evidence of sexual attraction – but then this regularity in turn would require explanation. However, our explanation is couched in different terms. In citing the force of sexual attraction, we are identifying a force familiar to us all by virtue of our nature as human beings. The sexual drive is an integral part of the human make-up – even when it is repressed. As such, it is a power (or a susceptibility) which acts as a causal mechanism in producing particular and identifiable effects (such as pregnancy). From this perspective, cause is related to capabilities and liabilities; instead of being external and contingent, it is internal and necessary to the subjects of our study (cf. Sayer 1992: 103–116). We can understand how things happen if we can attribute them to the inherent capabilities and liabilities of social actors, be they individuals, agencies or whole societies. For example, we could also attribute the pattern of male-female connections to the capabilities inherent in certain types of media and advertising. Other media and forms of advertising (e.g. in gay magazines) might produce rather different results. In terms of such capabilities and liabilities, we can reach a qualitative understanding of how events are connected.

Although I have implied that we first look for regularities or variations, and then consider how they might be connected, this is a curiously indirect way of identifying how things interrelate. It is not that regularities are irrelevant, for they can provide a guide to analysing connections, even if potentially misleading and far from conclusive. However, the search for regularities has to be considered as a way of assisting rather than substituting for the analysis of connections between events. In the first instance, a *qualitative approach implies analysis of the inherent capabilities and liabilities* of social actors, and how these interact to produce particular effects.

A concern for capabilities in turn requires an analysis of social structure. By this, I mean the social roles, identities, agencies and institutions which create a network of interdependent relations between actors. These may have a decisive effect in creating or reducing capabilities for action. My power to influence events is subject to a variety of opportunities and constraints, reflecting my various identities (husband, father) and roles (lecturer, researcher), my status as an employee, the decision-making structure of my department and university, and so on. These relations may be variously economic, social or personal in character, but they all interact in ways which govern my actions and determine or influence my choices.

We can use graphic tools to represent chronological or narrative sequences within the data, contributing to the construction of an overall case study (Figure 3.7). Another connection between concepts is through structural or causal analysis. For example, we may have some ideas about what makes for successful contacts. These can be easily graphed, at least where only a few factors are involved (Figure 3.8).

Graphic representation is an especially appropriate method for qualitative analysis (cf. Miles and Huberman 1984), for it provides an effective way of coping with complex interactions, indicating the key concepts employed and their inter-relation. Pictures provide a powerful tool for capturing or conveying meaning.

How we analyse our data will reflect the hunches or hypotheses which inform our research. This is so, regardless of whether our chief purpose is the development of academic theory or the evaluation of a particular policy. Nor does it matter particularly if we have developed some theoretical ideas prior to analysis, or develop hunches and hypotheses through analysis of the data. Either way, we cannot classify or make connections

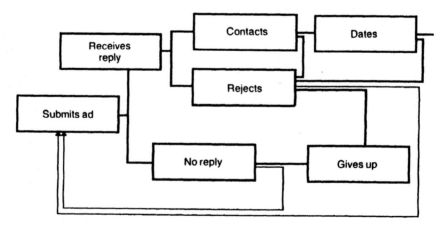

*Figure 3.7* Connections between chronological or narrative sequences

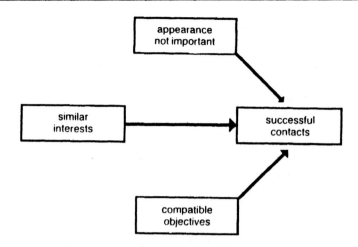

*Figure 3.8* Causal connections between concepts

without developing some more systematic ideas about the data. Indeed, our overriding concern will be the development of an overall view of our data.

In this respect, we need to extend our analogy from blocks and mortar to include a plan of what we are constructing. Depending on our aims and the stage of our research, this plan may be simple or complex, implicit or explicit, dimly perceived or closely articulated. It makes a difference if we are constructing the equivalent of a simple wall or a complicated palace. But even the equivalent of a wall imposes some discipline and direction, with one block being placed on top of another; otherwise the result will simply be a chaotic mess. The analysis must be informed at least by some sense of what our overall research objectives may be.

If we think of theory simply as an idea about how other ideas can be related (Dixon *et al.* 1988: 23), then theory can provide the design through which we can construct our wall. It can provide the necessary direction and organizing framework through which to bring together the different concepts used in our analysis. A sense of direction or design implies a role for theory in conceptualizing experience, in much the same way as our concepts convey meaning (Sayer 1992: 49–65). For example, we may entertain a theory that dating and mating through the personal ads is related to either very extrovert or very introvert behaviour. This is a psychological conceptualization of behaviour, by comparison with alternative theories which might stress, for example, the influence of social or spatial factors.

On the other hand, we can also think of a theory as a complex system of ideas through which we conceptualize some aspect of experience. Such theories are the equivalent of a palace, and as we all know, theories of this type in social science have a similar scarcity value. Ideologies and prejudices can accommodate (or deny) the inconsistencies and contradictions which characterize our everyday thinking. A complex system of ideas that conceptualizes experience – that's something else! A system is a set of logically interconnected parts which together constitute a whole. A few loosely related propositions about causal interconnections do not constitute a theory in this sense, though they may contain elements of one. A problem with complex systems of ideas is that they often relate concepts which are poor conceptualizations of experience. More attention is given to 'systematizing' ideas than to conceptualizing experience – a characteristic most familiar in the more quantitative disciplines such as economics.

The traditional emphasis in qualitative research has been on generating theories rather than testing them. This reflects a concern with developing adequate conceptualizations of the social world before we develop elaborate theories. As Bliss (1983) puts it, we are often at the stage where the problem is to know what the problem is, not what the answer is. The qualitative analyst is cast in the role of a discoverer who unearths problems, identifies indicators and formulates hypotheses rather than investigating predetermined problems within an established theoretical framework (Becker and Geer 1982). This image is an attractive one, providing we do not insist that our discoverer must completely disregard any existing maps of the ground being explored! Also, in social research the dividing line between formulating and testing theories is barely discernible (Sayer 1992: 204). It is difficult to separate the process of discovering theory from the process of evaluating it. Much of the task of qualitative analysis is not just to develop conceptualizations but to examine their adequacy in the light of the data.

Given its predominantly exploratory character, and its emphasis on the problems of meaning and conceptualization, qualitative analysis is more likely to result in the construction of walls than the creation of palaces. It can enrich our descriptions of the empirical world and sharpen our conceptual tools, even if it does not result in highly abstract theories. Even so, it is important in qualitative analysis to be theoretical and systematic, in the sense of articulating and working towards some overall objectives rather than just trying to muddle through. The over-riding objective of analysis is to produce an intelligible, coherent and valid account.

---

- In classifying we establish logical connections between categories
- Once categorized, we can look for patterns in the data
- Statistics can help identify singularities, regularities and variations
- Regularities can be suggestive but not conclusive evidence of connections
- To establish connections requires a qualitative analysis of capabilities and liabilities
- Capabilities can be analysed in terms of social structure
- Graphic representation is useful in analysing concepts and their connections
- Theories can contribute direction and order to the analysis

I have presented these various aspects of analysis sequentially, as though analysis proceeded straight through the various facets of description and classification to connecting concepts and producing an overall account (Figure 3.9).

Describing                                    Connecting
Data ——————————————————————————————————▶ Account
                        Classifying

*Figure 3.9* Qualitative analysis as a single sequential process

However, analysis is iterative and is better represented by a spiral than a straight line (Figure 3.10).

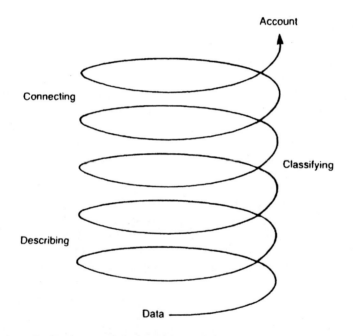

*Figure 3.10* Qualitative analysis as an iterative spiral

To change the analogy somewhat, we can compare qualitative data analysis with climbing a mountain to see the view. First of all, we must insist that our mountain rises above the plain world of common sense to afford a more 'scientific' perspective. The common sense world tends to take meanings for granted; it tends to reify the social world, i.e. to treat as 'things' structures and relationships which are produced and sustained through meaningful social action. Social science is redundant if it does not transcend a common sense view of the world – we cannot interpret or explain social action without also critically evaluating it (Sayer 1992: 39–40).

This requirement accepted, we can allow our mountain to be of any size and shape: the small hill of a short undergraduate project, or the precipitous peak of a large-scale research project. The latter may present some absorbing technical difficulties manageable only by an experienced team, but ·for the most part much the same tasks are required of both novice and expert. In both cases, our interest is in the view, and our purpose in climbing the mountain is to obtain it. The mountain is climbed bit by bit, and while we are climbing, we focus on one step at a time. But the view we obtain is more than the sum of the sequence of steps we take along the way. Every so often, we can turn and look to the horizon, and in doing so we see the surrounding country from a fresh vantage point. It is the climb that makes this possible, but we only obtain a fresh perspective if we remember to look as well as climb.

We can push this analogy a little further. By looking, we obtain fresh views, not just of the surrounding country, but also of the path we have just taken, and of the climb ahead. We may see the path we have taken so far in a new perspective, as detail is lost and new patterns emerge. Or looking ahead, we may plan, given a closer view, to take a different route from that first intended. We may find some bits of the climb easy and straight-forward, others difficult and requiring considerable care. We may have to take devious paths, not always going straight or always going up; at times we may even retrace our steps. This climb, with its circuitous paths, its tangents and apparent reversals, and its fresh vistas, reflects the creative and non-sequential character of the analytic process. Progress may be slow and laborious, but it can be rewarded with some breath-taking revelations. In practice, of course, weather conditions may obscure the view – reflecting the contingent character and potential frustrations of any analysis: un-fortunately nothing can guarantee results! Not even a computer.

# Chapter 4

# Introducing computers

'No one is completely unhappy at the failure of their best friend'
(Groucho Marx)

Computers make good friends. No matter how stupid, dull or dumb we may feel, we can still feel smarter than our computer. Computers can do many things, but they cannot think – and we can. Unfortunately, that also means the thinking is up to us. A computer can help us to analyse our data, but it cannot analyse our data. This is not a pedantic distinction: we must do the analysis.

I am writing this book with the help of a computer. I don't write in the same way with a computer as I do without one. For one thing, as I write I am much more careless over spelling and punctuation than I would be if I were using pen and paper; I know it will be easy to correct errors afterwards. The powerful editing facilities allow me to bash on regardless; I can change things later if I want. In fact, I can easily move whole passages of text around, altering the sequence and sense of what I write now in the light of what I write later. The software I am using supports an 'outlining' facility which allows me to structure and restructure my text. So I no longer need to write sequentially; I can outline a structure for the book and flesh out the various parts of this skeleton with detail as I please. I can continually arrange and rearrange the body of text in a systematic way.

A new technology supports a new way of writing. The computer cannot think, but it can help me to think, and even to think differently from how I used to think. Some things I have always done, I can now do quicker, and more efficiently; such as correcting mistakes. Some of things I now do, such as continually restructuring the text, I wouldn't dream of doing without the computer. In general, we can think about the computer as helping in these two ways: in enhancing what we already do, and in opening up new possibilities.

First let us consider how the computer can enhance what we do.

Our first consideration must be how to record our data. There are various ways in which the computer can make this task more reliable and efficient. Keyboard skills can speed up the process of inputting data. Editing facilities allow mistakes to be easily located and corrected. More sophisticated technology, such as scanners, may allow data to be read into the computer without typing. Laptop computers allow data to be input 'in the field' and then transferred to the desktop. The day has not yet come when computers can record data directly from audio, but even present progress represents a significant advance over pen and paper or the traditional keyboard.

The computer provides an excellent medium for storing data. As qualitative data is notoriously voluminous, this is an important contribution to managing data efficiently. The vast filing cabinet is replaced by the small box of disks. The sheer volume and variety of data which can be conveniently stored for analysis is increasing exponentially. Optical storage technology will allow notebook sized computers to carry millions of pages of information. Improvements in capacity and compatibility are rapidly extending computer access to stores of graphic, audio and video as well as textual information. Computers also facilitate access to stores of data held elsewhere. Disk data can be readily transported from one location to another, whether physically or by phone, facilitating collaborative research and cooperative use of data. Computers with notebook-sized satellite receivers already (as I write in 1991) allow communication between computers without connecting wires.

Computers provide notably efficient filing systems which allow quick and easy access to data. Files can be opened, closed, copied, printed, created and amended by a few simple procedures. Through hierarchical file systems users can manage data in a logical manner. Files can be located together within folders, folders within folders, in a systematic and meaningful order. That lost file, crucial of course to the whole analysis, should be a thing of the past. Unlike us, so long as it continues to function the computer never forgets. That mislaid file can be readily located using the computer's list or search facilities.

Of course, this paradise has pitfalls, and it will be a perfectionist indeed who does not sometimes fall into them. A hierarchical system facilitates but does not compel a logical approach to filing. It is as easy to delete files as to create them. And computers sometimes break down. However, the ease with which data can be copied provides a crucial safeguard against major disasters. Beyond its utility in backing up files, efficiency in copying data has a special significance for qualitative analysts concerned to retain their original data in pristine condition. In days gone by, copying files for use in analysis was a time-consuming chore. Now files can be copied in seconds, and bits of data can be repeatedly reproduced as often as required for analysis.

The indexing of data was another laborious chore which dissipated the energies and taxed the enthusiasm of the most committed pen-and-paper analyst. Every time a file was copied or a bit of data reproduced, a thorough approach required recording of an index of information such as title, location, and date. Now the computer can automatically index information of this kind.

These aspects of managing data may seem trivial; they are anything but. Given the sheer volume and complexity of qualitative data, failure to manage the data efficiently means failure to analyse the data effectively. It may be that some of the aims (perhaps it might be better to say 'ideals') of qualitative analysis can only be achieved now computers have provided efficient methods which eliminate much of the tedium and time-consuming chores involved in managing data. This is perhaps one reason why the introduction of computers has been associated with renewed calls for rigour in qualitative analysis.

At the core of qualitative analysis lies a twofold task: to select a bit of data, and assign it to a category. This has become known as 'coding' data (more on that later). In the far-off days when I was working on my Ph.D., this involved copying bits of data on to cards, and filing each card under an appropriate category. If the data had to be filed under more than one category – then tough! No, there were no xerox machines or other labour-saving devices available in those days. The computer now allows this task to be accomplished with amazing rapidity. Most of the software packages designed for qualitative analysis provide procedures for coding data quickly and easily.

There are, of course, significant variations in what the software offers (Tesch 1990). Let us consider some of the ways a computer can make life easier. It can make it a simple matter to select the relevant bit of data, whether by line number or (more appropriately for qualitative analysis) by selecting meaningful bits of text. It can record automatically the text location, the file reference, and any other information you want to note about this bit of data (e.g. who is speaking). It can keep an up-to-date list of categories from which you can easily choose those you want to assign to the data. It can store the selected data and category (or categories) automatically in a new and easily accessible file together with all the other relevant information. It can allow ready access to all the data previously assigned to a particular category or categories. It can retrieve all the data assigned to a particular category or combination of categories, and file or print out the results. In these ways, the computer can enormously enhance the speed and thoroughness with which data are coded and retrieved.

---

**Computer enhancements**
- Recording and storing data
- Filing and indexing data
- Coding and retrieving data

Although 'coding' has become an accepted term for categorizing data, it has misleading connotations and is singularly inappropriate for qualitative analysis. In common usage, 'codes' are legal statutes arranged to avoid inconsistency and overlapping. They can also refer to symbols used for brevity (or secrecy) in place of ordinary language. Both usages are relevant in the use of 'coding' as a term for analysing data resulting from research where structured responses can be assigned unambiguously to pre-defined categories. But neither usage is appropriate for qualitative analysis, where much of the data is unstructured. In categorizing unstructured data, inconsistencies and overlaps are unavoidable, since at least in the initial stages of analysis, categories are inclusive rather than exclusive. As for the use of codes (i.e. brief symbols) in place of categories, advances in computing technology have rendered this procedure redundant; it is now possible (and in some respects, desirable) to categorize data with terms whose meaning is immediately intelligible. We may retain 'coding' as a term for replacing full category names by brief symbols, but we should not confuse this with the analytic process of creating and assigning the categories themselves.

The term 'coding' has a rather mechanical overtone quite at odds with the conceptual tasks involved in categorizing data. This arises from the association of coding with a consistent and complete set of rules governing the assignment of codes to data, thereby eliminating error and of course allowing recovery of the original data simply by reversing the process (i.e. decoding). Qualitative analysis, in contrast, requires the analyst to create or adapt concepts relevant to the data rather than to apply a set of pre-established rules. It is ironic that one of the foremost exponents of a theoretical approach to qualitative analysis should also have popularized the language of 'coding' as a way of describing this process (Strauss 1987; Strauss and Corbin 1990).

This may seem an unduly long digression, but it can be justified if it signals some of the dangers which have been ascribed to the introduction of computers in qualitative analysis. But before considering some of the potential drawbacks of the computer, let us look at some of the ways in which it promises to transform the analytic process.

The computer is a powerful tool for searching data. Even a simple word-processing package will have facilities for finding all examples of a user-specified 'keyword' (or phrase). More sophisticated procedures will allow an analyst to search for related forms or synonyms, and use wild card characters and exclusions. Even using the simplest search procedure it is possible for an analyst to read through the data in a variety of ways. One of my colleagues aptly describes this as taking different 'cuts' through the data. Reading the data in a sequential way then becomes only one possibility amongst many.

Using the computer's search facilities, we can not only read the data differently, we can extract information from the data relevant for our analysis. We can find out how often a keyword appears in the text. We can list information about where each keyword appears. We can extract the contextual data for each keyword: for example, a number of characters either side of the keyword, or each sentence or paragraph in which it is located.

Search procedures are useful not only with unstructured data, but also with data which we have categorized in some way. We can search the categorized data for all the bits of data assigned to a category or combination of categories. We can organize these searches on logical lines, to test out various hunches or hypotheses we may have about the data. We can compare how one category varies with another and check for associations between them. For some analysts, the ability to interrogate data and revise conceptualizations through searching and retrieving categorized data promises to introduce a new flexibility and rigour into qualitative analysis (Richards and Richards 1991).

The computer also allows us to create new pathways through our data. Using the computer we can create links between different parts of our data. Let us take an example which is very simple to understand. Suppose you want to check on what I mean by 'links' in a glossary of concepts used in the text. In this book you would have to turn to the glossary and look up the word 'links'. Using the computer, I can create a computer link between the word 'links' in the text and the word 'links' in the glossary, so that you can go directly from one to the other just by selecting the word 'links' in the text.

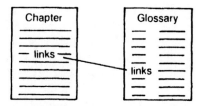

*Figure 4.1* A link between text held in separate locations

This kind of link is known as a 'hypertext' (or 'hypermedia') link, and with it you can do all sorts of clever tricks, linking information in one place with relevant information held elsewhere in the data. Early visionaries believed hypertext systems would transform the way we handle information, liberating us from traditional logical and sequential forms and permitting a more creative and associative reading of texts. Many people have found hypertext intriguing, but it has one critical limitation: most people still read books, not computers!

Nevertheless, hypertext links are very useful during qualitative analysis, even if we cannot incorporate them into a printed report of our research (Cordingley 1991). For example, we can link data indexes directly to the relevant data, so that it can be located easily. We can link categories used in the analysis to a dictionary of definitions, so that we can always have direct access to how a category has been defined. We can link any 'bits' of data we are analysing to the part of the text from which they have been extracted, so that when making comparisons between different bits of data we can always check on the data in its original context. We can link summary results of analysis (e.g. a cell in a cross-tabulation table) with the data to which the summary refers.

Linking data provides a powerful tool for identifying empirically re-lationships between different parts of the data. We can link data which seems related in some way; for example, we might link actions to conse-quences; or premises to conclusions. Or we might link actions which seem inconsistent, or assumptions which seem contradictory. We can then compare all the bits of data which have been linked in some way, and perhaps refine our analysis or infer some connection between categories from the results. Linking data in this way provides a powerful method of grounding connections between categories in an empirically based analysis of relationships within the data. Linking can also provide a useful tool for narrative description and the analysis of processes within the data.

The results of qualitative analysis may be persuasively presented and vividly documented, while the procedures upon which these results are based remain cloaked in mystery. The sceptical reader is therefore unable to review critically the relation between the original data and the final results. Computer-based analysis offers the prospect of new standards in the reporting of qualitative research. The computer can be programmed to take note of all the main decisions made during analysis. For example, the evolution of key concepts can be 'audited'; so that instead of being presented with a conceptual *fait accompli*, readers can see for themselves how concepts have been created, adapted or refined through the analytic process. Because the computer can audit the analysis, the analyst can account more readily for the main strategies pursued and shifts in direction which have occurred as the analysis unfolds. Whereas earlier studies tended to present a pre-packaged finished product, ready-made for consumption, a computer-based approach allows the analyst to chart the interplay between data and concepts and preserve some sense of other analytic possibilities.

---

**Computer transformations**
- Searching and interrogating data
- Electronic links between data
- Auditing analysis

In the evolution of policy, the solutions of one generation become the problems of the next. The computer has provided some solutions for qualitative analysts, particularly with regard to managing and coding data efficiently. It also provides a new set of tools, in the form of facilities for searching and linking data. What problems can we anticipate will follow the use of computers for qualitative analysis? Or are these problems already upon us?

One point is plain; reservations about computer-based analysis are not attributable simply to the prejudices of those who believe that because computers are for counting they have no role to play in qualitative analysis. Anxiety is not confined to the prejudiced. Indeed, those contributing to software development have been amongst the most vocal in emphasising the drawbacks as well as the potential of computer-based analysis.

One problem is that the computer may become for this generation what the motor car was to the last. One of my relatives was so obsessed with his car that he would not walk to the shop at the end of our road – a distance of some 100 yards. In the same way, people may become so obsessed with the computer that they forget that there are other technologies, e.g. pen and paper. Analysis then reduces to what the computer can do; if the computer cannot do it, then it no longer gets done. The technology takes over from the task, and data which cannot be analysed by computer are ignored.

The problem of expecting too much of the computer also finds expression in unrealistic expectations of the volume of data which can be analysed. The computer may be able to handle an enormous volume of data; but the analyst may not!

Another reservation often expressed is that use of a computer can encourage a 'mechanistic' approach to analysis. In this nightmare scenario, the roles of creativity, intuition and insight in analysis are eclipsed in favour of a routine and mechanical processing of data. All that is required of the analyst is to provide the computer with a catalyst, in the form of a list of categories which can be readily put together through a brief review of relevant literature and a quick scan through the data. The computer can then break the data down into bits, and put these bits together again. All that remains is to write up the results.

In contrast to the vices of this mechanistic manipulator of data, we could set the virtues of the dedicated and dextrous theoretician. But it is enough to emphasize the conceptual character of categorization: categorizing data is never a 'routine' process. The computer cannot break the data down into bits, or put the bits together again; only the analyst can do that. There are limits, therefore, to how 'mechanistic' even the most atheoretically inclined analyst can be. If this provides some comfort, there remains a danger that an obsession with the technology and technique will blind the analyst to the crucial conceptual problems and assumptions of his or her research (Seidel 1991: 112–113).

There are more radical criticisms of the role of the computer. For example, it is sometimes argued that the computer encourages 'data fragmentation'. Computer-based analysis can be likened to dissection – to the irony of trying to understand the living by dissecting the dead. Instead of studying the data *in situ*, the data are 'fragmented' into bits and the overall sense of the data is lost. A related complaint is that the computer encourages a quantitative mentality orientated to 'computing' frequencies and cross-tabulations in place of more qualitative forms of analysis. But these criticisms relate more to the continuing contest between rival epistemologies than to the role of the computer *per se* in qualitative analysis.

It should be clear by now that these problems lie less in the technology than in the use (or abuse) we make of it. There is no need to throw out the (technological) baby with the (unrealistic expectations) bathwater. All that is required is to retain a sense of proportion about the role of the computer; to recognize its limitations; and to keep a firm focus throughout on the analytic as well as the technical tasks to be accomplished.

# Chapter 5

# Finding a focus

A Zen story tells of an American professor interested in Zen who was once visiting Nan-in, a Japanese master. Nan-in invited the professor to take tea. He filled the professor's cup; but instead of stopping when the cup was full, he carried on pouring. The tea overflowed; but Nan-in continued to pour. When the professor remonstrated, Nan-in said: 'Like this cup, you are full of your own opinions and speculations. How can I show Zen unless you first empty your cup?' (Zukav quoted in Praverand 1984: 14).

In less dramatic form, the injunction of the Zen master is commonplace in the literature on qualitative analysis: beware of bias! Do not let assumptions blind you to the evidence of your data. Avoid preconceived ideas. Before you start to analyse your data, make sure your cup is empty.

These exhortations seem eminently reasonable. To produce an account, we have to search, select, and summarize data. We also have latitude in choosing which analytic procedures to use as well as what problems to address and how to interpret results. There is no lack of opportunities for bias in selecting and interpreting our data. All the more important, therefore, that in qualitative analysis we do not 'impose' our ideas upon the data.

However, the exhortation to beware of bias should not be interpreted as an injunction against prior thought. The scientist and the Zen master in fact follow different routes to different kinds of knowledge. In Zen, religious revelation is the aim, intuition and insight the path to it. In science, systematic knowledge is the aim, and observation and inference the way to achieve it. While the world as experienced by the mystic may perhaps accord with the world as analysed by the modern scientist (Capra 1983), their purposes and paths differ. The scientist who 'empties his cup' is a scientist no longer. He may be more open to religious experience; but he is no longer equipped for scientific analysis.

In short, there is a difference between an open mind and empty head. To analyse data, we need to use accumulated knowledge, not dispense with it. The issue is not whether to use existing knowledge, but how. Our problem is to find a focus, without committing ourselves prematurely to a particular perspective and so foreclosing options for our analysis. The danger lies not in having assumptions but in not being aware of them; in qualitative analysis we should try to suspend beliefs in familiar convictions and examine evidence in a new and critical way (Edson 1988).

Finding a focus is not something we consider as an afterthought, once we have embarked on our research and already produced our data. It is a process initiated in the very moment we first conceive of a research project. It is more or less explicit in the articulation of our research objectives, in the design of the project, in the kind of data we have decided to collect and what we anticipate doing with it. As we begin to analyse our data, we need to review (and perhaps revise) our analytic focus given the implications of earlier decisions for the development of our analysis.

One way of finding a focus for our analysis is to reflect upon the data we have to analyse. What kind of data has the research produced? Sometimes, we don't get what we expected. Even if the data does conform to our initial expectations, we have to be sure that our focus is in tune with the data. We need to know what we are going to analyse. At this stage, this is more a matter of forming some general impressions and intuitions, than making a detailed study of the data.

Let us explore this through the example of humour. Suppose we have chosen as our subject the humour of a pre-eminent comedienne, Victoria Wood. Following up our interest in dating and mating, Illustration 5.1 is a sketch in which Sheila hopes to find a mate through video dating. Victoria is discussing with Sheila some of the (un)likely prospects they saw on her video tape.

Looking at our example, what kind of data is this? The first point we may note is that we are dealing with text rather than video. Although this sketch is the basis for a performance, we have only the text before us. There are aspects of humour, to do with visual clues, timing, and setting, which we cannot analyse unless we have access to the complete performance. This immediately draws some boundaries around what we can achieve in our analysis.

*Illustration 5.1* 'The library'

| | |
|---|---|
| *Victoria* | So who did you fancy? |
| *Sheila* | Oh I'm no judge of character, Victoria. |
| *Victoria* | Do you think *I* am? I've had my drive tarmacked eight times. |
| *Sheila* | Give me your views on Rodney. |
| *Victoria* | Well, Rodney had white towelling socks, didn't he? Which in my book makes him unreliable, untrustworthy and prone to vaseline jokes. Mark ... |
| *Sheila* | The solicitor. |
| *Victoria* | He was OK – but, as he says himself, he does a lot of conveyancing so that'll be seventeen phone calls just to meet him for a cup of coffee. |
| *Sheila* | I was rather taken with Simon – the gynaecologist. |
| *Victoria* | No – too inhibiting. You can't flirt with someone who can visualise your Fallopian tubes. |

| Sheila | Now Malcolm – what do you think he meant by 'lively social life'? |
|---|---|
| Victoria | Drink. |
| Sheila | He wants a breezy, uninhibited companion. |
| Victoria | To drink with. |
| Sheila | And what do you think he meant by 'life peppered with personal tragedy'? |
| Victoria | Hangovers. |

*Source:* Wood 1990: 39 (abridged)

What kind of humour is this? Well, it is not slapstick comedy, nor joke-telling. The humour is woven into an ordinary conversation between two women discussing men. The conversation is 'ordinary', but the images are 'extraordinary' – the drive tarmacked eight times, the seventeen phone calls. The subject may be mundane, but the style is distinctive, with an obvious leaning towards hyperbole. There is also a deflationary element to this humour, with male pretensions punctured by Victoria's cynical comments. This sketch has an obvious target. Even on a first and superficial impression, then, we can identify some lines for analysis. We could explore the use made of the contrast between the ordinary setting and the extraordinary images, or how the humour targets certain victims. Even at this stage, our general knowledge of the data can shape our thinking, suggest some main themes, and impose some parameters on our analysis.

Why analyse this kind of humour? To answer that question, we have to ask another: why humour in the first place? Before we plunge headlong into the analysis, this is the point at which to reflect upon our reasons for undertaking the research. This is a useful exercise, even if means going over old ground. No matter how well thought out our initial research aims, in the interim, our ideas may have developed or changed. Why are we interested in humour? Are we simply interested in what makes people laugh? Are we interested in how the humorist achieves her effects? Are we interested in the substance of humour – the general social expectations and assumptions it reveals, or the particular groups it targets? Do we want to look at humour from a philosophical, psychological, sociological, anthropological, semantic or literary perspective, or some combination of these? Addressing or re-addressing such basic questions can help to develop a focus for the analysis.

Another way of finding a focus is through a review of the decisions we have made in selecting material for analysis. Why have we selected the particular sites, individuals or events we have included in our observations? If they are in some way 'typical' or 'exceptional', then how are they 'typical' or 'exceptional' – and why is this important? Why choose Victoria Wood as an example? How, if at all, is Victoria Wood 'representative' of a wider population? Is it because she is successful? Does it matter that she is a woman? Is it important that she is a contemporary comedienne? Is it significant that she works in television and radio as well as in print? How we answer these questions may help to focus our analysis. For example, we might concentrate on issues of gender, taking Victoria Wood as a significant figure amongst contemporary female humorists. Thinking through the reasons we have selected our data can give us clues about the direction our analysis should take.

We also have to think about our potential audience: who is going to read the results of the research, and what would be interesting or useful to report? We can ask ourselves bluntly: who cares? If we are conducting a study of gender and humour for a television network, for example, we might identify a rather different set of analytic interests and concerns, than if we are hoping to produce a Ph.D. in media studies. We also have to ask ourselves another blunt question: so what? Trying to anticipate what our audience may value as a worthwhile analysis can help to shape our thinking even at a preliminary stage. In some cases, such as policy-oriented research, it may be possible or indeed necessary to discuss research aims and analytic objectives with others with a stake in the project's outcomes.

---

**Questions to help find a focus**
- What kind of data are we analysing?
- How can we characterize this data?
- What are our analytic objectives?
- Why have we selected this data?
- How is the data representative/exceptional ?
- Who wants to know? What do they want to know?

---

Rather than start the analysis from scratch, we also need to consider what resources we can call upon. In trying to clarify our interests and aims, we may want to reflect upon our own experience of humour. For example, one factor stimulating my own interest in the humour of Victoria Wood was the laughter one of her sketches provoked when we watched it during a discussion of interviewing in a methods class. Humour is part of everyday life, and we probably all have our favourite humorous programmes, books, anecdotes and incidents. Reflection on personal experience can be a rich mine of insights and ideas which may prove useful in directing our analysis.

The general culture may provide another rich source of ideas for analysis. There is a 'non-academic' literature on humour, to be found in newspaper reviews, comedian biographies and the like. There may also be non-literary sources, such as radio and TV interviews. I write in a city which is fortunate to have an annual book festival devoted to literary issues, such as the social functions of humour. Academics thankfully have no monopoly over the dissection of humour. Indeed I suspect discussion of what was 'funny' or 'not funny' on last night's TV may run the weather a close second as a topic of everyday conversation.

As we have seen, accumulated knowledge need not refer only to the results of previous research and scholarship. But undoubtedly the academic literature may prove one of the most useful sources of analytic strategy. This is because previous research or scholarship may have examined issues in a thorough and systematic way. Some of the concepts and relationships observed or hypothesized in previous work may suggest questions which require further exploration. Of course, replication is seldom on the agenda in social science research, since novelty has a strong career value; and it is even less likely to commend itself to qualitative researchers. On the other hand, plagiarism is rife. In a research context, it makes sense to 'borrow' freely from other authors, providing we acknowledge our sources and subject their ideas to a critical assessment through examining evidence.

In this case, we could review the existing literature on humour. Fortunately, computer-based bibliographies now allow us to track down relevant literature through a few interactive exchanges at the computer terminal. We can locate immediately all the texts catalogued under humour, or related subjects such as wit or comedy. We can explore other parts of the bibliography, using search facilities to find texts which include relevant words in their title, such as 'laughter'. Our search may take us across different disciplines, for example, to texts on the psychology or anthropology of humour. It may take us through the nooks and crannies of the bibliography to unsuspected texts.

We may begin with an eclectic approach to the literature, but we must quickly sort out what texts seem promising and which seem irrelevant. Here we cross our first Rubicon, for the literature tends to be organized along disciplinary lines. Do we adopt a literary approach, and explore issues of style, idiom and the use of irony? Do we take a linguistic view, and investigate the communication of humorous intent through language? Do we want to take a psychological, anthropological or sociological perspective? Do we want to confine ourselves to a particular perspective, or attempt a more inter-disciplinary analysis? No doubt our background, training and inclinations will influence this decision. But we should try to articulate, as clearly as possible (and on paper), our reasons for deciding one way or another. In these reasons, we may find some clues to how we may begin to analyse the data.

As an example of the value of literature in sign-posting different directions for the analysis, consider the comments in Illustration 5.2 on women's comedy, taken from an article by Merrill in a recent collection exploring perspectives on women and comedy (Merrill 1988). In the space of one short article, we have a rich range of potential topics for analysis. These statements and questions may spark off any number of ideas about how to proceed. We can identify some questions or even some hypotheses which can be explored through our analysis.

*Illustration 5.2* Comments on feminist humour

> Because humor depends upon a perception of events or behaviour as unexpected or incongruous, the individual who publicly points up such inconsistencies risks making a statement about the status quo. Consequently, satire, irony and comedy pointedly directed can wield enormous social and political power. 272
>
> Because of conventional sex roles, women have had to be practical; pragmatists rather than idealists. The mundane day-to-day business of life has been women's domain . . . Women's comedy is infused with these realistic associations. 274
>
> . . . the point-of-view represented in feminist comedy is one that affirms women's experience, rather than denigrating it . . . Oppressive contexts and restrictive values would be ridiculed, rather than the characters who are struggling against such restrictions. 275
>
> Comedy depends on perspective. A certain aesthetic distancing or tension between empathy and judgement is needed for one to view the irrational or incongruous as comic. 276
>
> Tomlin's characters display insight and integrity which allows them to be self-critical without being self deprecating. 277
>
> Comedy is both an aggressive and intellectual response to human nature and experience . . . (feminist humor) addresses itself to women and to the multiplicity of experiences and values women may embody. 278
>
> Humor addressed to women; comedy that recognizes the value of female experience may be an important step in developing a culture that allows women to self-critically question the stereotypes that have governed our lives. 279

*Source*: Merrill 1988

For example, here are some questions about Victoria Wood's humour which we might ask inspired by the comments in Illustration 5.2.

Is it infused with 'realistic associations'?

Does it affirm women's experience, rather than denigrate it?

Does it ridicule oppressive contexts and restrictive values?

Do Wood's characters display insight and integrity, being self-critical without being self-deprecating?

Does it address itself to women, their values and experiences?

Does it allow women to question self-critically the stereotypes that have governed their lives?

We can also identify some questions about humour in general rather than women's humour in particular. We could frame these in the form of hypotheses (Figure 5.1).

The virtue of expressing questions in this form is that it focuses enquiry on the nature of the concepts employed and on the character of the relationships between these concepts. For example, in formulating these hypotheses, should we distinguish the 'unexpected' and the 'irrational' from the 'incongruous', as Merrill does, or are these merely variants of the same concept? What does an 'aesthetic distance between empathy and judgement' mean? How would we recognize one if we saw it? By formulating hypotheses, we force ourselves to clarify our concepts, because we have to think in terms of how these concepts can be observed or measured.

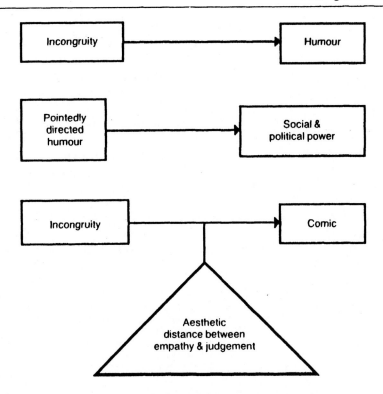

*Figure 5.1* Deriving hypotheses about humour from the literature

The same is true of relationships between concepts. Take the hypothesis relating 'congruity' and 'humour'. What is the nature of this relationship? Is 'incongruity' a cause of humour, as I have implied, or merely a condition of it? And if 'incongruity' is a cause of humour, does it require as a condition an 'aesthetic distance between empathy and judgement?'

One article is hardly an exhaustive review of the literature; but already we have acquired some sense of what questions we might ask, and what we could look for in the data.

**Resources to help find a focus**
- Personal experience
- General culture
- Academic literature

In developing a focus we are less concerned with the detail of individual concepts and relationships than with the identification of general themes.

What are the central issues for the analysis? From the various questions we address and resources we can call upon, we need to select those which look most promising. We have to consider what we can hope to accomplish in the time available. We also need to consider whether our main themes can be related, to produce a reasonably concise and coherent analysis.

Keeping with our example of humour, let us briefly consider some general themes for analysis, and how these might be related.

Even a cursory glance through the literature is enough to indicate the crucial role attributed to incongruity in humour. Incongruity can be achieved through a variety of techniques, such as exaggeration, puns, or the unexpected transposition of characters or situations. Incongruity involves a disruption of expectations: a situation is suddenly not what it seemed. We can recognize incongruity in Victoria's exaggerations about the tarmac and the phone calls. Incongruity is also the stuff of everyday jokes, for example in stock question-and-answer routines where misunderstanding produces an unexpected reply.

| | |
|---|---|
| Transposition: Doctor: 'I'm afraid I can't diagnose your complaint. I think it must be drink.' Patient: 'All right then, I'll come back when you are sober.' | Pun play: A man was worried about his sex life. 'How often should I have sex, doctor?' he asked. 'Infrequently,' said the doctor. 'Is that one word or two?' asked the man. |

The references to health and sex in the above examples raise another theme. Catharsis – which we can think of as humour giving an outlet to repressed emotions – is another often-cited aspect of humour. Laughter giving emotional release can act as a social as well as a psychological safety valve. Topics which tend to be anxiety laden or taboo – sex, race, work, health, death – provide excellent sources of comic material. The more sensitive or sacrosanct the subject, the greater the effect. This is the province of the 'sick' joke, which may gratify even as it appalls us. But cathartic humour can also have a more positive aspect.

| | |
|---|---|
| 'Is sex dirty? Only when it's done right' (Woody Allen) | 'Don't knock masturbation – it's sex with someone I love' (Woody Allen) |

Criticism is another ingredient we can readily recognize in humour. This aspect is emphasized in Merrill's discussion of women's comedy. Humour can deflate, or denigrate. It can puncture pretensions. In the form of subversive satire, it can mock the vanity and ridicule the vice of the powerful. Lives have been lost because of witticisms 'out of season'. But humour can also function as a means of oppression, of maintaining the status quo. Merrill (1988: 270) cites a study by Rose Laub Coser of jokes in a psychiatric institution, which found a hierarchy of humour: those with power could publicly enjoy a joke at the expense of those without – but not vice versa. Nor is it always the powerful who seek to confirm the position of the powerless. Telling jokes against oneself can be a form of social defence, through which one denies any threat of disruption to established order. Merrill (1988: 273) goes on to discuss comediennes whose humour is based on self deprecation, ridiculing and demeaning themselves and other women.

Who are the targets or victims of criticism? Andrew Brown (1991) reports that the wave of humour currently (i.e. in 1991) sweeping southern England has as its target the 'Essex Girl' (and 'Essex Man'), apparently representative of a newly emergent stratum of the working class with high household incomes.

- How can you tell the difference between Essex Girl and a supermarket trolley (the supermarket trolley has a mind of its own).
- How does an Essex Girl turn on the light afterwards? She kicks open the car door.
- What did the Essex Girl ask when told she was pregnant? 'How do you know it's mine?'

This humour has a savage streak, and Brown comments that these are jokes which 'no one would dare to tell' against traditional targets of humour. As social mores change, so do social scapegoats. A recent example was an intended joke made by a panellist on a satirical TV programme when asked to explain the difference between four people, one of whom was black. The comment 'Well, one of them is coloured' was greeted with a stony silence on all sides, and the panellist had to be rescued from his embarrassing predicament. Colour is no longer a 'funny' issue.

Despite its penchant for disrupting expectations, humour may function to confirm rather than undermine stereotypes. Women as a butt of humour often involves confirmation of male conceits: the female as sexually avaricious, the wife as a pain in the neck. The Essex girl is stereotyped as brainless, promiscuous, and incredibly stupid. The doctor is typecast as a drunk. Men with white socks are stereotyped as unreliable, untrustworthy and prone to vaseline jokes. Humour trades in such stereotypes, affirming rather than subverting existing values.

Finally, we can ask how humour treats its victims. Are we invited to laugh at them, or laugh with them? Is there, as Merrill suggests, a 'distance between empathy and judgement', such that criticism is softened by empathy? Or are the victims subjected to unmitigated ridicule? Is comedy self-critical without being self-deprecating? Is humour critical without being cruel?

> **Main themes in analysis of humour**
> • Disrupting expectations: incongruity
> • Releasing emotions: catharsis
> • Affirming or subverting values
> • Laughing with or at victims
> • Trading in stereotypes

We have identified a number of themes which can form the main threads of our analysis (Figure 5.2).

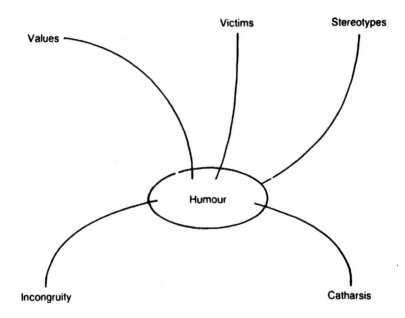

*Figure 5.2* Main themes for analysing humour

Now we can consider how these can be woven together. For example, we could distinguish between style and substance in humour, drawing a contrast between process and content (Figure 5.3). How are humorous effects achieved? And what are the subjects of humour? Around this distinction we can organize the various themes we have discussed so far.

These ideas may seem vague, but that is not unreasonable given that we have not yet undertaken a detailed analysis of our data. Finding a focus is not, of course, a single stage in the development of our analysis. It is not something which is completed before we begin. It is a recurrent task, which informs the whole analysis from start to finish. The important point is that our analysis throughout should be animated by an endeavour to identify

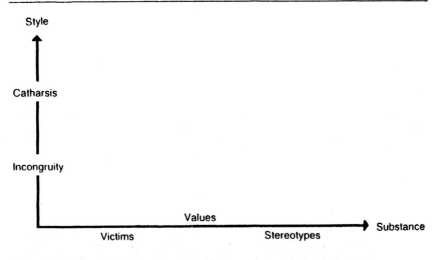

*Figure 5.3* Integrating themes around issues of style and substance

and develop key themes, to which all the individual details of analysis can be related. We need to set boundaries, and map out the main features of our topography, or we can easily get lost in the mass of data.

# Chapter 6

# Managing data

Piles of papers spilling from the desk across the floor and strewn over every available surface: such is the archetypal image of the qualitative analyst at work. Of course, this shrewd paragon of academic virtue knows exactly where everything is and can always find a particular paper within moments: the supposed chaos is more apparent than real. This image is comforting, but hardly credible. In the real world, a chaotic mass of papers spread across the room is a recipe for confusion, error and frustration; finding that particular paper may take not moments but hours or even days. In practice, therefore, the analyst depends on storing and filing data in an organized and systematic way. In any case, the image of the paper-strewn room has been superseded by that of the desktop computer. The data which once occupied a room now occupies a small disk no larger than a thick notepad. The scramble through endless papers is replaced by the search through innumerable files held on the computer.

Good analysis requires efficient management of one's data. The opportunities for error are, in Gibbon's words, 'various and infinite.' Data must be recorded fully and accurately, and that may be easier said than done, as anyone who has tried transcribing audio tapes can verify. For example, try to decipher a group interview with a dozen very animated respondents, all speaking rapidly in broad dialect and sometimes several speaking at once! Apart from 'technical' difficulties, there are problems in ensuring data is of consistently high quality where observations have been directed at more subtle aspects of social interaction.

Take the sketch in Illustration 6.1 for example. The dialogue can be recorded with relative ease, but we may also want to record other details, such as what Thelm and Pat are wearing (bikini 'overalls' over their everyday clothes), what they are doing (chain-smoking while supervising the baths) and other aspects of their interaction apart from the dialogue. The more complex the data, the more risk that some information will be overlooked or not recorded accurately and that as a result the quality of the data will be uneven. Our first concern, therefore, is to check the data for accuracy and to look for possible gaps and inconsistencies. Where the data is of uneven quality, it may be possible to 'repair the damage' by further research. Where this is not possible, our anxieties and reservations about the quality of the data should be recorded for future reference.

*Illustration 6.1* 'Two attendants at a Turkish Bath'

| | |
|---|---|
| *Thelm* | My God, if her bum was a bungalow she'd never get a mortgage on it. |
| *Pat* | She's let it drop. |
| *Thelm* | I'll say. Never mind knickers, she needs a safety net. |
| *Pat* | She wants to do that Jane Fonda. |
| *Thelm* | That what? |
| *Pat* | That exercise thing – nemobics. |
| *Thelm* | What's that? |
| *Pat* | Our next-door does it. We can hear her through the grate. You have to clench those buttocks. |
| *Thelm* | Do you? She'll never get hers clenched – take two big lads and a wheelbarrow ... |

*Source:* Victoria Wood 1985: 107

Since some of this data is held in video rather than text format, we need to find ways of recording such data for analysis. Unfortunately computer storage of significant amounts of video data is not yet possible, though the computer can cope with static images (e.g. pictures and diagrams) providing substantial memory resources are available. However, most of the software available at present for analysing data is oriented to analysing text, and while some can accommodate graphics, analysis is still based on textual description of the material. This translation of pictures into text is also likely to pose problems for achieving a consistent and complete recording of relevant data.

Data should be recorded in a format which facilitates analysis. Decisions made at this stage can have repercussions later. Suppose we have conducted some interviews and we have to record responses to a large number of open-ended questions. Do we file the data as a complete interview for each case, or as a set of responses for each question? The former allows the interview to be recorded and read as a whole, but inhibits ready comparison between related responses; the latter facilitates comparison between responses, but makes it difficult to see the interview as a whole. Fieldwork notes pose similar problems. Do we file the data chronologically, by setting, by source or by topic? Whatever basis we choose for filing data, it is likely to facilitate analysis in some directions and inhibit it in others.

In filing the data, we already have to address issues which are fundamental to our analysis. What is the focus of our research? If we are conducting a case study, then what constitutes the case? If we intend to make comparisons across a number of cases, what is the 'population' we are studying? Our answers to these questions will determine what we can say about our data at the end of the day.

A decision need not be difficult just because it is fundamental. We may have no problem in deciding what constitutes a case, for example, where our data results from a set of unstructured interviews, and our research aim is to analyse the perceptions and attitudes of our respondents. Each respondent can be regarded as a 'case' and each interview filed under a reference to the appropriate case. Matters become more complicated where our data derives from a variety of sources, and our analysis has multiple foci, such as groups and agencies as well as individuals.

How should we record the material for our analysis of humour? How we answer this question depends on what we want to draw conclusions about at the end of the analysis. Do we want to discuss and compare each of the TV programmes, for example? Or do we want to focus our inquiry on each of the several sketches which taken together constitute a programme? If we split the data up into sketches, it may be more difficult to relate the data to the overall programmes. We may lose important information about how one sketch leads into another, how sketches of different types are put together, and so on. On the other hand, if our main interest is in how the humour works within individual sketches, there is no point in filing the material by programme. This will make it more difficult to make comparisons between the different sketches.

Fortunately, these are not either/or decisions. One virtue of the computer is that it may provide facilities for reformatting data. For example, we may decide to file by programme, but still be able to reformat the data so that we can take the sketches as our basic cases – or vice versa. We can amalgamate files to make new ones, bringing all the relevant sketches together to make a programme file; or we can disaggregate files, splitting programme files up to make files for their constituent sketches. If one reformatting procedure is simpler than another, this may influence our initial decision about how to file the data. As well as considering the central focus of the analysis, we also have to consider the ease and efficiency with which we can file and reformat the data. We may opt for sketches as our basic cases because they are convenient in terms of length and content; by comparison, programmes may be too complex and unwieldy. Decisions in terms of convenience can be justified if they coincide with or at least don't contravene our analytic interests.

In formatting data, we must ensure that the data is fully referenced. This may mean no more than specifying a reference for each case included in our study: 'Sketch01' or 'Programme01' for example. However, we may want to reference the data more fully, by including details of who recorded the data, how, when and where it was recorded, and so on. This information may provide important contextual material and may also be useful if we want to make comparisons between cases in terms of how the data was obtained. For example, we may want to compare sketches we have seen 'live' in the theatre with those seen on video or those which we have only read, but not seen performed. Nevertheless, unless this reference information may illuminate the data in some way, or promises to provide a useful basis of comparison, there is no point in recording it.

As well as reference information about cases, we may also want to record reference information about the data in each case. We might reference the 'Turkish Bath' sketch as 'Case 001', and record some further information about when, where and how this was observed. But in addition to information about the case, we also have information about the data itself. We know who is speaking at any one point in the data, and can therefore record the source of the data as it varies through the case material. Most interview data will contain at least two sources – the respondent and the interviewer. Other forms of data – group discussions, meetings, informal conversations – may include several sources. Referencing the data by source is useful, but only if it sheds light on the data, or provides a basis for future comparison. If we have no interest in 'Pat' or 'Thelm' as individuals, we may dispense with the information about sources and concentrate entirely on the dialogue itself.

The computer has a capacity to locate and retrieve information which is remarkable by human standards. For example, we can ask it to collate all the contributions which Pat (or Thelm) makes to the dialogue. The computer can hunt through all the cases for contributions which Pat has made, and record these in a separate file.

The computer can also improve our efficiency in managing data. The trick is to file information only once, and then obtain access to it as required. If we file information about different speakers (e.g. 'S1 is Pat, S2 is Thelm') then we can reference the data more economically and retrieve the full reference whenever required. Anyone who has obtained qualitative data through a standardized questionnaire will immediately see the value of this facility. The questions can be filed once, and then it is sufficient to record a brief reference (e.g. Q1) for the data. The full question can be displayed on screen as required. Take Illustration 6.2 as an example.

*Illustration 6.2* Recording data fully but inefficiently

| | |
|---|---|
| *Interviewer* | Maybe you think it's not worth being qualified as there are so few jobs in Liverpool . . . ? |
| *Jeanette* | There is lots of jobs. The Government wants to keep us unemployed so we won't smoke on the buses . . . I could have been in a film but it was boring . . . |
| *Interviewer* | What film was that? |
| *Jeanette* | Documentary on child prostitution. |
| *Interviewer* | You've actually been a prostitute? |
| *Jeanette* | Yeah but it was boring. The sex was all right but they kept wanting you to talk to them . . . |
| *Interviewer* | Is there much sleeping around amongst young people? |
| *Marie* | No, it's boring. |
| *Jeanette* | It's like for your Mums and Dads really, isn't it? |
| *Marie* | Like drinking. |

| | |
|---|---|
| *Interviewer* | Don't you and your, er, mates drink? |
| *Jeanette* | We used to drink battery acid. |
| *Marie* | But it burns holes in your tights. |
| *Interviewer* | Do you sniff glue? |
| *Jeanette* | That's for snobs, really, isn't it? |
| *Marie* | Grammar school kids sniff glue. |
| *Jeanette* | We sniff burning lino. |

*Source*: Victoria Wood 1985: 25–26 (abridged)

If this was one of a set of interviews, they can be recorded more efficiently by recording all the full reference information in separate files. For the sake of efficiency, we may want to record questions in a standard form even though the way they are asked may vary slightly from interview to interview. If the variation is trivial, it can be safely ignored (Illustration 6.3).

*Illustration 6.3* Filing reference information – questions and sources

| | |
|---|---|
| *Q1* | Not worth being qualified as there are so few jobs? |
| *Q2* | Is there much sleeping around amongst young people? |
| *Q3* | Do you drink? |
| *Q4* | Do you sniff glue? |

| | |
|---|---|
| *S1* | interviewer |
| *S2* | Jeanette |
| *S3* | Marie |

There is no point in filing separately information which only appears once in the text, such as the questions about filming and prostitution. These may be properly regarded as part of the data. By filing repetitive information separately we can record our data much more economically. We can still have access immediately to the full reference: if we have forgotten that Q1 is about qualifications and jobs, we can ask the computer to display Q1 in full. So the loss of intelligibility, which may seem a significant problem on paper, in practice is negligible (Illustration 6.4).

*Illustration 6.4* Data filed efficiently

| | |
|---|---|
| *Q1 S2* | There is lots of jobs. The Government wants to keep us unemployed so we won't smoke on the buses … I could have been in a film but it was boring … |
| *S1* | What film was that? |
| *S2* | Documentary on child prostitution. |
| *S1* | You've actually been a prostitute? |
| *S2* | Yeah but it was boring. The sex was all right but they kept wanting you to talk to them … |
| *Q2 S3* | No, it's boring. |
| *S2* | It's like for your Mums and Dads really, isn't it? |
| *S3* | Like drinking. |
| *Q3 S2* | We used to drink battery acid. |
| *S3* | But it burns holes in your tights. |
| *Q4 S2* | That's for snobs, really, isn't it? |
| *S3* | Grammar school kids sniff glue. |
| *S2* | We sniff burning lino. |

There is obviously a trade-off here between efficiency and intelligibility. However, the computer, by giving us instant access to the appropriate reference information, helps to improve the former without unduly sacrificing the latter. Where we want to treat questions as part of the data, however, obviously they must be recorded fully.

Apart from reference data, we may have other information about the case which we want to record. For example, the interviewer in the above dialogue is male. Suppose we want to record this as a 'face-sheet' variable (so-called because this kind of background information is often recorded on the first page of an interview). We should only need to record such information once. Then, when we want to analyse all cases where the interviewer is male, the computer can identify these cases for us, and create a subset within the data.

It will probably be most convenient if all this information – the case references, the data references and the 'facesheet' variables, and the data itself – is held separately by the computer, but filed together in one place. How can it be held separately and yet kept together? The computer operates a hierarchical filing system, which allows files to be 'nested' together within 'folders'. So cases can be kept in folders, with the data and related information stored in a family of documents or files within the folder (Figure 6.1).

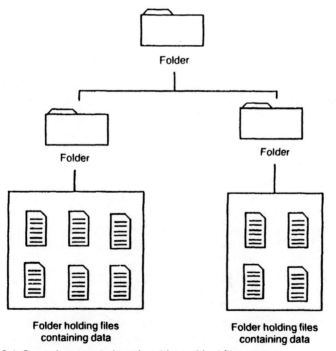

Folder

Folder

Folder

Folder holding files
containing data

Folder holding files
containing data

*Figure 6.1* Case documents kept in a hierarchical file system

The hierarchical file system will be familiar to anyone remotely acquainted with a computer. Perhaps less familiar is an alternative method of storing data, based on cards rather than files (Figure 6.2). Here data can also be stored 'separately and yet together', with a case being held on a card and the data, facesheet variables, etc., stored on 'fields' within the card. The card is the equivalent of a folder, and the field is the equivalent of a file. However, the card/field system is a very flat hierarchy, as it is not possible to nest cards within cards, as one can nest folders within folders.

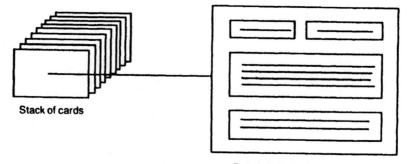

Stack of cards

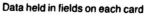

Data held in fields on each card

*Figure 6.2* Data stored in fields on a card-based filing system

On the other hand, the card/field system has advantages which can make our analysis much more efficient. Fields are designed for managing databases rather than word processing. Compared with files, they allow the analyst to control and manipulate information more effectively. For example, we can tell the computer to display the information held at particular places in the field. Suppose we want to check on the gender of the interviewer, and we have stored information about gender on the third line of our field containing 'facesheet' variables. We can instruct the computer to display the third line of the field, and it will tell us that in this case the interviewer is male. We can make these instructions very specific, and we can choose to do a variety of things with the data: for example, we can instruct the computer to 'copy the first character of the third word of the fourth line'. This gives us a very powerful tool for managing information, because we can ask the computer to do jobs (like looking up the information held on the third line of the 'facesheet' variables field) which we would otherwise have to do ourselves.

We have already touched on this facility in relation to data references, where we can store reference information common to all cases in one file, and then instruct the computer to display this information as required. Instructing the computer perhaps sounds unduly intimidating, since it usually means nothing more complicated than choosing from a menu list. The menu might contain an item 'Show the full reference for the selected question' – or words to that effect – typically menu items are rather less verbose.

Another area where this facility can save work is indexing cases. Rather than compiling our own index of cases, the computer can do it for us. If we decide to amend a case reference, the computer can locate the appropriate reference in the index and amend it accordingly. We don't have to do a thing. A case index is useful, of course, for keeping track of data; but with the computer, we can also use it to locate cases immediately within the filing system. Once again, the computer does the work, and we no longer have to rummage through the filing cabinet looking for the right file.

One way of making data more manageable is to reduce it. This is another procedure which provokes a certain amount of anxiety amongst analysts. If we can reduce the amount of data we have to work with, then we can concentrate on what is important and our analysis should become more efficient. There is little point in reading through more than once any data which is clearly irrelevant to the analysis. Why not eliminate it – or at least, summarize it? The reason lies in a natural reluctance to 'tamper' with the data, and concern over what may or may not become relevant as the analysis unfolds. Today's irrelevant digression may contain tomorrow's illuminating insight. This uncertainty encourages a natural caution when it comes to dispensing with data.

Once again, the computer can come to our rescue. Using the computer, we can reconcile our interest in efficiency with our concern over relevance; we can reduce the data without risk. Data which is clearly irrelevant at the outset of the analysis can be summarized; a page of tangents can be reduced to one pithy synopsis. The computer allows us to do this 'without risk', because we can instantly locate or restore the original data if we wish. This is possible because the computer can make a direct connection between our summary and the original data, assuming that we always work with a copy of the data and keep the original material stored on a separate disk.

The virtue of summarizing data is not only in the greater efficiency with which we can subsequently deal with the data. Summarizing is not just an investment: it can have an immediate pay-off, for it also obliges us to consider the question of relevance at the very outset of our analysis. In deciding whether or not data is 'relevant' we have also to decide what it is (ir)relevant for. The purposes and parameters of the analysis are implicit in these decisions, and we can clarify them by considering carefully the criteria upon which decisions about relevance are based. From this point of view, there may be analytic benefits from summarizing data irrespective of how much data we have or how relevant it all appears. It is only if we ignore the underlying analytic issues that summarizing may seem a tedious and mechanical chore.

This eulogy extolling the virtues of managing data on the computer must be coupled with a warning and a reservation. The reservation relates to the memory limitations of existing card/field systems, which can require compromises in how data is stored. The card/field system offers more control over the data, but it is not designed to handle the massive volumes of data typical of qualitative research, and the amount of data which may be stored in any one field may be limited.

The warning is a familiar one: data held electronically must be 'backed up' in case something goes wrong. The analyst's nightmare of a crashed hard disk, with all data lost, can and does happen. The only safeguard is to ensure that all the data held on disk has been copied. The time this takes is trifling; the discipline it requires is tremendous!

# Chapter 7

# Reading and annotating

According to Edmund Burke, 'to read without reflecting is like eating without digesting' (quoted in Peter 1982). Reading and annotating are processes which aid the 'digestion' of our data. Although I discuss them separately, they are two facets of the same process of absorbing information and reflecting upon it. Reading our data is akin to 'reading' a situation – it is a process of interpreting what the data may mean (Sayer 1992: 35–6). This process should not be reduced to the indispensible task of recognizing the meaning of the symbols through which information is conveyed. It encompasses integration – relating various parts of data to other parts, or to the data as a whole. It involves assimilation – relating the data to previous knowledge. It requires retention and recall – storing the understanding we gain through reading in an accessible form. And it culminates in communication – the use we make of our reading in producing an account (cf. Buzan 1982: 28). If reading and annotating the data are to contribute effectively to our analysis, we have to consider how each of these elements can be facilitated and sustained.

## READING

We cannot analyse our data unless we read it. How well we read it may determine how we well analyse it. Reading in qualitative data analysis is not passive. We read to comprehend, but intelligibility is not our only nor even our main goal. The aim of reading through our data is to prepare the ground for analysis. We can compare the action of reading the data with a bit of gardening. By digging over the ground, we loosen the soil and make it possible for the seeds of our analysis to put down roots and grow. It may help to have some fertilizer (organic, naturally) in the shape of a few ideas; the fruits of our digging may not be seen straight away, but when the results do show, the resulting shoots will be stronger and more profuse.

How do we read in an active, or perhaps one should say, an 'interactive' way? One technique is to develop a set of questions to ask of the data. These need be no more than the interrogative quintet 'Who? What?

When? Where? Why?' – questions which are the stock-in-trade of any analyst. These questions can lead in all sorts of directions, opening up interesting avenues to explore in the data. The emphasis should be on exploration of potential themes and topics, but not entirely without some discipline or direction. 'So what?' is another stock question which is always worth asking, since it forces us to consider why some aspect of the data seems so interesting.

A further source of ideas can be identified in the substantive issues with which the researcher is concerned. These substantive concerns usually reflect the researcher's disciplinary perspective and the kind of problems with which they are working. A psychologist or an economist may have quite different substantive concerns from a sociologist, for example.

A good example of how substantive concerns can help in generating ideas is provided by Bogdan *et al.* (1982). These authors identify a variety of areas in which ideas can be generated reflecting distinctively sociological concerns:

- Settings: describing the setting/context
- Definitions: perceptions of situation, objects
- Processes: sequences, changes, transitions, turning points
- Activities: regular patterns of behaviour
- Events: specific happenings or incidents
- Strategies: how people get things done
- Relationships/structure: friendships, cliques, coalitions, etc

Anselm Strauss (1987) provides another example, in his suggestion of a 'paradigm' in terms of which to analyse data. The paradigm alerts the analyst to theoretical issues which can inform the analysis:

- Conditions
- Interactions
- Strategies and tactics
- Consequences

These are sociological preoccupations with analysing social processes. We might draw up a different checklist if we were interested in, for example, the processes of policy implementation. The following checklist is derived from a review of the extensive literature on factors influencing the success and failure of policy implementation (Sabatier 1986):

- Causal adequacy
- Financial resources
- Legal powers and constraints
- Political/interest group support
- Official/bureaucratic commitment
- Social/economic environment

There is no particular virtue in one checklist over another; one checklist is merely more or less fruitful than another in generating ideas for the analysis. Their value and relevance depends upon the preoccupations of the analyst and the nature of the data. None of the checklists we have mentioned, for example, seems especially relevant to our analysis of humour.

Even if we plagiarize other checklists, we have to construct one which is appropriate to our own purposes. Suppose we draw up a checklist for analysing humour on the basis of our earlier discussion of finding a focus. It might look like this:

**Humour checklist**
- Incongruity
- Catharsis
- Values
- Victims
- Stereotypes

We can look out for these aspects of humour in the data. This may be helpful, but we should also be mindful of the contingent character of any checklist and the need to adapt it to the data.

As an example, take the conversation in Illustration 7.1. Our checklist may alert us to different aspects of the humour of this sketch. An element of incongruity is evident, for example, in the unexpected use of bricks and tumbler driers to get to sleep; and in the sandwiches filled with soap powder and coconut matting. The checklist also suggests some interesting questions. Beattie and Connie are the ostensible 'victims' of this humour, but who do they represent? Does their gender matter? Is it significant that they are working (obviously secretaries) 'in the office'? And are they being ridiculed or is the criticism softened by empathy? What values are targeted through this shifting preoccupation with sleeplessness, deodorants, diet, and dress? And are these values affirmed or subverted? Is there an element of catharsis here, for example in the reference to 'body odour'?

*Illustration 7.1* 'In the Office'

| | |
|---|---|
| *Beattie* | You look tired, Connie. |
| *Connie* | I couldn't get off last night . . . I even had Dick throw a brick at my head to stun me but . . . |
| *Beattie* | Have you tried jamming your head in the tumble-drier and switching on? |
| *Connie* | No? |
| *Beattie* | It worked for me. Then of course the body gets accustomed. |
| *Connie* | Like deodorants. They work for a certain amount of time and then bang – people are backing away with handbags over their noses. |
| *Beattie* | You're not ponging too badly at the minute, Connie. |
| *Connie* | I've had my armpits stripped. A peel-off paste. Quite simple to apply though it has marked my cork flooring . . . |
| *Beattie* | What's in your sandwiches? |

| Connie | Soap powder. I think it's these drugs I'm on. Quite nice though. What's yours? |
| Beattie | Coconut matting. I'm doing the high fibre. |
| Connie | Did you watch the news? |
| Beattie | The nine o'clock? |
| Connie | Yes. Nasty blouse. |
| Beattie | We stayed up for News at Ten. Three bangles and a polo-neck, thank you. |
| Connie | No, her ears are in the wrong place for a polo-neck. |
| Beattie | You need to be Princess Di, really. |
| Connie | They've got the length of bone, haven't they, royalty? |

*Source:* Victoria Wood 1985: 33/4 (abridged)

Checklists can help but they can also inhibit. Part of the charm of the dialogue is in the language and the delivery. This delights in a different way from any discussed on our list : the kind of humour that resides in a recognition of authenticity – that that's just how things are. Perhaps we can think of this in terms of a 'creative' humour, did it not seem closer to a form of parody. Reading the data means rethinking and redeveloping our ideas.

Another useful technique for generating ideas is transposition. This involves asking 'What if' questions. What if this dialogue was between two men? What if the women were management rather clerical workers? What if the setting was a hospital rather than an office? Such transpositions can clarify the assumptions implicit in the situation and the dialogue, and our own reaction to it. They can generate quite new perspectives on the data. Would this sketch be less convincing and authentic were it presented as a dialogue between two male doctors in a hospital, and if so, why?

Transposition is a form of comparison, and this is another resource in responding creatively to the data. We can compare different sketches, for example: how does the 'In the Office' sketch compare with the 'Turkish Bath' sketch? The similarities and differences between the two sketches may be suggestive. But we can also stimulate our thinking by making comparisons outwith the data, such as with other types of humour, or situations which we ourselves have found amusing. Nor is there any need to confine ourselves to relatively analogous experiences; there is a place too for 'far-out' comparisons, as Strauss and Corbin (1990) put it.

Free association is another technique of value in literally setting the mind free of fixed assumptions and encouraging a more sensitive and critical response to the data. Take the key elements in the above dialogue: sleeplessness, odour, diet, dress – and free associate. Write down all the images that spring to mind. With humour, this is an especially useful exercise, for its power often lies in the whole baggage of assumptions and expectations which we as audience bring to bear.

In reading data we should be aware of the need to shift our focus between different levels within the data. We may use our attention as a telescope, considering the universe as a whole, or as a microscope fixed on a particular detail. Thus we can think about the sketch overall, or the use of one line or even one word within it. Of course we cannot attend to all the data in equal detail – we need to be selective, focusing on what seems 'outstanding', for example in the shape of key characters or especially funny lines. Thus we might take the discussion of the news as a 'key' point in the sketch, as it makes explicit the contrast between the supposedly serious world of public affairs and politics and the apparently ordinary – or petty? – concerns these women profess.

I say 'supposedly' and 'apparently' because we should be wary of first impressions; it is not at all clear that in making this contrast between the serious and the trivial, we are intended to endorse the former at the expense of the latter. This, of course, is the male stereotype of a female world, obsessed with the mundane and ignorant of vital public concerns. There is a converse stereotype, which contrasts the male's obsession with the vain and vacuous world of politics with the female's involvement in the real and personal issues of everyday life. This brings us neatly back to the contrast between the female comic who ridicules women, and the feminist comic who encourages women to think critically about the stereotypes that govern their lives (Merrill 1988).

As well as shifting focus, we can stimulate our thinking by shifting sequence. By this I mean reading through the data in various sequences, and not adopting a single and 'linear' approach. There may be circumstances in which a linear reading is useful if not indispensable – especially when looking at the unfolding of an historical process within the data. But often the sequence in which data happens to be stored is fairly arbitrary. Cases may be ordered, for example, according to when individuals were interviewed, or alphabetically. Yet the analyst remains wedded to an arbitrary order, and this may encourage bias, since almost inevitably attention may focus on those interviews (or in our example, sketches) which happen to come first. Incidentally, the computer may help to counter this bias by providing facilities for reading and analysing the data in random order.

Shifting sequence may involve more, though, than simply reading through material in a different order. Using the computer's search facilities, we can take different tacks through the data, focusing on key words or phrases and reading around these to produce a different perspective. This opens up a variety of pathways through the data. For example, we could take 'Victoria' as a key word, and explore the way Victoria Wood appears as herself in these sketches. We could pick up on issues like sleep or diet and ask the computer to look for other examples. Note that in doing so, it is essential to search for the terms used in the data, and not the terms in which we may have been thinking about it. A search for other examples of 'pong' may have more success than a search for 'body odour'! This is another virtue of shifting sequences in this way: it encourages the analyst to become familiar with the language used in the data, and acquire some sense of which terms are rare and which are prevalent.

We may be able to set up quite sophisticated searches for a family of related terms; if not, we can look sequentially for each member of the family. Either way, searches of this kind have inherent limitations, because the computer can only do what it is told. Since we cannot devise exhaustive searches for every item, we can never be sure that we have found all the relevant data that pertain to a topic. For example, there may be many interchanges about diet where the word itself is not mentioned explicitly. Nevertheless, as a springboard for thought and a guide to analysis, this can be a very useful way of exploring the data.

I have discussed briefly a number of techniques for reading data in an interactive way. These have not exhausted all possibilities, but readers can look for further guidance to discussions by Buzan (1982), Riley (1990) and Strauss and Corbin (1990).

The richness of qualitative data demands an equally rich response from the analyst. These techniques can provide a surprisingly straightforward and rewarding way of opening up lines of thought and lubricating the analysis. Without such lubricant, the analysis may not go very far.

---

**Techniques for interactive reading**
- The interrogative quintet
- The substantive checklist
- Transposing data
- Making comparisons
- Free association
- Shifting focus
- Shifting sequence

---

## ANNOTATING DATA

Elizabethan gallants or inns-of-court men carried 'table-books' about with them, to note down interesting anecdotes, witty jests, memorable remarks and the like (Wilson 1936: xli). The qualitative analyst likewise needs a version of the Elizabethan table-book, or perhaps of its modern equivalent, the Filofax, to help him or her to annotate their data. Annotating goes hand in hand with reading the data. We need to record our observations and ideas about the data in order to prepare the ground for further analysis. And we need to record them now, while we have them; and not even five minutes later, when that flash of insight has literally flashed out of existence!

Using field work techniques and even interviews, much of our data may take the form of notes. Annotating data involves making notes about the notes. To distinguish the two, we can call our notes about notes 'memos'. Memos may relate to any aspect of the data. They may record pedantic points of information – or brilliant leaps of imagination. They can encompass a panoramic sweep of the data, or pinpoint minutiae. It doesn't matter. They are simply a useful way of enriching our analysis.

It may be helpful to think of memos as essentially private, like diary entries. We don't have to justify them to anyone. We may record our first impressions of the data: 'I laughed here'; 'This isn't funny'. We may put down a jumble of confused ideas. We may ask naïve questions. Memoing should be a creative activity, relatively unencumbered by the rigours of logic and the requirements of corroborating evidence. Memos should be suggestive; they needn't be conclusive.

There are some tasks for which memos are particularly well suited. One is to comment closely and critically on the quality of the data. Suppose I didn't find a sketch funny, but the TV audience laughed uproariously. Was it a live audience? These are points worth noting. If the data is uneven, where are the strong and weak points? Where do we have most confidence in the data? Where is there evidence of bias? Memoing is another road to 'thorough' description: What is the context? What is meant? What happens? Can we clarify or elaborate on the data? Answering these questions provides a basis for well grounded interpretation.

Memoing can also be more analytic. What is this sketch about? Is this dialogue typical? Why is that a 'key' episode? Here we can bring into play the reading techniques outlined above, with the aim of stimulating ideas and developing new lines of inquiry (Illustration 7.2).

*Illustration 7.2* Using memos to open up lines of enquiry

| Data | | Memos |
| --- | --- | --- |
| *Beattie* | What's in your sandwiches? | 'Drugs' – we are not told what drugs, but I imagine valium etc. rather than cocaine. The implicit reference is surely to drug dependency. The humour |
| *Connie* | Soap powder. I think it's these drugs I'm on. Quite nice though. What's yours? | is in the effects – not just eating soap powder sandwiches, but finding them 'quite nice'! This is an example of incongruity – we don't expect people to eat and enjoy soap powder sandwiches. What kind of incongruity? Not exaggeration. Absurd, unbelievable. |
| | | Why soap powder – a hint of domesticity here? |

How should we record memos? The back of an envelope will do! But there are more reliable methods. Suppose as we are reading through some data we want to add a memo. On paper, we can either write the memo on the same sheet as the data – perhaps in the margin – or we can write it on a separate sheet. Neither method may seem very satisfactory. If we write on the same sheet, we make a clear connection between the data and our memo, but we may feel unduly intrusive and in danger of disrupting the flow of information. And suppose we change our minds and decide our comment is no longer appropriate, perhaps even misleading? On the other hand, if we write on a separate sheet, we leave the data undisturbed, but then the connection between our comment and the data is less apparent. We may overlook the comment, or lose it. Perhaps the paper clip provides a partial solution: we can write our comment on a separate sheet, and clip it to the sheet with the data. But this is a clumsy method of doing what the computer can achieve with elegance.

This is another way in which the computer allows us to keep things 'separately and yet together'. Using the computer, we can file our memo separately, leaving the data undisturbed, while at the same time linking our memo directly to precisely that part of the data we are commenting on. Then when we are analysing that part of the data, we can ask the computer to locate and display our memo. Or if we are reading our memos separately, we can ask the computer to locate and display the part of the data we are commenting on. We can keep the data pristine, without losing the connection between data and memo; the computer allows us to do both. In Illustration 7.3, for example, I have used an asterisk to link memos to particular points in the data. By selecting the word preceding the asterisk, the computer can immediately locate the appropriate memo which may be filed elsewhere. Similarly, by selecting the memo number, the computer can immediately locate the data to which the memo refers.

*Illustration 7.3* Linking memos and data

| Data | | Memos |
|------|---|-------|
| Connie | Like deodorants* They work for a certain amount of time and then bang – people are backing away with handbags* over their noses. | 1. I remember how we used to jeer at 'S.T.' in primary school. Body odour is a taboo topic – hence that advert whispering 'B.O.'. So the humour here is cathartic.<br><br>2. Also element of 'incongruity' in sudden handbag retreat. This is stuff of farce – a 'ludicrously improbable event'. Is farce one aspect of incongruity? Note that 'handbags' underlines 'body odour' as a female preoccupation. |
| Beattie | You're not ponging* too badly at the minute, Connie. | 3. We don't expect people to make frank comments on how we smell. And what kind of reassurance is this? 'Ponging' is good – 'smelling' wouldn't work nearly as well; in fact it might not work at all. Why not? |

Another advantage in recording memos this way is that we can retain the spontaneity which is a feature of creative endeavour. Without the computer, a separate memo might mean writing out the date, the references for the file and the data, and perhaps even extracts from the data being commented on. With the computer, we can escape this chore and concentrate entirely on recording what we are thinking.

Don't be misled by my reference to spontaneity in memo writing. We should not confuse spontaneity and simultaneity. Like Archimedes and Newton, we can expect ideas to make a sudden and unexpected appearance. But ideas rarely come on cue. There is no need to panic if we are not overwhelmed by stimulating insights the moment we work through part of the data. They may come later – in my experience usually when they are least welcome, in the wee small hours of the morning! Hence the back of the envelope.

We can relate our memos to the data. How do we relate them to our analysis? If we have to explore an unknown desert island, one thing we might do, as we traverse the island this way and that, is draw a map. We may want to acquire some sense of the island's topography – to outline its main physical features, to locate barren and fertile areas, to identify various paths across it – and to find the hidden treasure. However crude it may be, our map becomes our guide to further exploration. Much the same applies to exploring data. By mapping out our observations and ideas, we can provide a guide for further and more systematic analysis.

A map is a diagram based on our memos. It integrates disparate elements to make a common theme; it pulls together different themes to

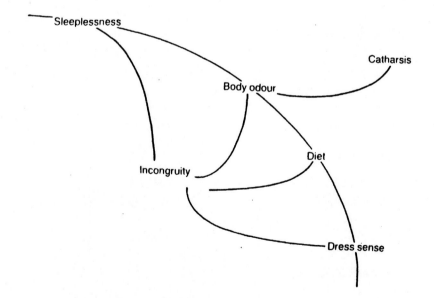

*Figure 7.1* Relating data to key themes

make a composite picture. Graphic representation allows us to see and question the connections between different parts of the whole. At this stage, it is a tentative business, oriented to puzzles and possibilities, not to a finished product.

Suppose we want to map out our memos of the 'In the Office' sketch. We might consider how various aspects of the sketch relate to the idea of humour as incongruity or catharsis (Figure 7.1).

Through mapping we can relate data systematically to particular ideas. Suppose we want to explore the use of incongruity a bit further. In one of our memos, we noticed a farcical element in the data. We can connect all the elements in the sketch which rely on farce for effect. We can use the same technique to map our ideas to data across different cases. Take the dialogue about the news. This evokes several stereotypes of women: they don't take public and political issues seriously, being immersed in mundane everyday concerns; they are obsessed with appearance – clothes, hair, make-up; they are prone to gossip at the expense of other women. We can begin to see ways of analysing this data in terms of stereotypes in humour. When we encounter similar examples in other sketches, we can recognize them more readily. Here for example is Kitty drinking her fifth cream sherry and talking affably to Morag:

> 'If I was Prime Minister, and thank goodness I'm not, because I've been the length and breadth of Downing Street and never spotted a decent wool shop. But if I were, I would put a hot drinks machine into the Houses of Parliament and turn it into a leisure centre. The income from that would pay off the national debt, and meanwhile we could all meet in Madge's extension.'
>
> (Victoria Wood 1985: 112)

Already we are on familiar ground: the important eclipsed by the mundane, political issues domesticated (Figure 7.2).

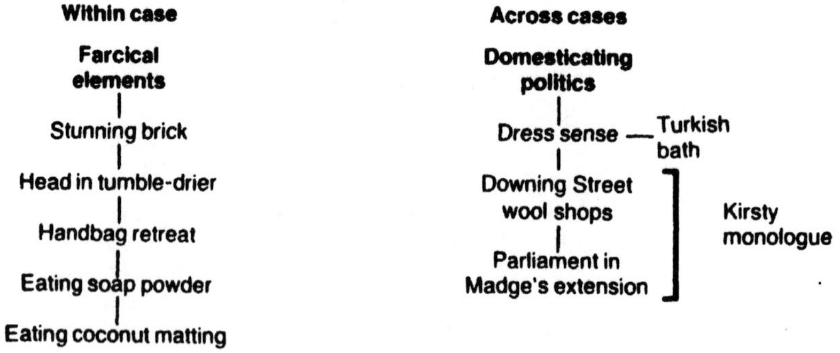

Figure 7.2 Mapping ideas to data within and across cases

As well as relating particular ideas to data, we can begin to sketch out possible relationships between ideas. For example, suppose we relate the stereotypes about women to the use of farce. We might map out the values which are assumed in this sketch – a series of stereotypes about women, some but not all of which are ridiculed through farcical images (Figure 7.3).

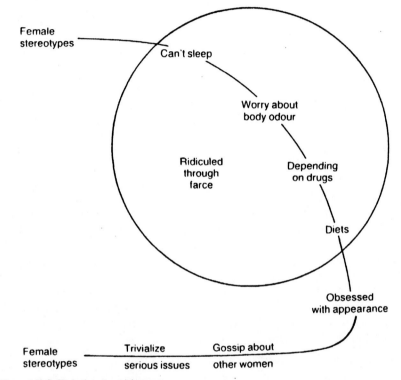

*Figure 7.3* Relating two ideas

Note that these diagrams remain close to the data, though they begin to point beyond it towards some ways of analysing the information. Note also how open-ended this mapping is. It is exploratory and suggestive – drawing out the threads of analysis, rather than organizing or classifying data in any systematic way.

Annotating data is a way of opening up the data, preparing the ground for a more systematic and thorough analysis. But the task of generating and developing ideas is not confined to one particular stage in the process. Even once we have embarked on a more organized and disciplined analysis, through categorizing and linking data, we may return again and again to the freer and more creative mode of annotating. In this way we can continue to capture the impressions, insights and intuitions which provide us with fresh perspectives and new directions for analysis.

# Chapter 8

# Creating categories

'We think in generalities, we live in detail'
(Whitehead quoted in Peter 1982: 493)

We have to interpret our data in order to analyse it. But analysis can go beyond interpretation. We can try to create conceptual tools to classify and compare the important or essential features of the phenomena we are studying. This involves a process of abstracting from the immense detail and complexity of our data those features which are most salient for our purpose. For example, the chemist focuses not on 'water' but on $H_2O$, stripping away the many connotations of the term to isolate those characteristics essential for analysis (Brooks and Warren 1967). Abstraction is a means to greater clarity and precision in making comparisons. We can focus on the essential features of objects and the relations between them. However, it is important to remember what we are abstracting from. The Taoist Chuang Tzu wrote:

> Fishing baskets are employed to catch fish; but when the fish are caught, the men forget the baskets; snares are employed to catch hares, but when the hares are got, men forget the snares. Words are employed to convey ideas, but when the ideas are grasped, men forget the words.
>
> (Quoted in Capra 1983: 36)

Abstractions are powerful means of making comparisons, but we must also remember their origins and limitations.

In making comparisons, it is helpful to distinguish between two forms of relation between objects or events (cf. Sayer (1992: 88). On the one hand, we can identify 'substantial' relations of connection and interaction. When we laugh at a joke, for example, there is a substantial connection between the joke and our laughter. On the other hand, we can identify purely 'formal' relations of similarity and difference between things. Thus we can distinguish between jokes and laughter, as different types of phenomena. This type of comparison involves categorizing phenomena according to their similarities or differences. In this and the following two chapters, I focus on how we can categorize qualitative data, before considering issues raised by substantive connections.

In this chapter, I shall look at the problems of generating categories for the analysis. In the following chapter I turn to the issues raised in assigning these categories to the data. Then in Chapter 10, the last dealing with categorizing data, I consider how we can 'split and splice' categories – in other words, subdivide or integrate categories as ways of refining or focusing our analysis. Naturally, we have to create categories before we can assign them, and we have to assign them before we can split or splice them. But despite this logical precedence, in practice we may find ourselves shifting backwards and forwards between these different aspects of categorizing data.

The very quality of qualitative data – its richness and specificity – makes for problems when we try to make comparisons between observations. For what are we comparing? There are no standard categories in terms of which to compare observations. Indeed, there are no clear boundaries as to what constitutes an observation.

To compare observations, we must be able to identify bits of data which can be related for the purposes of comparison. How can this be done? The answer is deceptively simple. In principle, we could organize the data by grouping like with like, so that any observation which seems similar to or related to others can be grouped with those observations. We can put all the bits of data which seem similar or related into separate piles, and then compare the bits within each pile. We may even want to divide up the items in a pile into separate 'sub-piles' if the data merits further differentiation. We can then compare observations within each pile or sub-pile, looking for interesting similarities or differences within the data. We can also make comparisons between the different piles or sub-piles, again looking for patterns or variations in the data.

However, this procedure begs two important questions. First, what is an observation? We referred above to 'bits' of data, but how are these bits to be identified or distinguished from the rest of the data? There must be some criterion or criteria which allow us to distinguish one bit or observation from another. Second, how can an observation be judged similar to or related to some other observations? Why put a bit of data into one pile, but not into another? Because they are alike, or related? But things are not just alike or related – they are alike or related in some respect or another. Although we may say that observations are alike or related without explaining why this is so, nevertheless there must be some respect or other in terms of which this judgement is made. If we distinguish between an employer and an employee, for example, we implicitly refer to a variety of social and economic features which characterize the difference between them. Distinctions are always conceptual as well as empirical – they reflect some criterion or criteria in terms of which observations are distinguished and compared. In data analysis, we can try to make explicit (or at any rate, as explicit as possible) the conceptual criteria in terms of which distinctions are made between observations.

Grouping data in this way therefore involves developing a set of criteria in terms of which to distinguish observations as similar or related. Typically, this is done through the development of a set of categories, with each category expressing a criterion (or a set of criteria) for distinguishing some observations from others, as similar or related in some particular respect(s). The development of a set of categories allows the data to be organized through a variety of different distinctions. Data within each category can then be compared. If necessary, further distinctions can then be drawn within each category to allow for a more detailed comparison of data organised within a set of sub-categories. Conversely, data assigned to different categories can be compared and interrelated to produce a more encompassing analysis of the data. This process can continue until the analyst is satisfied that all relevant distinctions between observations have been drawn, and observations can be compared effectively in terms of an established category system.

In categorizing data, we are not simply bringing together observations which are similar or related. A comparison is already implied in the adoption of a particular category. The data is being classified as 'belonging' to a particular group and this already implies a comparison between this data and other observations which do not 'belong' to the category in question. Categorizing involves differentiating between the included and excluded observations. The process of categorization may seem akin to naming observations, and in the literature is sometimes referred to as 'labelling' data and categories are sometimes referred to as 'labels'. However, this may be confusing and misleading if we think of 'naming' in terms of proper names rather than classes of objects. We may name a baby 'Rebecca' and this name distinguishes her from her siblings 'Katie' and 'Paul'. However, naming here simply aims to provide a label sufficiently unique (for practical purposes) to designate an individual person. It is not a label which stands for a class of objects – it is not a concept. There is a role for labelling in this sense of designating names for unique bits of data, as we shall see later. But where we are 'labelling' in order to group data, it may be less confusing to use the term 'categorization' for this process of making and applying distinctions within the data.

Creating categories is both a conceptual and empirical challenge; categories must be 'grounded' conceptually and empirically. That means they must relate to an appropriate analytic context, and be rooted in relevant empirical material. Categories which seem fine 'in theory' are no good if they do not fit the data. Categories which do fit the data are no good if they cannot relate to a wider conceptual context. We could say that categories must have two aspects, an internal aspect – they must be meaningful in relation to the data – and an external aspect – they must be meaningful in relation to the other categories.

It is not by accident, therefore, that we refer to creating categories in the plural. A category cannot be created in isolation from the other categories we want to use in the analysis. When we devise a category, we are making decisions about how to organize the data in ways which are useful for the analysis – and we have to take some account of how this category will 'fit' into this wider analytic context. It is usual, therefore, to think in terms of generating a set or list of categories through which to organize comparisons between observations. The formal relations between the categories are important in defining the relation between any particular category and the data. In generating categories, therefore, we have to think systematically and logically as well as creatively.

How does one begin to generate a category set? This is a question which researchers have had some difficulty in answering, in part because there is no single or simple answer. Obviously the methods of generating a category set will reflect the type of data being analysed, and also the aims, inclinations, knowledge and theoretical sophistication of the researcher. The theoretically-inclined participant observer with voluminous field-notes and the policy evaluator with a set of open-ended interview responses to analyse may have quite different starting points and quite different resources upon which to call. The theorist may be able to draw upon existing theoretical perspectives. By contrast, the policy evaluator is more than likely to generate a category system around an established set of policy issues, and specific categories may already have been anticipated in the methods used to collect data. That said, there are some considerations which may apply to the generation of categories, whatever the specific aims and circumstances of the analyst. This becomes clear if, rather than trying to characterize and contrast different approaches, we consider instead the common resources which can be utilized in any approach to generating a category set.

One source of ideas for generating categories is the data itself. Qualitative methods often involve the acquisition of data which cannot be accommodated within pre-existing categories. This is, indeed, usually part of the rationale and justification for using a qualitative approach. It is assumed that the researcher cannot establish all (or perhaps any) of the important categorical distinctions at the outset of the research. In some forms of research, such as participant observation or ethnography, the analyst may be reluctant to adopt any prior conceptions before entering the field, and may therefore depend almost entirely on inferring distinctions from the data. In less unstructured research, though some categories may be established in advance, these may still require confirmation in the data, while other categories or subcategories may be derived from distinctions suggested in the data. Even with a relatively structured technique, such as a structured interview schedule with open-ended questions, all the responses produced cannot be assigned to categories in advance of analysing the data. At the very least the adoption of a pre-existing set of categories requires confirmation that these are indeed the important distinctions within the data. In any case, these distinctions are more than likely to be preliminary rather than exhaustive. Further differentiation within each category will almost certainly draw upon distinctions made within the data.

Thus distinctions within the data can generate new categories, or contribute significantly to refining or modifying the original categories. Amongst those using qualitative techniques, there is usually a strong emphasis on creating categories based on distinctions in the data, most especially where these are recognized or used by the research subjects themselves. Qualitative research is often concerned to elucidate the ways in which subjects experience and perceive situations and events. It would certainly be difficult if not impossible to convey these experiences and perceptions without taking account of how the subjects themselves distinguish situations and events.

At the same time, qualitative researchers often employ observational methods which may produce data inconsistent with how subjects experience, perceive or explain events. A subject's 'explanations' of events may involve assumptions or preconceptions which s/he only dimly recognizes, if at all; and 'explanation' can serve a variety of purposes, including self-justification and exculpation, which have little to do with providing an accurate or truthful account. Thus some distinctions may be drawn by the subjects of the research, while others may be suggested by the data, though not recognized explicitly or even implicitly by the subjects themselves.

Categories should not be imposed upon the data arbitrarily; the categories adopted should reflect the data. The distinctions established through categorization should be meaningful in terms of the data being analysed. However, reflecting the data does not mean that categories merely reproduce distinctions which are made or are apparent in the data, although these distinctions can sometimes provide some useful ideas for categorization. A 'reflection' (i.e. mirror image) involves a new view of the data – that of the researcher; and this view can only emerge through 'reflection' (i.e. thought) on the part of the analyst, since the distinctions drawn must be those of the analyst, and related to the overall direction and purpose of the research. Distinctions must serve some analytic purpose which the analyst brings to the data. The actor acts; the analyst analyses – this is integral to their respective roles as subject and researcher. This dictum is not the whole truth, for its inversion may also be applicable – the actor may also analyse and the analyst may also act. But the analyst cannot escape responsibility for the analysis, which must be based on his or her own ideas about the data.

Categorization of the data requires a dialectic to develop between categories and data. Generating and developing categories is a process in which one moves backwards and forwards between the two. It is this interaction of category and data which is crucial to the generation of a category set. To try to generate categories in the absence of both these resources would be premature. Although we can consider these as separate resources, in practice the generation of categories is an interaction between the two. For example, even if we have not read a single line of data, any ideas we have prior to the analysis must still anticipate the kind of data we will want to analyse.

A rich source of ideas for categories can be found in the questions in terms of which the research originated and developed. These questions, perhaps vaguely formed and poorly articulated at the outset, may already have been considerably redefined and reformulated by the time the final stage of data analysis has been reached. The process of research, whether through interviewing, documentary analysis, or observation, inevitably involves selecting data. This selection is made by the researcher in terms of what seems significant, puzzling or problematic, and the criteria used in selecting data can provide a rich source of ideas for generating a category system.

In documentary analysis, for example, the criteria for selecting documents, or for focusing on particular extracts, should reflect the issues on which the researcher is seeking evidence. There must be some criteria for inclusion and exclusion of documentary data, even if these are broadly defined and refer mainly to the boundaries rather than the substance of the subject being researched. With interviewing, the researcher will have some idea in advance of what questions to ask and which topics to pursue – no matter how non-directive the interviewer may be, the interview has to be conducted with some research purpose in mind. With observation, the observer must make decisions about which sites, situations and events to observe. Often these decisions will be affected by the data emerging from observation and new priorities will develop through the course of the research. In each of these approaches, initial or emergent issues, more or less explicitly defined by the researcher, will provide some guidance to the categories worth developing in the analysis of data. While, in the nature of qualitative research, such questions are not likely to be either comprehensive or exhaustive, they may nevertheless provide a vital starting point for generating categories for analysis.

The process of finding a focus for the analysis, and reading and annotating the data, leads on naturally to the creation of categories. In practice, a sharp distinction cannot be drawn between these processes. The techniques we discussed earlier for generating ideas also provide fertile ground for the generation of categories. However, compared with browsing and annotating data, creating a category set requires a more disciplined and systematic approach. Ideas must be sifted, their import assessed, their relevance evaluated. Some may be discarded. Others may suggest key concepts through which to understand the data.

---

**Resources for generating categories**
- Inferences from the data
- Initial or emergent research questions
- Substantive, policy and theoretical issues
- Imagination, intuition and previous knowledge

---

Any or all of these resources can be brought to bear in the task of generating categories for analysis. It is not possible to predict in advance which will prove most useful in developing a category set. That will depend both on the richness and complexity of the data being analysed, and the range and relevance of the experience and ideas which the researcher can bring to the analysis.

Suppose we want to derive a category set from our ideas on humour. Through our initial efforts to find a focus for the analysis, we identified some key ideas to use in the analysis:

- Incongruity
- Catharsis
- Values
- Victims
- Stereotypes

These ideas were inspired by a prior reading of the relevant literature, and their relevance to our analysis has been established through our review and annotation of the data. Do they provide a useful basis for distinguishing differences and similarities in the data? We have found sufficient elements of the different styles of humour to be confident in the general utility of these ideas. We can treat them tentatively as the first approximation of a category set through which to analyse the data.

At the same time, we may want to modify the categories in the light of our knowledge of the data. We might note an element of exaggeration in the sketch 'In the Office', in the references to tarmacking the drive eight times, or receiving seventeen phone calls. There is also an element of transposition, where the women discuss dress instead of the news. We may want to modify our categories in the light of these observations, by adding to our list or perhaps by incorporating them as elements of existing categories. For instance, we could see both exaggeration and transposition as interactive elements in incongruous humour, the latter confirming our expectations only for the former to confound them.

- Incongruity (exaggerating, transposing)

- Catharsis
- Values
- Victims
- Stereotypes

While annotating the data, we noted the role of stereotypes in creating humorous effects. The humour invoked stereotypical views of women's problems with sleeplessness, diet, drugs, their concerns with appearance and body odour, and an inclination to frivolity and gossip. We may therefore want to develop some categories to capture the kind of stereotypes being used. There is no one way to categorize this data: we must chose between different alternatives. When we create a category based on the data, we address the general question: 'What is this data about?'. We also address more specific questions inspired by our analytic concerns: e.g. 'How is this funny?' 'What kind of stereotypes are used here?'. Categories express ideas about the data. The categories we use will reflect the kind of questions we ask. For example, we could try either of the two category sets listed in Table 8.1

*Table 8.1* Alternative category lists

| Detailed category list | Broad category list |
| --- | --- |
| Sleeplessness | Health |
| Odour | Appearance |
| Diet | Character |
| Drugs | |
| Dress | |
| Gossip | |
| Frivolity | |

The first list of categories is longer and more refined; the second is shorter and more general. One list stays close to the data; the other is at one remove, already implying an implicit categorization (Figure 8.1)

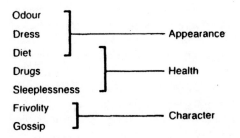

*Figure 8.1* Alternative category lists for analysing female stereotypes

We might amend our category set to incorporate these ideas, for example by including the shorter, more general categories in our category list:

- Incongruity (exaggerating, transposing)
- Catharsis
- Creativity
- Values
- Victims
- Stereotypes (appearance, character, health)

There are at least three questions we might ask of this list of categories. What do these categories mean? Is this list sufficiently refined? And what about relationships between the categories? Let us take each of these points in turn.

First, let us take the question of what the categories mean. We noted above that categories must denote bits of data, and relate this data conceptually to the wider analysis. The meaning of a category is therefore bound up on the one hand with the bits of data to which it is assigned, and on the other hand with the ideas it expresses. These ideas may be rather vague at the outset of the analysis. The meaning of a category is something that evolves during the analysis, as we make more and more decisions about which bits of data can or cannot be assigned to the category. To make these decisions, we need not just a category but also a developing set of criteria in terms of which we can decide when and where to assign the category to the data. In other words, we should always try to define and redefine our categories by specifying and modifying the criteria for assigning them to the data. Without such criteria, our analysis may seem arbitrary and impressionistic. At the same time, we must recognize that any definitions we develop at the outset are liable to be rather general and contingent in character. In defining categories, therefore, we have to be both attentive and tentative – attentive to the data, and tentative in our conceptualizations of them.

Take the category 'catharsis' as an example. We introduced this category to refer to humour which involves some sort of emotional release, and related it to topics which are anxiety-laden or even taboo. Now we need to 'operationalize' this category in terms of observations in the data. We might start with sex and violence as subjects which are often sensitive issues. 'Often' is not 'always' and not all references to sex and violence will be 'cathartic'. We might also start to think about what 'sensitivity' involves. Suppose we try to make preliminary 'definitions' of the main categories we have created so far (Illustration 8.1).

This is only a starting point. Our 'definitions' are notably vague, reflecting the rather abstract nature of the categories we have chosen. We

*Illustration 8.1* Preliminary definitions of categories

| Incongruity | Include any data where expectations are disrupted. |
|---|---|
| | Disrupted expectations are not always humorous. Identify elements involved in humorous disruption: farce, absurdity, exaggeration. |
| Catharsis | Include any data which can be seen as sensitive in some way. |
| | Possible topics: sex, violence. |
| | Sensitivity: associated with discomfort, embarrassment, humiliation, guilt. |
| Values | Include any data which relates to the affirmation or subversion of social values. |
| Victims | Include any data where humour has an identifiable human target, but only where this target may be representative of a wider group or institution. |
| | Include any such targets, regardless of whether or not the humour ridicules or criticizes with empathy. |
| Stereotypes | Include any data which seems to invoke stereotypical images. |
| | A stereotype is an 'unduly fixed' image which may or may not be accurate but is applied regardless. |
| | Note that not all fixed images are stereotypes. |

must be ready to extend or modify our criteria as the data demands. We shall therefore return to the problem of defining categories when we consider the process of assigning them to the data.

Meantime let us turn to the question of whether our initial category list is sufficiently refined. Our category set is short, and the categories are very general. Is this satisfactory? Should it be nearer eight categories, than eighty, or eight hundred? There is no single answer to this question. Data analysts who emphasize the importance of 'grounding' categories in the data sometimes advocate a 'line-by-line' approach to generating categories (see Strauss 1987). Perhaps more accurately, this is a 'bit-by-bit' approach where each bit of data can be as small as a single word. Each bit is considered in detail, to identify aspects which may be relevant to the analysis. The significance of a bit of data can be considered by contrasting it with other bits, by imagining this bit in alternative contexts, or by drawing on relevant theoretical or policy issues. In this way a variety of distinctions may emerge, some of which may eventually prove fruitful in analysing the data. The aim is to generate theory which is fully grounded in the data. Once categories have been developed in this detailed way, the analyst can identify the most relevant categories for further elaboration, and finally proceed to a more integrated analysis around the core categories which emerge from this process.

By contrast, it is possible to begin with categories which are based on a general comprehension of the data and proceed to a fuller and more detailed categorization (Jones 1985). The emphasis here is on a 'holistic' approach, attempting to grasp basic themes or issues in the data by absorbing them as a whole rather than by analysing them line by line. Broad categories and their interconnections are then distilled from a general overview of the data, before a more detailed analysis fills in and refines these through a process of subcategorization. This approach is more feasible where the analyst already has a fair idea of what s/he is looking for in the data.

Most data analysis probably falls some way between these two extremes. Perhaps the most flexible approach is to develop 'middle-order' categories, which draw some broad preliminary distinctions within the data (cf. Becker and Geer 1982). Often these distinctions may be based on fairly common sense categories, around which the data can be organized quite effectively, without implying commitment to any particular theoretical approach. This approach also fits well with policy-oriented research where a policy agenda already provides a source of categories for analysis. Once the data has been organized into broad categories, the analysis can move in either direction, towards more refined distinctions through subcategorization or towards a more integrated approach by linking and integrating the 'middle-order' categories.

A middle-order approach offers a flexible compromise which allows the analysis to develop in a more detailed or holistic way as time and inclination permits. A middle-order approach is also attractive if the data, although qualitative, is not entirely lacking in structure. Policy issues and programme conditions in evaluative research, for example, can provide a framework for generating a middle-order category set which can already be anticipated in the identification of 'key issues' used in collecting data. Our choice may be as much influenced by our confidence in the organizing power of our initial categories as by any considerations of time or purpose, significant though these may be. For example, if our ideas from other sources at the outset of data analysis are very limited, we may find a bit-by-bit approach applied to at least part of the data is most useful in generating categories for the analysis.

None of these approaches has a monopoly of virtue, and whether one takes a holistic view, begins with middle-order categories or starts with a bit-by-bit analysis must be a question of pragmatism rather than principle. There is no sense in undertaking a bit-by-bit analysis, for example, if time does not permit such a detailed and laborious approach, with the result that some parts of the data are never properly analysed. Where time is tight, a middle-level or holistic approach may provide a better method of selecting data for categorization. On the other hand, a bit-by-bit approach may be better suited to data analysis where the overriding aim is to use the data to generate theory rather than bringing it to bear on existing policy or theoretical concerns.

In any case, the contrast between these different approaches can be overdrawn, since we are only discussing where to begin. In categorizing the data, the analyst has to work at each of these levels. A holistic approach has still to be rooted in the data, through middle-level categories and bit-by-bit analysis. A middle-level approach has to be geared from the start to the development of a more detailed and integrated analysis. With a bit-by-bit approach, the analyst must become more selective and integrative in subsequent phases of the analysis.

One good reason for adding categories to a set is to ensure that our category list is sufficiently comprehensive. Obviously the length of a category list will depend in part on the range of issues and the breadth of the data being analysed. However, we can also add categories by developing a more refined category set. Would this not save time going over the same material again later to make further distinctions within it? Or would a more extensive category set depend on making further subdivisions than seems desirable at this point in the analysis?

Why not make distinctions now, if it saves us work later on? If categories are too broad, too much data would be included within each category for useful comparisons to be possible. The data would cover too many distinctive topics, and still require further differentiation along the broad lines which we can already identify as relevant at this point in the analysis. Why not assign the data immediately to the more refined category, reducing two operations to one? Why produce an enormous and unwieldy mass of data under a single category, if the data can already be more differentiated amongst several?

Against a concern with efficiency, however, we must balance the issue of confidence. The introduction of more refined distinctions at this stage should only contemplated if we are confident that these distinctions are sufficiently grounded conceptually and empirically to form a useful framework for analysis. In general, we may prefer to use broad categories at the outset to avoid prejudicing subsequent analysis and perhaps even precluding particular lines of development. It is important not to close off options at this stage by making distinctions which are not based on a thorough review of all the relevant data. This will only create more work later on. 'Errors' in initial categorization also exact a price in terms of subsequent efficiency.

There are advantages in leaving the task of refining categories until later. One is that all the data for a category can be brought together and examined as a whole before deciding upon any refinements. This may be useful in identifying the weight attached to particular issues and establishing the connections between them. A detailed inspection of the data may suggest a rather different way of refining the analysis. Rather than make precipitate judgements at this stage, it may be better to wait until all the data has been categorized under the broad category. The main purpose of a middle-order category set is to make possible a more detailed inspection of the data by extracting and ordering observations through some broad preliminary distinctions.

Another difficulty with using too many detailed categories is simply remembering all the relevant categories in terms of which the data can be distinguished. So long as categories are broad, this need not be a major problem, as it will generally be fairly obvious whether the data can be distinguished under one heading or another. But if a category list becomes lengthy through being excessively detailed, it may be difficult to recall all the relevant distinctions when working through the data. An unduly long and cumbersome category list would be difficult to apply to the data.

The degree of refinement at this stage in the analysis may therefore reflect the volume of data to be analysed and the degree to which categories can be readily identified. In developing an initial category set, we may as well take account of distinctions which are already clearly relevant, providing always that this does not preclude the possibility of developing the analysis later on in a variety of directions. Obviously the degree of refinement required is difficult to determine, since we have to balance some competing considerations in devising an initial category set. How this balance is struck may affect the reliability, efficiency and flexibility of the analysis. Too few categories, and later flexibility may be ensured, but at a high price in terms of efficiency, since distinctions still have to be made which could have been applied in the initial categorization. Too many categories, and efficiency may be enhanced, but at the expense of reliability and later flexibility. Striking a reasonable balance is a matter of judgement, reflecting the range, complexity and volume of data to be differentiated (Figure 8.2).

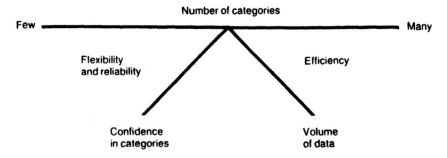

*Figure 8.2* Weighing up the degree of refinement in initial category set

Returning to our categories for stereotypes, we must weigh up the virtues of using a more or less refined list. The more refined, the more categories we shall use. A single sketch has generated several possible categories – drugs, diet, etc. – and we have to beware of being overwhelmed by the sheer number of similarly refined categories generated by the data, which includes many other sketches. We may benefit by using the more general categories – health, appearance and character – which also express more interesting conceptual distinctions. Even these distinctions could be dispensed with, if we opted instead for a very general category 'stereotypes'. But at this level of generality, we may be overwhelmed by the sheer volume of data which would be categorized under such a general category. At a minimum we may want to differentiate between different kinds of stereotypes, and we may also start to refine other categories to produce a much more extensive category list (Illustration 8.2).

At this point, we can turn to our third question and consider relationships between the categories we use. This raises two basic issues. First, are categories inclusive or exclusive? And second, how many levels of classification do we want to use?

*Illustration 8.2* Developing a more extensive category list

Catharsis–sex
Catharsis–suffering
Catharsis–other
Incongruity–exaggerating
Incongruity–transposing
Incongruity–other
Values–confirming
Values–subverting
Victims–ridiculing
Victims–empathizing
Stereotype–appearance
Stereotype–health
Stereotype–character

Categories can be either inclusive or exclusive. If two categories are inclusive, then we can assign them both to the same bit of data without being inconsistent. If two categories are exclusive, then we can only assign one or other to the bit of data. Categories which are exclusive are always related in some way to an underlying concept or overarching category. In Figure 8.3 I have differentiated between inclusive and exclusive categories by using different ways of depicting the way categories interrelate. I have used a long bar with short arms to bracket those categories which are inclusive, and a short bar with longer arms to indicate those which are exclusive. Thus the category 'victims' includes two exclusive categories 'ridiculing' and 'empathizing', while the category 'stereotypes' embraces three categories which are inclusive. Because the categories 'victims' and 'stereotypes' are inclusive rather than exclusive, we could assign 'ridiculing' and 'appearance' to the same bit of data. It doesn't matter how you choose to depict these different relations between categories, so long as they are consistently noted in some way.

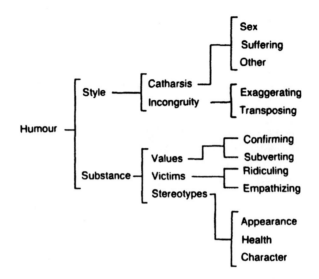

*Figure 8.3* Developing a more refined category list

Second, we have to consider levels of classification. Figure 8.3 already involves four levels of classification, with some categories 'nested' within others. But in terms of our category set, some of these levels can be deemed redundant when it comes to categorizing the data. There is simply no point in using the category 'humour' – nor of distinguishing between 'style' and 'substance'. These are distinctions which may be useful conceptually, but have little analytic power when it comes to organizing the data. They do not discriminate sufficiently between different aspects of the data. At most we might opt for a couple of levels, using the subcategories of style and substance, and their own subcategories. It is important to keep track of these different levels of classification, and the easiest way to do this is graphic representation. Some computer packages provide facilities to support this aspect of analysis.

Although conceptually our classification includes different levels, in practice we can operate as though we have an undifferentiated category set. This is more efficient since it saves categorizing the data at different levels. We do not want to have to assign overarching categories, where we have already used the relevant subcategory. For example, if we have used the category 'appearance' then we don't need to assign its overarching category, 'stereotype'. We know anyway that the data assigned to 'appearance' also belongs to the category 'stereotype'. Suppose later on we want to compare all the data implicitly assigned to the category 'stereotype'? How can we if we have not assigned the category? The computer provides a simple answer, since it allows us to locate or combine all the bits of data assigned initially to the separate subcategories.

In developing our category list, therefore, we can include only the most refined categories. To proceed in this way using a single category list is simpler and more efficient, but there are two requirements we must meet. Combining categories later on is only possible if we use a unique specification for each category in our category set. Our initial category set must therefore contain no duplicates. We have to designate each subcategory uniquely, and not assume that the computer will differentiate between two identical subcategories which belong to different overarching categories.

The second requirement is that our categories must be exhaustive. Where the subcategories are exhaustive, there is no need to include the over-arching category in the list, since it is entirely included within the subcategories. Where the categories are not exhaustive, a residual category is required to pick up data which cannot be assigned to the appropriate subcategories. This decision may be taken in establishing an initial list, but the question of 'exhaustion' is one which really can be answered only in relation to the data. At any point, we may have to amend our list if we encounter data which does not fit within the existing subcategories. In practice, therefore, it may be convenient to use an overarching category, such as 'stereotype', as a residual category for data which cannot be readily assigned initially to one of its subcategories. This allows us to retain flexibility in the development of the analysis and avoid premature judgements for the sake of efficiency.

So far, we have looked at the resources upon which we can draw in creating categories, and the issues which arise in creating an initial category list. To conclude this discussion, let us consider some common injunctions applied to the process of creating categories. This process can take a variety of forms, depending in part on the purpose of the research and in part on the time and resources available for the analysis. While qualitative data analysis is not an endeavour subject to 'rules', there are several points worth considering in developing a category system. These provide some general guidelines which can be adopted (or adapted) as appropriate, rather than an established set of procedures to be followed mechanically.

Category development requires the analyst to become thoroughly familiar with the data, and it is worthwhile acquiring this familiarity at an early stage in the analysis. Although this may seem a rather innocuous point, in practice becoming thoroughly familiar with the data can prove quite an onerous undertaking. When observations are voluminous, as is often the case with qualitative data, the temptation to take short-cuts is considerable. Given the constraints imposed on research budgets and timetables, and the limited aims of some data analysis, some short-cuts may also be to some extent unavoidable. However, time spent becoming thoroughly absorbed in the data early in the analysis may save considerable time in the later stages, as problems are less likely to arise later on from unexpected observations or sudden changes in tack.

Perhaps the most common injunction to would-be analysts is that data must always be considered in context. One of the major concerns of qualitative analysis is the observation of opinion or behaviour within a 'natural' setting. From this perspective, meaning depends upon context, and the interpretation of action or opinion must take account of the setting in which it is produced. An observation cannot be fully understood outwith the context in which it is made. To consider this fully, it is often essential to regard the researcher as part of the context being studied. This is obviously relevant in interviews, where the respondent is responding to some sort of stimulus on the part of the interviewer. It is also relevant in observational research where the researcher interacts socially with the subjects of the study. How subjects perceive and respond to the observer can then have a significant effect on what they say or do. The researcher's own actions and perceptions therefore become part of the social interaction, and need to be observed and analysed as such.

The injunction to consider context may seem somewhat paradoxical, however, since for the purposes of comparison, it is necessary to abstract data from its immediate context, and consider it from a point of view which transcends that context and allows the data to be compared with observations made in a different context. For example, a stereotypical comment may be made in the context of specific sketch, and yet I may want to compare these stereotypical comments across a range of different sketches. These observations must therefore be abstracted from their immediate context. However, confirmation is required that these comments can be meaningfully compared. In practice, this confirmation can be established partly through comparing how stereotypical comments have been used in different contexts. We saw earlier how much observation depends upon implicit classification, or, in other words, implicit comparisons. Thus comparison is itself a useful method of identifying and understanding the specific context within which observations occur. This does not remove the tension between analysing meaning in context and analysing it through comparison, but it does imply that both processes are necessary for an adequate elucidation and interpretation of the data. This is why categories have to be meaningful both internally, in relation to the data understood in context, and externally, in relation to the data understood through comparison.

A third point concerns alternative ways of categorizing observations. Our category set cannot be entirely arbitrary, for it must make sense of the data. But there is no single set of categories waiting to be discovered. There are as many ways of 'seeing' the data as one can invent. Any distinction has to be considered in relation to the purpose for which it is drawn. With respect to that purpose, it may be more or less useful, but one distinction cannot be considered more or less valid than another independently of the reasons why it is made. It is better to be profligate in producing alternative categories than to foreclose analysis by adopting one particular set too early on in the analysis.

A related point is that flexibility in extending, modifying and discarding categories is important in developing an effective category system. The fit between data and categories is subject to continual adjustment. Flexibility is required to accommodate fresh observations and new directions in the analysis. Categories may be extended or modified to cope with data which does not quite fit, but at some point categories which cannot cope with the range and complexity of the data must simply be discarded in favour of more promising alternatives. It is also likely that the analysis will shift in emphasis or direction as initial assumptions are modified in the light of the data. New categories may be needed which more accurately reflect the changing aims of the analyst.

Categories can be considered, not just in terms of the data but also in terms of their connections with other categories. While the same observations may be categorized in several different ways, reflecting different aspects of the analysis, too much overlap between categories leads to an inefficient and cumbersome analysis. As far as possible, categories reflecting the same dimension of the analysis should not overlap unduly. If categories do overlap, then this should reflect significant differences in the distinctions being made about the data.

Developing categories usually involves looking forwards towards the overall results of the analysis as well as looking backwards towards the data. It is worth working towards a holistic view, even if this may not be feasible at the outset. It is not the case that a more holistic view will somehow simply emerge from an accumulation of detailed categorization. Perhaps if we plant a sufficient number of individual trees, we do create a wood, but to see the trees as a wood still requires a shift of vision. To pursue the analogy, it is also necessary to plant trees whose type and location are related, for otherwise there will be no wood but simply a jumble of scattered trees. Therefore it is as important to consider the relation between categories as it is to consider the relation between a particular category and the data.

The process of developing categories is one of continuous refinement. Inevitably, the criteria for including and excluding observations, which may be rather vague at the outset, become more precise during the course of the analysis. These criteria need to be set out as clearly as possible if observations are to categorized in a reliable way. It is worth trying to spell this out as far as possible at the outset. If nothing else, this will indicate where ambiguities exist which one can try to clarify or remove during the process of categorizing observations. Decisions about what to include and exclude are themselves part of the process of clarifying the criteria involved. In developing categories, therefore, it is useful to keep track of the criteria which are being adopted in making such decisions. Recording these criteria provides a running commentary on how a category is being used and provides a basis for developing a more precise statement of what distinctions are being drawn. Where the research is a cooperative activity and more than one person is involved in analysing the data, this is essential if categories are to be applied on a consistent and uniform basis. But much the same point applies even where only one analyst is involved, since even here there is a need to secure a consistent approach and avoid arbitrary and ad hoc decisions.

Since categorizing observations is a crucial phase in data analysis, there is some virtue in regarding this as a public rather than private activity. In other words, we may consider how decisions about categorizing data can be explained and justified to others. This can help to sharpen our approach and ensure sufficient rigour in decisions about categorization. It may also help to clarify the relationship between observations, interpretation and the overall results of the analysis. We may be better placed to explain why a particular tack has been taken in analysing the data, why some distinctions have come to be regarded as crucial while others have been discarded, and just how comparisons resulting from categorization are rooted in the available evidence.

---

**Some common injunctions in creating categories**
- Become thoroughly familiar with the data
- Always be sensitive to the context of the data
- Be flexible – extend, modify and discard categories
- Consider connections and avoid needless overlaps
- Record the criteria on which category decisions are to be taken
- Consider alternative ways of categorizing and interpreting data

---

The categories that we create become the basis for organizing and conceptualizing our data. Categorizing is therefore a crucial element in the process of analysis, and as well as considering how to create categories, we also have to consider the issues involved in assigning them. This will be the focus of the following chapter.

# Chapter 9

# Assigning categories

Having established an initial category set, we can turn to the task of categorizing the data. For clarity I consider these as distinct activities. In practice, there is no need to develop a complete category set in advance of categorizing the data. As the ensuing discussion makes clear, the process of assigning categories will almost certainly lead us to modify whatever categories are employed at the outset.

What does categorizing the data involve? At a practical level, it involves the transfer of bits of data from one context (the original data) to another (the data assigned to the category). The bits of data are not actually transferred: they are copied, and the copy filed under the appropriate category (Figure 9.1)

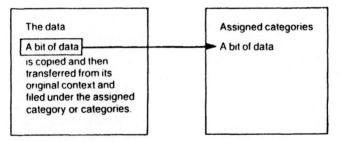

*Figure 9.1* Categorizing data – 1

The mechanical aspects of this process are so simple – copying and filing – that it is no surprise that computer software has been designed to facilitate this task. The conceptual aspects are more complex – but more of that later. Meantime, let us give our computer a bit more work to do by complicating the mechanical process a little. We may want to note where the categorized bit of data is in the text, so that we can return to the right place in the data after a break. We may want to assign more than one category to the data. We may want to file some reference information, such as the case reference, or reference information (e.g. question, source) about the particular bit of data being categorized. We may want to file the exact location of the data in the original text. We may want to denote our bit of data in some way, perhaps supplying a brief synopsis ourselves or using the first few words as a way of indexing the data. We may want to record the date at which this category was made. We may even (in joint research) want to record which analyst has done the categorizing (Figure 9.2).

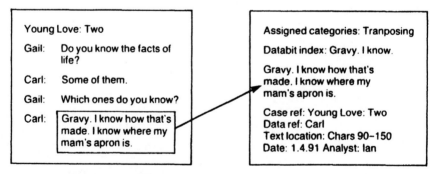

*Figure 9.2* Categorizing data – 2

Though in essence our task remains a simple one, we have managed nevertheless to produce a fairly formidable set of requirements. To fulfil these requirements each time we want to categorize a bit of data is a rather long and tedious process (Figure 9.3).

*Figure 9.3* Categorizing data – 3

Time spent on mechanical routines is time wasted. Fortunately, computer software is available which can automatically accomplish most if not all of these tasks, leaving the analyst to concentrate on the task of selecting categories to assign to the data.

Before we leave the mechanics of categorizing data, there are some other aspects worth noting. Assuming any additional information can be recorded automatically, the mechanical task of categorizing reduces to two selections. We must select a bit of data, and we must select a category (or categories). The computer allows these selections to be made with the minimum of physical effort. No more rummaging around for that mislaid category list. The computer will present the list whenever we need it. No more copying data and categories by hand – the computer will copy any selection for us. Incidentally, this facility makes the use of 'codes' in place of categories rather redundant. The rationale for using codes is to abbreviate category names and so reduce to a minimum the task of writing (or typing) out long names. The drawback is the loss of intelligibility. Such codes are no longer required, although there may still be some virtue in abbreviating category names to make them shorter, providing they remain intelligible.

Another software facility to support the process of categorization is 'linking' through Hypertext procedures. We shall consider the use of Hypertext 'linking' to analyse substantive relations within the data in a later chapter. Meantime, we should note that linking can give us immediate access to information which may be useful in assigning categories. For example, suppose we have a 'dictionary' containing conceptual 'definitions' of the categories we are using. By 'linking' the categories in our list to the categories in our dictionary the computer can give us direct access to our current definition for any category. We can also locate empirical examples of bits of data which we have previously assigned to the category. Both of these contribute to the meaning of our category, and the ability to review quickly the current definition and previous assignations of any category can help make categorization a more efficient and reliable process.

Let us turn now to some of the conceptual issues which arise when we assign categories to the data. The first question we encounter involves deciding what constitutes a 'bit' of data. Again, there is no 'right' answer to this question. We may want to categorize words, lines, sentences or paragraphs. Sometimes computer software may limit our options, for example where bits of data are identified through line numbering rather than free selection within the text. Whatever we decide, we should aim for some consistency in the size of the bits we categorize, especially if we want to assess later the weight of evidence supporting our analysis by considering the number of bits we have assigned to a category. At the same time, we need to be flexible, and take account of the varying character of the data. A long sentence may contain more 'bits' than a short paragraph. Grammar can only serve as a rule-of-thumb guide to selecting bits. Since ideas can be expressed succinctly or expansively, the number of words is less important than the meaning they convey. The underlying consideration should be the relevant 'unit of meaning' which is conveyed by content rather than form. Does the bit of data present an intelligible and coherent point which is in some sense self-sufficient, even if we cannot fully grasp its meaning out of context? We may look for natural breaks and transitions within the data – often but not invariably reflected in its grammar – which distinguish one 'unit of meaning' from another. This process of breaking up the data is inevitably to some extent arbitrary. But just as we would look askance at a jigsaw puzzle where some of the pieces were very small and some very large, so we are entitled to expect some consistency in the divisions which are drawn within the data.

To illustrate this process, let us look at a letter ostensibly written by Vincent Van Gogh to his brother Theo (Illustration 9.1), but actually one of ten written by Woody Allen (1978) in his article 'If the Impressionists had been Dentists' (see Appendix 1).

*Illustration 9.1* Two ways of identifying 'bits' of data.

Dear Theo

[Will life never treat me decently? I am wracked by despair! My head is pounding.] [Mrs Sol Schwimmer is suing me because I made her bridge as I felt it and not to fit her ridiculous mouth.] [That's right! I can't work to order like a common tradesman.] [I decided her bridge should be enormous and billowing with wild, explosive teeth flaring up in every direction like fire!] [Now she is upset because it won't fit in her mouth!] [She is so bourgeois and stupid, I want to smash her.] [I tried forcing the false plate in but it sticks out like a star burst chandelier.] [Still, I find it beautiful. She claims she can't chew! What do I care whether she can chew or not! ] [Theo, I can't go on like this much longer!] [I asked Cézanne if he would share an office with me but he is old and infirm and unable to hold the instruments and they must be tied to his wrists but then he lacks accuracy and once inside a mouth, he knocks out more teeth than he saves.] [What to do?]

Vincent

Dear Theo

[Will life never treat me decently? I am wracked by despair! My head is pounding. Mrs Sol Schwimmer is suing me because I made her bridge as I felt it and not to fit her ridiculous mouth. That's right! I can't work to order like a common tradesman. I decided her bridge should be enormous and billowing with wild, explosive teeth flaring up in every direction like fire! Now she is upset because it won't fit in her mouth! She is so bourgeois and stupid, I want to smash her. I tried forcing the false plate in but it sticks out like a star burst chandelier. Still, I find it beautiful. She claims she can't chew! What do I care whether she can chew or not!] [Theo, I can't go on like this much longer! I asked Cézanne if he would share an office with me but he is old and infirm and unable to hold the instruments and they must be tied to his wrists but he lacks accuracy and once inside a mouth, he knocks out more teeth than he saves. What to do?]

Vincent

*Source*: Woody Allen 1978: 188

No doubt we could argue over the fine detail of these decisions; the break between one bit of data and another is a matter of judgement, and alternatives might be equally plausible. However, there is some consistency in how the data is broken down within each example, and a sharp contrast between the two. In the first example, bits are narrowly defined in terms of relatively small 'units of meaning' with the break between one bit and another often – but not always – demarcated by the end of a sentence. Each bit conveys a distinct element within the narration. In the second example, bits are defined more broadly in terms of larger 'units of meaning' which embrace distinct episodes within the text, the first concerning the lamentable business of Mrs Schwimmer's bridge and the second the frailties of Cézanne.

Although I have presented a clear division between different bits of data, it is possible to overlap the different bits, so that one bit starts within another. In Illustration 9.2, for example, the second bit of data, demarcated by the double brackets, overlaps with the first.

*Illustration 9.2* Overlapping bits of data

[Will life never treat me decently? I am wracked by despair! [[My head is pounding.] Mrs Sol Schwimmer is suing me because I made her bridge as I felt it and not to fit her ridiculous mouth.]]

Whenever we divide data into bits in this way, meaning is lost because the data is abstracted from its context. This is true, regardless of the size of the bits of data we identify. For example, the import of the episode with Cézanne can only be understood fully in the context of the preceding account of the incident with Mrs Sol Schwimmer. Even if we had taken the whole letter as our bit of data, this can only be fully understood within the context of the series of letters which Vincent writes to his brother Theo. This loss of meaning is inescapable. On the other hand, the bits of data also acquire a new meaning, in relation to other bits of data with which we implicitly or explicitly compare them.

Our choice between alternative methods of breaking up the data may be dictated by how fine-grained we want our analysis to be, and how narrowly or broadly focused our categories are. We may be concerned not to include too much information within a single bit of data, leading to a proliferation of assigned categories for each databit. On the other hand, we may be reluctant to adopt too narrow an approach, if this means we lose some sense of the overall meaning of the data. When we break the date up too finely we may lose important contextual information about the data. This problem is less severe where the computer allows us to retrieve instantly the context of any bit of data, but we will still want to respect the 'integrity' of the data. However we choose, once having chosen a particular path we ought to follow it as consistently as we can right through our analysis of the data.

This does not mean, though, that we have to categorize every bit of data. Even if we have previously summarized our data and eliminated some of 'the dross', there may still be parts of the data which turn out to be less relevant than expected as the aims and direction of our analysis become more focused. There is no point in categorizing data which is not clearly relevant to the analysis as it develops.

So far we have only considered how to identify bits of data through judgements by the analyst which take account of irreducible 'units of meaning' in the data. This approach respects the integrity of the data and also ensures that bits of data are meaningful both internally and with respect to the analysis. Another approach is to allow the computer to create bits of data for us. For example, we could simply divide up the text on an entirely arbitrary basis, asking the computer to demarcate bits of data by a specified number of characters or lines. This would certainly ensure consistency in the size of databits, but at the expense of intelligibility. However, we can use this facility more selectively, by focusing on target keywords or phrases in the text, and asking the computer to extract all the bits of data which contain the specified target. The size of these extracts may be specified in different ways, according to the number of characters or lines before or after the target text, or (less arbitrarily) to include the sentence or paragraph in which it occurs. For example, the computer could extract for us all the sentences which contain the word 'Cézanne'.

This method of generating bits of data is quick, but it also has limitations. The boundaries which demarcate bits of data are arbitrary, even where the computer extracts the contextual sentences or paragraphs. The analyst no longer defines the appropriate 'unit of meaning', and has to make do with whatever results the computer produces. This disadvantage can be offset somewhat, if the computer allows us to retrieve the original context and modify the boundaries of the bits of data it has extracted as appropriate. The time gain may depend on how selective we can be in checking contexts and adjusting the boundaries of bits of data retrospectively.

Another drawback of this approach is that it identifies 'units of meaning' entirely in terms of key words or phrases in the text. These are unlikely to be the only bits of data relevant to the analysis as a whole, or even to the particular aspect of the analysis in which we are interested. Thus the computer cannot pick up any discussion of Cézanne where he is not explicitly mentioned in the text. Generating bits of data automatically is unlikely to exhaust all possibilities, and may therefore be better regarded as a way of complementing rather than substituting for judgements by the analyst.

Let us now turn to some of the problems of assigning categories. This is likely to prove the most challenging but also the most rewarding aspect of analysing the data. In general, it will involve going through the data case by case in a systematic way, and deciding whether and how bits of data should be categorized. This requires considerable concentration, in order to ensure that all the appropriate categories for all the data have been considered. Though the computer allows the mechanical aspects of this task to be performed expeditiously, so that all the analyst has to do is select the data and the appropriate category or categories, it is also likely, even with the aid of the computer, to prove a fairly long and demanding process.

Suppose we try to categorize the letters from Vincent to Theo. Let us try to identify the decisions we may have to make in order to assign a category to a bit of data. To do this, we must separate out and discuss sequentially decisions which in practice may be simultaneous and mutually dependent, or taken in a different order.

As we are focusing on the process of assigning categories, let us assume that we have already devised some general categories with which to begin the analysis. As a convenient starting point, let us use some of the categories we created earlier in relation to the sketches by Victoria Wood. A preliminary category list might include the categories in Illustration 9.3.

*Illustration 9.3* A preliminary category list

Catharsis–sex
Catharsis–suffering
Catharsis–other
Incongruity–exaggerating
Incongruity–transposing
Incongruity–other
Values–confirming
Values–subverting
Victims–ridiculing
Victims–empathizing
Stereotypes

Let us assume that these categories have been reviewed in the light of the data, and confirmed as a reasonable basis from which to launch our analysis.

The first thing we have to decide is where to begin. The overwhelming temptation is, of course, to begin at the beginning. We have ten letters from Vincent to Theo – why not begin with the first and then analyse each letter in chronological order? To 'begin at the beginning' seems so natural that we may take for granted our rationale justifying this decision; indeed, we may not realize we have already taken a decision. However, the rationale lies in the chronological order of the data. There may be elements in the sequence of events which are significant to our analysis. To understand the evolution of action and its history we should respect the order in which events are narrated by Vincent.

Although often characteristic of fieldwork notes and documentary material, not all data has a chronological order which justifies a decision to 'begin at the beginning'. For example, for data which has been collected through a one-off survey of respondents, a chronological order may apply to the data within each interview, but not between the interviews. It may be entirely arbitrary whether one starts with one interview or another, if random or pragmatic factors determined the order in which interview data was collected, transcribed and filed. There is a natural tendency to file such data in some 'meaningful' sequence, perhaps numerical or alphabetic, for ease of retrieval. We must be careful not to invest the essentially arbitrary order in which cases are filed with an unwarranted significance.

This point is not entirely trivial, as bias can arise simply from continually encountering some data more frequently because it is located first in some arbitrary – perhaps numerical or alphabetical, but not chronological – order. Those with names headed by a letter late in the alphabet will know all too well the injustices attendant on coming last in some convenient but arbitrary order. For data organized in this way, we may adopt the injunction: never begin at the beginning! Using the computer, we may be able to ensure that our analysis is based instead on a genuinely random sequence of cases.

The allure of working in sequence is as seductive in its way as the temptation to start at the beginning. Surely it is plain common sense to work through the data systematically, i.e. sequentially? But again, we should be aware that we are making a decision to analyse the data in this, and not some other way. There are alternatives. For example, we may have sufficient familiarity with the data, and feel sufficiently focused in our analysis, to analyse data in a selective rather than sequential way. We could focus on the analysis of responses to key questions. Or we could use the computer's search facilities to locate within the data key text significant for the analysis. Another option is to search through memos to locate key ideas. Whichever way we choose, categorizing the data can proceed through a variety of selective paths, rather than slavishly following the sequential route.

Our first decisions, therefore, are where to begin, and whether to analyse selectively or sequentially. In this case, let us begin at the beginning, and analyse the data in sequence.

Now let us decide how to break up the data into bits. To simplify matters let us select between the two options we outlined earlier. Shall we opt for individual points or whole episodes? Suppose we choose the former, perhaps because we want to develop a more fine-grained analysis. As there are less than a dozen fairly short letters in all, we can afford to develop a more detailed breakdown of the data.

Once we have opted for a more or less detailed breakdown of the data, we can turn to the problem of selecting and categorizing individual bits of data. Let us treat the first three sentences as our first 'bit' of data.

[Will life never treat me decently? I am wracked by despair! My head is pounding.]

There are three sentences here, each expressing a different point. Why treat this as one bit and not three? The latter would be equally plausible if we required a still more detailed analysis. But the three points are closely related and can be taken to express a common theme; they describe Vincent's state of mind. They express his mental anguish and physical suffering at the unfairness of life. In this sense, they can be seen as one 'unit of meaning'. By contrast, there is a sharp break in meaning between these sentences and the following sentence, which moves on from a description of Vincent's state to an explanation of what has happened. At this stage, it seems reasonable to treat this as a single bit of data. Later on, if need be, we can subdivide the data again if this seems required by further analysis.

Now that we have selected our first 'bit of data', let us for convenience call it a 'databit'. At some point, we must categorize this databit. This need not be done immediately. We could collect other databits, and then assign them to categories. If we proceed in this way, it may be convenient to index the databits we collect, so that we can identify and locate them more easily. We could label this first databit 'wracked by despair', for example, and use this label in an index of databits. An alternative which may be quicker though less intelligible is to allow the computer to index databits automatically, for example by using the first few words or characters of the databit. Either way, we should be clear that indexing or labelling the databit is not an equivalent of categorizing it. As I suggested earlier, we can think of a label as a proper name which denotes the individual databit. It does not identify it as a member of a class of objects.

The advantage of this approach is that we can make clearer comparisons between databits before we assign categories to them. The disadvantage is that in making such comparisons, we lose sight of the contexts from which the databits are taken. The computer allows us to retrieve contexts readily, but on balance it may be preferable to categorize the data in context, and then consider comparisons between the databits.

Let us consider whether and how to categorize this databit. On the face of it, it has nothing to do with the humour in Vincent's letter, which resides more obviously in his aesthetically inspired disfiguration of Mrs Schwimmer and his complaints of Cézanne's incompetence. First of all, we need to check whether we have annotated this data. Suppose we have already made a memo reading as in Illustration 9.4.

*Illustration 9.4* Checking memos prior to categorizing data

The letters open with Vincent's statement of despair. Does this not immediately suggest a stereotype of the artistic temperament, prone to exaggerated emotions? Is there not an element of self-pity suggested here in Vincent's complaint about life's unfairness – to him? (It hasn't been very fair to Mrs Sol Schwimmer.) Look out for similar displays of temperament.

This memo suggests a possible categorization in terms of temperament. Also, we need to read the databit in context. Vincent's despair is a result of Mrs Sol Schwimmer's search for legal redress following her disfigurement. If Mrs Sol Schwimmer's suit is reasonable, is Vincent's despair unreasonable? The databit takes on new meaning, if we recognize the absurdity of the action which has precipitated it. It is no longer just an 'innocent' statement of how Vincent feels. It is an expression of Vincent's fundamental folly in complaining because he cannot act as he likes regardless of the consequences for others.

We can run through our list of categories, and consider whether there is a category which obviously suggests itself at this point. We have a short category set (at least to start with) so there is no problem checking through all of it. But with a longer list of categories, it would obviously be more efficient to concentrate on likely prospects and discount non-contenders. We may be able to divide our list into probables and improbables, possibles and impossibles; and then consider whether any of the probables or possibles applies.

From our short list, the category 'stereotypes' is one possibility. But we should also consider other possibilities, not as yet included in our current category set. Our memo mentions 'stereotypes' but it is also more precise: it suggests that this is a specific stereotype, one which invokes the image of the over-emotional artist. Should we add a category 'temperament' to our category set and assign it to this databit? To make this decision, we must consider the existing category set and reflect upon the virtues and drawbacks of extending it.

Since we have a short and relatively undifferentiated category list, let us add 'temperament' to it. But before we assign this category, we should consider how we are using it. As we are categorizing our very first databit, there are no previous empirical examples to refer to. We must therefore concentrate on conceptual clarification of the category. This could take the form of a first attempt at defining the category in terms of criteria which may govern its assignation. Illustration 9.5 contrasts two such 'definitions'.

It should be apparent that these 'definitions' involve different conceptualizations of the category 'temperament' and would result in their assignation to different sorts of data. The first definition is more general and

*Illustration 9.5* Contrasting definitions of the category 'temperament'

Temperament – Use this category for any expression of emotion, regardless of whether or not we would judge this 'extreme' or 'unreasonable'. Although we are interested in temperament as an aspect of stereotyping, our first trawl through the data should collect all examples reflecting some aspect of temperament with a view to subsequent differentiation.

Temperament – Use this category for any expression of emotions which might be regarded as 'extreme' and/or 'unreasonable' and therefore illustrative of an artistic stereotype. Be careful not to include expression of emotions typical of an 'ordinary' rather than 'artistic' temperament.

requires less judgement on the part of the analyst. The second definition is more focused, but therefore requires a finer judgement about what data 'fits' the category. On a first run through the data, we may be tempted to stick with the more general definition and avoid more difficult judgements until we can view all the data assigned to the category. On the other hand, our interest is in the use of stereotypes and we may want to confine our attention to this aspect of the data from the start. The choice between different definitions requires a fine judgement on the part of the analyst.

As well as defining the scope of the category, we shall have to consider in more detail the criteria for its assignation. In this databit, Vincent explicitly states that he is 'wracked by despair'. The data may not always be so helpful. Suppose we encounter a bit of data where there is no explicit statement concerning Vincent's emotional state, but there are reasonable grounds for inferring from his behaviour that he is governed by an artistic temperament? For example, take the bit of data in a later letter (Illustration 9.6).

*Illustration 9.6* Inferring an emotional state from behaviour

As if that was not enough, I attempted some root-canal work on Mrs Wilma Zardis, but half-way through I became despondent. I realized suddenly that root-canal work is not what I want to do! |I grew flushed and dizzy. I ran from the office into the air where I could breathe! I blacked out for several days and woke up at the seashore.| When I returned, she was still in the chair. I completed her mouth out of obligation but I couldn't bring myself to sign it.

We may want to assign the category 'temperament' to this databit also. If so, we may amend our definition accordingly by adding the following criterion:

Use 'temperament' even where there is no explicit statement of emotions, where there are reasonable grounds for inferring an emotional state from Vincent's behaviour.

If we cannot judge clearly in terms of existing criteria whether or not to assign a category, we may want to extend or modify our criteria in the light of the new data.

Returning to our initial categorization, we have now selected a databit and also a category. Our next decision concerns whether or not other categories might also be assigned to the databit. We may discount other categories, but we should do so consciously and not simply assume that one category exhausts all possibilities. For example, is there a cathartic element in the reference to Vincent's suffering through life's iniquities? Cathartic humour offers emotional release by making a joke of situations which make us uncomfortable because they are unpleasant, threatening, embarassing. We may doubt whether this criterion applies to Vincent's suffering – do we obtain 'emotional release' because his suffering is ridiculed? On the other hand, his suffering is certainly unpleasant. To be on the safe side, perhaps we should assign the category 'suffering', while noting our doubts for later analysis. The suffering Vincent goes through is ridiculed because of the incongruity in presenting a dentist with an artistic temperament. In this case, there is also an element of 'transposing' in this data. We could assign the category, 'transposing', to indicate this aspect of incongruity. Again, we have to define our terms and indicate the criteria for assigning the category.

We are ready for our first categorization. Now we can hand over to the computer, which should be able to finish the job in a matter of seconds. Most if not all of the tasks involved should be accomplished automatically once we have selected a bit of data and the relevant categories. The mechanical aspects of categorization should be so straightforward that they do not distract attention from the conceptual issues. The exact format through which this information is stored will vary with the type of software used, but it is reasonable to expect computer software to hold most or all of this information in some shape or form. Some software packages may allow you to access this information directly, while with others you may need to ask the computer to retrieve it for you before you can look at it. Illustration 9.7 is an example of the information which might be held by the computer for our first databit.

Categorizing the data is anything but mechanical, for it requires a continual exercise of judgement on the part of the analyst. This judgement concerns not only how to categorize the data but also whether and how to modify categories in view of the decisions being made. As we encounter more data we can define our categories with greater precision. It is important to note and reflect upon decisions to assign – or not to assign – a category, especially where these decisions are problematic, and to use this as a basis for defining criteria for inclusion and exclusion more explicitly. Even an established category set is not cast in stone, but subject to continual modification and renewal through interaction with the data.

*Illustration 9.7* Data stored following categorization of a databit

| Index | Will life never |
|---|---|
| Databit | Will life never treat me decently? I am wracked by despair! My head is pounding |
| Categories | Temperament Transposing Suffering |
| Case | Letter01 |
| DataRef1 | Vincent |
| DataRef2 | Theo |
| Date | 19.1.91 |
| Analyst | Ian Dey |
| Text location | Vincent's letters Letter01 characters 1–80 |
| Comment | 'Suffering' should involve 'emotional release' through ridicule etc. – does this databit meet this criterion? |

We seem to have spent a surprisingly long time over one bit of data. However, the first stages of any initial categorization of the data are bound to be rather slow and tentative. It is a case of learning to walk before we can run. As we progress with categorizing, our decisions should become more confident and more consistent as categories are clarified, ambiguities are resolved and we encounter fewer surprises and anomalies within the data. This should improve considerably the speed and efficiency with which we can categorize the data.

---

**General decisions in assigning categories**
- What generally constitutes a 'bit' of data?
- Whether and what to use as an initial category set?
- Where to begin? Cases by order or randomly?
- Whether to categorize sequentially or selectively?

---

**Specific decisions in assigning categories**
- What constitutes this 'bit' of data?
- Are there any relevant memos?
- How does the context affect the meaning?
- Are any categories probables/possibles?
- Which is the most likely category?
- What are examples assigned to this category?
- What is current definition of this category?
- Is this consistent with assigning this category?
- If there is ambiguity, can the category definition be modified?
- Should we assign this category?

---

**Further decisions in assigning categories**
• Should we assign other categories?
• Should we create a new category?

---

Let us conclude this discussion with an illustration of how the first letter could be categorized (Illustration 9.8). It should be obvious by now that there is no one 'right way' to do this. The categories we use are not 'right' or 'wrong' but simply more or less equal to the task. I have already assigned the category 'temperament' to the first databit. I have also devised new categories for other bits of data in this letter. Where the humour relies on stereotypical images of artistic work, I have referred to this by the category 'task'. Where the humour relies on catharsis through the emotional release associated with our fears of the dental chair, I have referred to this by the category 'suffering'.

In categorizing this letter, I have modified or refined some of our original categories, and ignored others. I have focused on incongruity and catharsis as well as stereotypes as these are prominent elements in the humour. However, these categories have been adapted to suit the character of the data. I have not explored the less central but perhaps no less interesting question of who the intended 'victims' of Woody Allen's humour may be, and what values if any he may be affirming or subverting through his humorous presentation of artists as dentists. Thus this is one possible categorization, and it is by no means exhaustive or conclusive.

For illustrative purposes I have numbered the databits in these examples, but it doesn't really matter how the databits are identified so long as the computer can recognize each databit uniquely.

By now, in addition to our original data, the computer should hold the following information:

1. A list of categories which we can access, modify and extend at any time.
2. A record of how each category has been and is currently defined.
3. A databit assigned to a category or categories, with all other relevant information.

What do we produce through this process of categorization? Arguably the most important product of categorization is a category set which is conceptually and empirically 'grounded' in the data. Categories are created, modified, divided and extended through confrontation with the data, so that by the end of this initial categorization we should have sharpened significantly the conceptual tools required for our analysis.

Three new resources are also created for the analysis through this first categorization of the data. First of all, categorization extracts from the mass of data those observations which can be distinguished with respect to a

*Illustration 9.8* Categorizing Vincent's first letter

| Databits | Categories |
|---|---|
| 1. Will life never treat me decently? I am wracked by despair! My head is pounding. | Temperament Transposing Suffering |
| 2. Mrs Sol Schwimmer is suing me because I made her bridge as I felt it and not to fit her ridiculous mouth. | Task Transposing |
| 3. That's right! I can't work to order like a common tradesman. | Task |
| 4. I decided her bridge should be enormous and billowing with wild, explosive teeth flaring up in every direction like fire! | Task Transposing |
| 5. Now she is upset because it won't fit in her mouth! | Suffering |
| 6. She is so bourgeois and stupid, I want to smash her | Temperament |
| 7. I tried forcing the false plate in but it sticks out like a star burst chandelier. | Task Suffering |
| 8. Still, I find it beautiful. She claims she can't chew! What do I care whether she can chew or not! | Task Suffering |
| 9. Theo, I can't go on like this much longer! | Temperament |
| 10. I asked Cézanne if he would share an office with me but he is old and infirm and unable to hold the instruments and they must be tied to his wrists but then he lacks accuracy and once inside a mouth, he knocks out more teeth than he saves. | Incongruity Suffering |
| 11. What to do? | Not assigned. |

specific criterion or set of criteria, the latter becoming increasingly explicit. The extracted data can now be inspected in detail, with a view to making further distinctions within the data or between these and other data. Secondly, this first categorization produces some ideas about whether and how to subcategorize the data. Finally, we should have clarified the boundaries between categories, and begun to develop some ideas about possible connections between them. Therefore categorization not only involves producing the data in a format convenient for further analysis; it can also contribute materially to the ideas needed to develop further comparisons both within and between categories.

Categorizing data is a powerful tool for organizing our analysis, both conceptually and empirically. Prior to categorization, the data is organized through our methods of collection and transcription rather than the ideas and objectives which inform our analysis. Once the data is categorized, we can examine and explore the data in our own terms. There is an irony inherent in this process, for in order to compare data within or between categories, we have to abstract the data from the context in which it is located. Without abstraction, comparison is not possible. And yet one of the most powerful injunctions of qualitative analysis is that data should be analysed in context. How can these contradictory requirements be reconciled? The computer provides a partial reconciliation, by allowing us to retain direct access to the context from which the data has been abstracted. Thus we can compare all the databits assigned the category 'temperament', while still being able to see each databit in context. Unfortunately we cannot accomplish these requirements simultaneously. But the ability to see the data one way, and then another, is perhaps the nearest we can hope to come to coping with this paradox.

# Chapter 10

# Splitting and splicing

The first thing we may do after creating and assigning categories to the data is consider ways of refining or focusing our analysis. To do this, we can shift attention from the 'original' data itself to the data as reconceptualized through the results of our labours. By this point, we have reorganized our data (or at least some of it) around a category set, which we may have created, modified and extended during our preliminary analysis. In the process we have also 'produced' a (probably very large) number of databits which have been assigned to one or more of the various categories used in our analysis. Therefore we can now organize and analyse our data in terms of the categories which we have developed. This shift in focus has been described as a 'recontextualization' of the data (Tesch 1990), as it can now be viewed in the context of our own categories rather than in its original context.

Depending upon the software we are using, in order to view the data in this new context we may have to 'retrieve' the databits which we have assigned to a particular category or categories. Most packages for analysing qualitative data involve a 'code and retrieve' process whereby codes (i.e. abbreviations for categories) are initially attached to bits of the data, and then these codes can be used to retrieve all the databits to which they have been assigned. In packages where codes are simply attached to the text, it is essential to retrieve the data in this way before we can have a look at it. Some software, though, allows you access to all the databits assigned to a particular category or categories without having to go through a retrieval process. This is achieved by copying all the databits to a separate file or files during categorization, so that as categories are assigned to the bits of data, the databits are simultaneously reorganized under those categories. This obviates the need to retrieve databits before we can examine the results of our categorization.

The format in which categories and databits are held is also likely to vary with the software we use. We may, for instance, put all the databits assigned to a category or categories together into a single file, or store each databit separately under its assigned category or categories and use the computer's search facilities to locate all examples belonging to a specified category or categories. But whatever the particular format, the important point is that we now want the computer to present our data in terms of the categories used in our analysis. For example, we want to be able to look at all the databits which have been assigned to a particular category (Illustration 10.1).

*Illustration 10.1* Comparing databits assigned to different categories

| Category 1 | Category 2 | Category 3 | Category 4 | Category 5 |
|------------|------------|------------|------------|------------|
| Databit 1 | Databit 2 | Databit 1 | Databit 3 | Databit 4 |
| Databit 7 | Databit 3 | Databit 5 | Databit 5 | Databit 6 |
| Databit 9 | Databit 4 | Databit 7 | Databit 8 | Databit 9 |
| etc. | etc. | etc. | etc. | etc. |

Returning to our example of Vincent's letters, let us take as an example the category 'suffering'. We can now look at all the databits which have been assigned this category during our initial analysis (Illustration 10.2).

This bald list of databits has its drawbacks. By abstracting the data from its original context, there is an obvious danger of misunderstanding or misinterpretation. For each databit, though, we may also hold information about the case to which it belongs, the date when it was categorized, the original context from which it comes and so on. This information may be vital to our interpretation of the data.

*Illustration 10.2* Databits assigned to the category 'suffering'

*Suffering*

1. Will life never treat me decently? I am wracked by despair! My head is pounding.

2. Now she is upset because it won't fit her mouth!

3. I tried forcing the false plate in but it sticks out like a star burst chandelier.

4. She claims she can't chew!

5. Then he lacks accuracy and once inside a mouth, he knocks out more teeth than he saves.

6. I grew flushed and dizzy. I ran from the office into the air where I could breathe! I blacked out for several days and woke up at the seashore.

7. When I returned, she was still in the chair.

8. God! I have not a penny left even for Novocaine! Today I pulled a tooth and had to anesthetize the patient by reading him some Dreizer.

etc. etc.

Using Hypertext linking, whenever necessary we can re-examine the databit within its original context. Suppose, for example, we forget what is meant by 'it' in the databit 'now she's upset that it won't fit her mouth'. We can go directly to the original text and check what 'it' refers to – the 'billowing bridge'. If we have become thoroughly familiar with our data, we may find that the occasions when we require to do so are surprisingly rare. We are not likely to forget that 'billowing bridge' in a hurry!

Nevertheless, in abstracting databits in this way we suffer a significant information loss. What do we gain by way of compensation? We gain the opportunity to think about our data in a new way. We can now make comparisons between all the different databits which we have assigned to a particular category. We can compare the databits assigned to one category with those assigned to another. On this basis, we can further clarify our categories and contribute to developing the conceptual framework through which we can apprehend our data. This process is likely to involve two main tasks, which I have called 'splitting' and 'splicing' categories. Splitting refers to the task of refining categories by subcategorizing data. Splicing refers to combining categories to provide a more integrated conceptualization. Let us consider each in turn.

## SPLITTING CATEGORIES

I described categorizing as a process of drawing distinctions within the data. This process is twofold. We divide up the data into bits, distinguishing one bit from another; and we assign a databit to one or more categories, distinguishing it thereby from databits assigned to other categories. In other words, categorizing involves subdividing the data as well as assigning categories.

With subcategorizing, we may no longer need to subdivide our data in quite the same way. Subcategorizing can be done using the existing databits without further subdivisions within our databits. We can split up our category into a number of subcategories which we can then assign to the databits which already belong to that category. The process of splitting up a category into subcategories is not just conceptual. It involves assigning the various databits to appropriate subcategories, and is therefore grounded in our analysis of these databits. However, we do not need to make any further subdivisions within databits as opposed to distinctions between them.

On the other hand, it is most unlikely that our initial categorization will have exhausted the distinctions we can draw within the data. If our data is at all voluminous or complex, it will almost certainly be necessary or desirable to develop further distinctions within the databits themselves. This will be especially true if we have chosen to undertake a very broad brush analysis on our first sweep through the data. But even if we have adopted a fine-grained approach, there may be particular parts of the text which we have deliberately categorized in a general way, leaving further refinement for a later stage in our analysis.

Not all categories will require or merit subcategorization. Subcategorizing will depend in part, too, on how far at this point we can identify some central concerns around which the analysis will revolve. By this stage, it may be possible to identify some areas where the further analysis is likely to prove most interesting and rewarding. We may be a bit clearer about the directions in which to go, even though there may still be some blind bends and cul-de-sacs on the route ahead. It might still ·be a matter of following up hunches and hypotheses, but these may by now be more informed, while some entertained at the outset may by now be discarded. Subcategorizing may therefore focus on those themes and issues which are emerging as the most significant for the analysis.

In relation to Vincent's letters, suppose we have become especially interested in the categories 'task', 'temperament' and 'suffering'. Following our initial categorization, we have decided that the bulk of our data falls within these categories, whereas other categories have proved much more marginal to the analysis. It has become clear that Woody Allen's humour in these letters relies mainly on the use of particular forms of incongruity – transpositions of task and temperament – and cathartic humour related to our fears of the dentist's chair.

Let us stay with the example of the category 'suffering' (Illustration 10.2). Suppose we want to develop subcategories which permit a more refined analysis of the cathartic elements this category conveys. Let us look therefore at the databits we have assigned this category in more detail. To keep things simple, let us cheat a little and imagine that these are all the databits assigned this category. This is necessary, for the whole point of categorizing is to ground our conceptualization in an analysis of all the relevant data.

Where do subcategories come from? As with categories, they express our ideas about the data. We can therefore look for inspiration to the data, and to the meanings and significance of the category we are using. The data is now organized in the form of relevant databits, while our ideas are reflected mainly in our category definition. But subcategories don't spring forth fully fledged from the databits, without our first having to recognize them and accord them significance. And they don't simply express ideas about categories, without reflecting also how these can apply to the data. As with categories, creating subcategories is an interactive process.

The first thing we might notice about these databits is that some refer to Vincent's own experiences, while others refer to the experience of his patients. The databits 1 and 6 both refer to Vincent's mental and physical suffering – headaches, suffocating, blackouts – which the author ridicules through exaggeration; hence the absurd image of Vincent waking up on the seashore after a blackout lasting several days. The other databits refer not to Vincent's own suffering, but to the suffering he inflicts on his patients.

We could distinguish between these, for example by distinguishing between 'dentist suffering' and 'patient suffering'. Again we have to be careful how we define our terms. We could use 'patient suffering' to refer to any suffering experienced by patients, or only to suffering inflicted by Vincent and other dentists upon them. It is important to determine as clearly as possible how we intend to use our subcategories.

Even if it makes sense to subcategorize the data, we have to decide whether it is worthwhile conceptually to do so. Does the distinction relate to or illuminate our main conceptual concerns? As it happens, we noted earlier some questions about victims of humour, and whether they are treated with sympathy or subjected to ridicule. If we wanted to pursue this line of enquiry, then this might justify the introduction of our subcategories from an analytic point of view. On the other hand, we may have already categorized the data according to who are the 'victims', for example using the categories 'dentists' and 'patients'. This subcategorization would then be unnecessary. Instead of subcategorizing the data, we could simply retrieve all the databits where either dentists or patients were identified as the 'victims' who suffered.

If the subcategories make sense, and seem valuable analytically, we still have to decide whether it is practically useful to subcategorize the databits. If we really had only eight databits, of which only two were deviant in terms of our main interest, then we might simply take note of the point without going to the trouble of actually subcategorizing the data. There are too few examples to require a formal division of the data into separate categories. Recalling and applying our distinction between the databits can be done in a matter of moments. There are always going to be some distinctions which, though not irrelevant conceptually, are too marginal in terms of the databits to justify subcategorization. If, on the other hand, there were far more databits – as would probably be the case in practice – then it might be useful to assign the databits to subcategories, where the data can be re-examined in a new context. In other words, it might be useful to take all the databits about 'patient suffering' and look at them separately.

In categorizing and subcategorizing we not only make distinctions, we also preserve them. The value of subcategorizing databits may depend on what we can do with the results. In this respect, we may not only want to compare databits within a subcategory; we may also want to compare databits between subcategories. Suppose we suspect that much of Woody Allen's humour relies on some incongruity in task or temperament which results in torture being inflicted upon the patient. In this event, we may anticipate a possible comparison between the databits we have assigned to the categories 'task' and 'temperament' and the databits assigned to the subcategories 'dentist suffering' and 'patient suffering'. We won't be able to make this comparison unless we so subcategorize the data.

Our distinction between 'dentist suffering' and 'patient suffering' was prompted initially by comparison between the databits, and confirmed by reference to our conceptual concerns. Now let us try to reverse this process, and start with some ideas about the category 'suffering'. There may be several different distinctions which occur to us in relation to this category. We can distinguish between physical and mental suffering, for example. Or we can focus on the kind of 'suffering' we associate with the dental chair, and reflect on its various aspects, such as the physical pain and discomfort, the (hopefully temporary) disfigurement, the more subtle sense of entrapment, the embarrassing invasion of personal space, or the appalling vulnerability to the dentist's drill. (No, I don't like going to the dentist!)

These distinctions make sense, but do they relate to the data? A review of the databits confirms that we can indeed distinguish between different forms of 'suffering' experienced by patients. For example, Mrs Sol Schwimmer seems to suffer in a number of ways. We can presume she suffers discomfort as Vincent 'forces' the false plate in; she suffers disfigurement because it 'sticks out like a star burst chandelier'; and she suffers disability because she 'can't chew' as a result. Mrs Wilma Zardis, on the other hand, suffers the fate of being left for several days 'in the chair' – a fate which plays at once upon our sense of entrapment in the dental chair, and our dread of delay while we are trapped there. Cézanne meanwhile 'knocks out teeth', behaviour which certainly implies discomfort and perhaps even subsequent disability and disfigurement. It certainly seems that the kind of distinctions we can draw conceptually have some relevance to the data. We could proceed to subcategorize 'suffering' into a number of subcategories, which are both conceptually and empirically grounded. Using 'discomfort' to refer to either physical or mental suffering, and including 'disability' as an additional dimension, we can identify three subcategories which might prove useful in the analysis (Illustration 10.3).

We could make finer distinctions than these, distinguishing, for example, between physical and mental discomfort, or within mental discomfort between entrapment, vulnerability, and the violation of personal space. Why not include these distinctions?

*Illustration 10.3* Subcategories of 'suffering'

| Category | Subcategories |
|----------|---------------|
| Suffering | Disability<br>Discomfort<br>Disfigurement |

One obvious reason might be that they are not empirically grounded in the data. However, the distinction between physical and mental discomfort does apply to the data, as we can see from the example of Mrs Zardis trapped in the dental chair. Why should this distinction be less significant than the distinction we also noted between discomfort and disability? This is not just a question of how many databits are assigned to a particular category or subcategory. We also have to consider the conceptual significance of our distinction. The subcategory 'disability' adds a new dimension to our analysis of 'suffering' whereas the subcategory 'entrapment' would add a new dimension to our analysis of mental discomfort. Because 'suffering' is nearer to the core categories in our analysis, its various dimensions are more analytically significant than distinctions between types of mental discomfort, which is a category much further from the heart of our analysis. Unless we want to explore this avenue in detail, and place a particular emphasis upon it in the analysis, it may be more economical to collapse the various distinctions we could draw into the single category 'discomfort'.

Taking this point a bit further, we might be inclined to include the subcategory 'disability' even if it had no empirical instantiation. There may be occasions when the absence of instances is as interesting and important as what is to be found in the data. Those familiar with the literature on agenda setting and 'non-decisions' will know that the exercise of power may be more apparent in the issues not discussed and the decisions not taken. With humour, the use of innuendo and irony may similarly depend precisely upon what is not said, but only implied. In addition, logic may sometimes lead us to look for observations which we do not expect to find. On conceptual grounds, we may want to include categories because they are integral to a logical classification. We could justify the inclusion of 'discomfort' in our list of categories, even if we could not find an empirical instantiation of it. This is because we may feel that any classification of the kind of 'suffering' inflicted at the hands of the dentist could not be complete without recognizing this dimension; if Woody Allen does not use it, that in itself may then tell us something about the data.

This point suggests a useful distinction between ideas and data as sources of categories and subcategories. Sometimes we can afford to dispense with empirical reference for a particular category or subcategory, but we cannot afford to disregard its conceptual significance. It is essential that categories make sense conceptually, but not essential that they must have a direct empirical reference. Being empirically grounded does not mean that in a mechanical way there must always be empirical instances for every category. A category can be relevant empirically if it reveals something important about the data, even where empirical instances of that category are few or even non-existent. At least in relation to particular categories, empirical relevance does not require empirical instantiation.

Note that in subcategorizing the data, we have used distinctions which have not been explicitly recognized or acknowledged by the subjects themselves. The distinctions we have used are suggested by the data, but they are not drawn in the data. Here again, empirical grounding should not be taken to mean some slavish obligation to reproduce only those distinctions which are meaningful to actors as well as analysts.

Though our subcategory list – arguably – makes sense conceptually and seems relevant empirically, we have not considered whether it also makes sense analytically, i.e. in terms of what we want from the analysis. Is there any point in distinguishing these subcategories? Here we have to consider the broader thrust of our analysis. Suppose we become interested in the interplay of the incongruous and cathartic aspects of humour. Different aspects of 'suffering' may then acquire significance because they allow a more detailed examination of the interplay between the two. For example, the 'knockabout' image of Cézanne with instruments tied to his wrists provides the element of incongruity which makes the knocked out teeth humorous and therefore cathartic. In general, we may be more convinced that cathartic and incongruous humour intertwine, if we can show that this point holds for the different subcategories of torture as well as for the category as a whole. Unless we can identify some analytic purposes of this sort, there is no point in subcategorizing the data just for the sake of it. We should 'play around' with the data, certainly, but by this stage our playing around should be informed by a more definite sense of purpose.

Note that the subcategories we have identified are inclusive rather than exclusive. In assigning one subcategory to the data, such as 'discomfort', we do not exclude the possibility of also assigning either of the other subcategories. We should not assume that subcategorizing involves the identification of logically distinct and mutually exclusive and exhaustive categories. Although our distinctions are more likely to approach this ideal, there is no reason to stipulate this as a requirement of subcategorization. In so far as qualitative data analysis involves an initial exploration of previously unconceptualized data, we may be modest in our expectations of what can be achieved. It is perfectly in order to adopt a set of subcategories which, like our categories before them, are designed to be inclusive rather than exclusive. Earlier I suggested that the patient whose teeth are knocked out may suffer (potential) disfigurement or even disability as well as (immediate) discomfort. Does it matter that our categories are not exclusive? No. What counts is whether we pick up all the databits where we think there is an element of disfigurement, disability or discomfort, or some combination of the three.

Within each of these subcategories, we may wish to develop a further set of subcategories to accommodate still further distinctions within the data. For the category 'suffering' we can easily identify several further levels of subclassification (Figure 10.1).

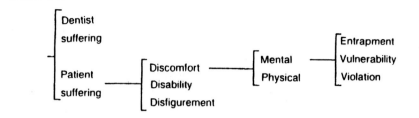

*Figure 10.1* Levels of subclassification of the subcategory 'suffering'

There is no limit to the levels of analysis we can develop other than our ability to draw distinctions between one databit and another. The more subcategories we use, the more refined or 'delicate' (Bliss *et al.* 1983) our analysis. Since no two databits are identical, there are always going to be differences between one databit and another. There is virtually no limit, therefore, to the subcategories we could create for analysing the data. However, we need only note those differences which are conceptually relevant and practically useful from the point of view of further analysis. Subcategorizing can let you see differences which would otherwise remain buried or blurred; but too many distinctions can lead to unnecessary fragmentation and loss of focus (Miles and Huberman 1984: 222). The databits need only be reorganized around our subcategories if this is going to make a difference to the comparisons we can make within our subcategories and between them and other categories.

---

**Issues in subcategorizing databits**
- Do the subcategories make sense conceptually?
- Are they instantiated empirically?
- Are the subcategories empirically relevant?
- Are the subcategories useful practically?
- Do the subcategories look useful analytically?

---

I have concentrated on the conceptual aspects of subcategorizing, because the mechanical aspects are so straightforward. The computer can streamline most of the mechanical aspects of subcategorizing data. The process should require no more than selecting the relevant data or databits and the appropriate subcategory or subcategories. For consistency, we should keep a list of subcategories and select from it as required. If we are subcategorizing data without subdividing databits, then all we have to do is assign subcategories from our list to the relevant databits. For the databits under the category 'suffering' we might assign subcategories as in Illustration 10.4.

*Illustration 10.4* Subcategorized databits for the category 'suffering'

| Disability | Discomfort | Disfigurement |
|---|---|---|
| 4. She claims she can't chew! | 3. I tried forcing the false plate in but it sticks out like a star burst chandelier. | 3. I tried forcing the false plate in but it sticks out like a star burst chandelier. |
| | 5. then he lacks accuracy and once inside a mouth, he knocks out more teeth than he saves. | |
| | 7. When I returned, she was still in the chair. | |
| | 8. God! I have not a penny left even for Novocaine! Today I pulled a tooth and had to anesthetize the patient by reading him some Dreizer. | |

Now suppose that as well as distinguishing between databits, we also want to subdivide data within databits. For example, the databit

[I tried forcing the false plate in but it sticks out like a star burst chandelier.]

could be subdivided in the light of our subcategories to distinguish the different bits of data (Illustration 10.5).

*Illustration 10.5* Subdividing databits between subcategories

| Discomfort | Disfigurement |
|---|---|
| I tried forcing the false plate in | but it sticks out like a star burst chandelier. |

If we had initially used broader distinctions within the data, for example treating the whole episode with Mrs Sol Schwimmer as a single databit, then the scope for making further distinctions within the data at this stage would obviously be that much greater.

The rationale for making further divisions between bits of data depends upon much the same factors as those we considered in relation to categorizing the data in the first place. If our databit is too extensive we may end up assigning too many subcategories to the databit, and the relation between the databit and the subcategory may be obscured by the presence of irrelevant data. It is certainly convenient if there is an immediately transparent relation between subcategory and databit and this may only be possible through subdividing the databit. On the other hand, we may be reluctant to subdivide data too far lest we lose important contextual information. Fortunately, this problem is reduced for subcategorized as for categorized data by the ability of the computer to locate the data immediately in the context from which it has been taken.

Subdividing databits does not require the assignation of subcategories, since we can subdivide databits using existing categories. In other words, we can split databits without splitting categories. We can think of this process as recategorizing rather than subcategorizing the data. How far we recategorize databits may depend on just how broad brush our initial analysis has been. If we have used very general, common sense categories in our initial analysis and assigned correspondingly large bits of data, we may want to recategorize in terms of more specific categories and more narrowly defined bits of data. This may or may not go hand in hand with splitting our initial categories into subcategories.

## SPLICING CATEGORIES

When we splice ropes, we join them by interweaving different strands. When we splice categories, we join them by interweaving the different strands in our analysis. We split categories in a search for greater resolution and detail and splice them in a search for greater integration and scope. The fewer and more powerful our categories, the more intelligible and coherent our analysis.

The most straightforward example of splicing categories is simply the reverse of splitting them. Suppose we had begun with a fine-grained analysis involving the categories 'disability' 'discomfort' and 'disfigurement'. Then we could splice these categories together by integrating them under the over-arching category 'suffering'.

Like splitting categories, splicing is likely to be an increasingly focused activity. We do not want to include every strand in our analysis. We want to concentrate our efforts on the central categories emerging from our preliminary analysis. How do we decide what is central? As always, we have to pay heed to both the conceptual and empirical relevance of the categories we have employed so far. Conceptual relevance can be established in terms of our main interests and objectives as these emerge from our preliminary analysis of the data. By this stage our ideas may be taking shape and we may be able to identify the main directions in which we want the analysis to go. Ideas which seemed interesting at first may no longer seem so; while other issues, apparently marginal at first, may now assume centre stage. The data provides the anvil upon which we can shape and sharpen our ideas. Some categories may apply to the data much more effectively than others. This is likely to be evident in the amount of data which is encompassed by our categories. Those which become central are likely to encompass most of the data, while those which become marginal may be weakly represented in the data.

Likely – but not necessarily. We have to avoid a mechanical approach and allow empirical relevance pride of place over empirical instantiation. We must judge whether the extent to which a category is represented in the data indicates its relevance to our understanding of the data. A small point may mean a great deal. For example, imagine we have a scene of two people meeting, and one person is holding something and pointing with outstretched arm towards the other. What the person is holding may matter a great deal in our interpretation of the scene. Is it coke – or cocaine? Some points, apparently small details in themselves, may be pivotal to our comprehension of the rest of our data.

Nevertheless, it would be a strange analysis which failed to encompass the bulk of the data upon which it is based. The small point can only be pivotal if we have also grasped the rest of the scene. Then and only then can we understand its implications. So although not all our central categories need to be richly represented in the data, some must. Overall, we can expect the categories which are central to encompass the bulk of the data.

Once we have selected the main strands of our analysis, we can begin to interweave them. Here we shift from making comparisons within categories to making comparisons between them. How can such comparisons be made?

At a conceptual level, when we first create our categories we may already have identified, implicitly or explicitly, some possible relationships between them. Recall our discussion of humour, and the logical relationships which we identified between the various categories we created. When we create and define categories, we have to consider the boundaries between them. We also have to consider whether the relationships between categories are inclusive or exclusive, and the different levels of classification in our category set. Even before we begin our analysis, therefore, we may have a rough idea of some of the logical relationships between the categories we are going to use in our analysis (Figure 10.2).

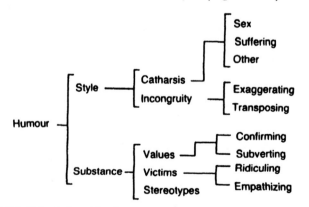

*Figure 10.2* Initial relationships between categories

We need to think in terms of a category set rather than an unrelated and haphazard collection of individual categories. When we assign categories, we may have to reconsider the boundaries of categories and relationships between them. Applying our ideas more systematically or to new data may oblige us to adapt old categories or adopt new ones. All this contributes to the emergence of new conceptual comparisons and connections between our categories. We can map out these changes in our category set as they develop. We can also indicate which are the more important aspects to emerge from our analysis of the data (Figure 10.3).

Once we have categorized the data, we are in a better position to review the boundaries and relationships between the categories used in our classification. We can do this by comparing systematically the databits which have been assigned to the categories used in our analysis. To do this we need to examine the databits which we have assigned to each category. The computer should allow us to retrieve the databits for any combination of categories in which we are interested.

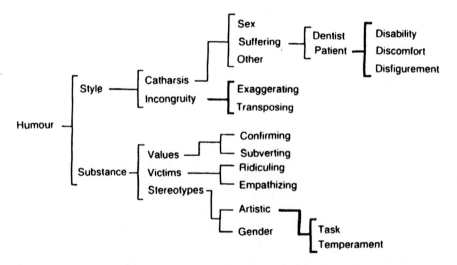

*Figure 10.3* Incorporating categories, and distinguishing more and less important lines of analysis

As an example, let us take the category 'task'. We have used this category to categorize data expressing stereotypical images of work. Suppose we have also used another category, 'occupation', to refer to general differences between the two occupations. Drilling a tooth or painting a canvas is a task, while the amount of income this generates is an occupational characteristic. Now we want to clarify the connection between our categories 'task' and 'occupation' and how these relate to our interest in the style and substance of Woody Allen's humour.

The first thing we may want to consider is whether or not the distinction between these categories is worth making. Have the categories discriminated effectively between databits in a way which contributes to our analysis? This question can be posed at both conceptual and empirical levels. Conceptually, we may doubt whether the distinction we have drawn makes much sense, at least in the terms in which we have drawn it. We began with the category 'tasks' to capture differences between occupational tasks because these differences made an overwhelming impression on our first encounter with the data. It was very obvious that Vincent entertained conceptions of his dental tasks inspired by artistic concerns and quite at odds with the tasks we expect dentists to perform. Closer analysis during categorization obliged us to create another category, 'occupation' to encompass other occupational differences to be found in the data.

Now we may doubt whether this conceptualization is very satisfactory, as 'task' may be more logically regarded as one aspect of occupation. In other words, we might be better to regard 'task' as a subcategory of 'occupation' rather than regarding them as two categories of equal status (Figure 10.4).

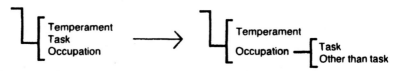

Figure.10.4 Reassessing relationships between categories – 1

If we want to make this change, it is not enough to change the place of categories on the map. We must also change the name of the categories assigned to the data. The category 'occupation' must now be assigned to all the databits, including those previously assigned only to the category 'task'. The category 'other than task' must be assigned to all the databits which were previously assigned to 'occupation'. Fortunately the computer can facilitate this task by automatically finding the relevant databits and renaming the categories assigned to them. This should be as easy to accomplish as our initial categorization, or we may be encouraged by technical constraints to be less flexible than we should be in the subsequent development of our analysis. In other words, it should be as easy to correct our mistakes as it was to make them in the first place!

Although we have clarified our distinction conceptually, we may still doubt its empirical value. Does it distinguish usefully between our databits? To compare the categories, we must look at the databits which we have assigned to each category (Illustration 10.6).

Here we may receive some reassurance from the fairly even distribution of the data between the two categories. This suggests that differing conceptions of task are more central to the analysis than the various other occupation characteristics which we have rather crudely lumped together under the 'other than task' category. At this point, we may decide that it would be worthwhile discriminating more effectively amongst these databits, perhaps dividing occupational characteristics into such aspects as recruitment, remuneration, retirement etc. where expectations clearly differ as between dentists and artists! On the other hand, the empirical power of our category 'task' may encourage us to focus on this data instead and set aside (at least for the moment, and possibly for good) any further different-iation amongst other occupational characteristics. At any rate, we may want to retain the category and not collapse it into a less differentiated category such as occupation.

*Illustration 10.6* Comparing databits between categories

| Other than task | Task |
|---|---|
| 1. I can't work to order like a common tradesman. | 1. I made her bridge as I felt it and not to fit her ridiculous mouth! |
| 2. (Cézanne) is old and infirm and unable to hold the instruments and they must be tied to his wrists. | 2. I decided her bridge should be enormous and billowing, with wild, explosive teeth flaring up in every direction like fire! |
| 3. Once again I am in need of funds. I know what a burden I must be to you, but who can I turn to? I need money for materials! | 3. I find it beautiful. She claims she can't chew! What do I care whether she can chew or not! |
| 4. I have not even a penny left for Novocaine! | 4. I took some dental X-rays this week that I thought were good. Degas saw them and was critical. He said the composition was bad. All the cavities were bunched in the lower left corner. |
| 5. (Gauguin) is a fine dentist who specializes in bridgework | |
| 6. (Gauguin) was very complimentary about my work on Mr Jay Greenglass. | 5. I explained to him that's how Mrs Slotkin's mouth looks, but he wouldn't listen! He said he hated the frames and mahogany was too heavy. |
| 7. Greenglass was adamant and we went to court. There was a legal question of ownership, and on my lawyer's advice, I cleverly sued for the whole tooth and settled for the filling. | 6. I completed her mouth out of obligation but I couldn't bring myself to sign it. |
| 8. Well, someone saw it lying in the corner of my office and he wants to put it in a show! They are already talking about a retrospective! | 7. I am working almost exclusively with dental floss now, improvising as I go along, and the results are exciting! |
| | 8. I filled his lower seven, then despised the filling and tried to remove it. |
| 9. (Toulouse-Lautrec) longs more than anything to be a great dentist, and he has real talent | 9. my old friend Monet refuses to work on anything but very very large mouths |
| 10. (Toulouse-Lautrec is) too short to reach his patients' mouths and too proud to stand on anything. | 10. Seurat, who is quite moody, has developed a method of cleaning one tooth at a time until he builds up what he calls 'a full fresh mouth.' It has an architectural solidity to it, but is it dental work? |

So far we have considered in the light of our retrievals whether and how to divide these categories. Now we may want to consider what kind of relationship holds between them. We can look at all the databits which we have assigned, not just to one or the other, but to both categories. We can do this by inspecting the databits assigned to each category to see whether there are any duplicates. With substantial amounts of data, this process would be very time-consuming and we may use the computer to speed the process up by looking for us. This involves boolean retrievals, which we shall consider in Chapter 12. Meantime, as we can see even without the help of the computer, it so happens that there are no databits which have been assigned to both these categories. Sometimes negative results can be very positive! This particular result suggests that we have been able to distinguish clearly in the data between occupational characteristics related to 'task' and occupational characteristics 'other than task', even though initially we regarded these as inclusive rather than exclusive categories. We may want to check this by a thorough review of the data; but if we are satisfied that these databits can be divided unambiguously between the two categories, then we can reasonably regard them as exclusive rather than inclusive (Figure 10.5).

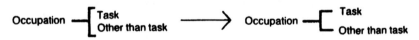

*Figure 10.5* Reassessing relationships between categories – 2

We can now treat 'occupation' as a nominal varible, with two categories which are exclusive and exhaustive.

We have considered whether or not these categories are exclusive, because this question fairly jumped out at us from our retrieval of the data. Suppose a few databits had been assigned to both categories. It would still be worth asking whether these categories could be regarded as exclusive rather than inclusive. We would want to check whether the databits assigned to both categories could not be split between them, for example by dividing the databits. In general, we may want to review whether the relation between categories is inclusive or exclusive whereever the pattern of databits shows few if any databits assigned to the categories in combination. If we can develop nominal – or perhaps even ordinal – variables by developing on our initial categorization, we sharpen our conceptualization of the data and provide a better basis for subsequently examining connections between categories.

So far we have focused rather narrowly on the conceptual and empirical relationship between 'task' and 'occupation'. We can also consider how to splice categories from a wider analytic viewpoint. How do these categories contribute to our overall analysis? (Figure 10.6)

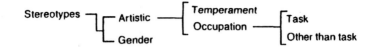

*Figure 10.6* Reassessing position of categories in analysis

Along with 'temperament', we introduced these categories to capture something of the substance of Woody Allen's humour in the stereotypes which he uses of dentists and artists. In subscribing to stereotypes we accept unduly fixed (and often false) images whose comfortable familiarity makes them easy targets of humour. The dentists Woody Allen presents are moody, poverty-stricken, and impractical; and in these respects, they conform to our stereotypical image of the artist. However, before we give undue weight to this category, we may reflect further upon its applicability. Does the data we have retrieved really sustain this conceptualization?

On reviewing the databits assigned to 'task' (Illustration 10.6) we may begin to entertain doubts. The databits are certainly concerned with differences between artistic and dental work, but it is less obvious that they also reflect stereotypes of artistic and dental tasks. When we associate artists and poverty, for example, we know that we are accepting a common image of artistic endeavour which may be misleading – hence the stereotyping. However, some of the databits we assigned to the category 'task' do not really invoke this kind of fixed imagery. They merely express the characteristics of artistic work – such as the priority of aesthetic considerations – which look ridiculous when transposed to a dental context. Take Seurat's method of cleaning one tooth at a time. Seurat's artistic method involved painting by placing individual dots of colour on the canvas. Transposed to a dental setting, this technique assumes an absurd character. However, although we may acknowledge that artists tend to develop individual styles and techniques, this hardly constitutes a 'stereotype' of artistic work. The same is true of specialization, improvization, revision, and signing or displaying artistic work. All become rather ridiculous when transposed to the dental context, but none really expresses 'stereotypes' in the sense of a fixed and possibly false image of what artists are about.

At this point, we might want to retrace our steps, and consider where this category came from. It emerged initially in our analysis of Victoria Wood's 'In the Office' sketch, with its succession of stereotypical images of women's concerns over diet, dress and so on. Then when we considered Vincent's first letter, the image of the depressed artist confirmed the relevance of stereotypes, which we went on to divide between 'temperament' and 'task', before including other occupational charactistics. If we review how we defined these categories, we find no clear distinction drawn between stereotypical and non-stereotypical characteristics. This may have

been partly because the category 'stereotype' was not defined with sufficient clarity.

---

Stereotype: Include any data which seems to invoke stereotypical images.

A stereotype is an 'unduly fixed' image which may or may not be accurate but is
applied regardless.

Note that not all fixed images are stereotypes.

---

Although we noted that not all fixed images are stereotypes, we didn't
spell out any criteria for distinguishing between 'fixed' and 'unduly fixed'
images; nor did we figure out how to categorize any data which fitted the
former rather than the latter. Also, many of the databits assigned to
temperament and to occupational characteristics 'other than task' do seem
stereotypical – our dentists are poor, moody and volatile. As our databits
often relate to temperament as well as task, perhaps the stereotypical
element in the former has coloured our interpretation of the latter?

We can see now how first impressions combined with indirect support
from related evidence could lead to our interpretation of the category 'task'
as an aspect of stereotyping. By retracing our steps, reviewing our definitions and reassessing our category assignments, we give ourselves the space
to reflect critically upon this interpretation, and if need be to modify or
discard it.

This reinterpretation of the category 'task' as dealing with occupational
differences rather than occupational stereotypes has wider implications for
our analysis. It shifts our attention from substance to style. Instead of
invoking or depending on stereotypical images, the databits assigned to the
category 'task' rely rather on the absurd results of transposing characteristics from one occupation to another. It is through the incongruity of these
images that Woody Allen achieves his humorous effects.

Before we consider the implications of this reassessment, let us consider
how we can choose between rival interpretations of the data. Our first
interpretation was sufficiently plausible that we could work with it over a
period, and yet we now want to discard it in favour of one which may give
a quite different tenor to our results. Perhaps at this point we might be
tempted to curse qualitative data analysis and invoke a plague on all
interpretations. On the other hand, we may derive some confidence from
the fact that we have been able to discriminate between different interpretations. By confronting the evidence critically, by making our categories and
decisions as explicit as possible, and by retaining scepticism even with
regard to categories central to our analysis, we have given ourselves the
space to review and recant. We have not simply looked for confirmation of
our initial categories by accumulating as much evidence as possible in
their support. In short, when we review our categories in the light of our

retrievals, we should be looking for confrontation with the data rather than confirmation of our categories.

If we accept this reinterpretation, then we have to modify our analysis accordingly. First we have to review all the databits assigned to the sub-categories of stereotype, to distinguish those which are stereotypical from those which are not. This will require us to be more precise about what we mean by a 'stereotype' and what criteria we can use for assigning the databits to the different categories. Thus we may distinguish between stereotypical and non-stereotypical images in terms of whether or not the assumption involved is reasonable. For example, it is not unreasonable to assume that an artist paints; but it is unreasonable to assume that an artist is poor. It is not unreasonable to assume that an artist works sometimes out of doors, but it is unreasonable to assume that an artist will be emotionally volatile. This criterion allows us to differentiate between 'fixed' and 'unduly fixed' images.

Suppose we find that almost all the databits assigned to the category 'task' are not stereotypical. We may decide to absorb those which do invoke stereotypes under 'temperament' and 'occupational' and discard the subcategories 'task' and 'other than task' altogether. We also need to check that the databits assigned to the category 'temperament' and 'other than task' all fit our stricter definition of a stereotypical image.

We have to decide what to do with those residual databits which we no longer want to characterize as stereotypical. We could create a new category or categories for those databits which no longer 'belong' to the subcategories of stereotype. We could create a new category 'not stereotypes', or simply call these 'residual' or 'problem' databits. Or, as they deal with differences between artists and dentists, whether of temperament, occupation or task, we could simply create a new category called 'differences'. But we may want to recategorize them in some way, if only as a temporary expedient, the alternative being to dispense with them altogether.

As the computer can identify all the databits assigned to our sub-categories, the mechanics of recategorizing the data should be very straightforward, whether it involves adding categories to databits or replacing old categories with new ones. These are tasks which can be accomplished by the computer automatically once we have made the relevant decisions. This leaves us free to concentrate on the wider implications of our reinterpretation.

Suppose we try to map out the relationships between our new categories, and consider their implication for our analysis overall (Figure 10.7). In particular, we may ask what to do with our residual category, 'differences', and whether the category 'stereotypes' retains the importance we attached to it in our analysis. How should we integrate such newly coined or newly defined categories into our analysis? A reflex reaction might

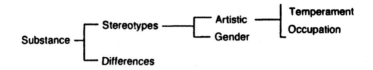

*Figure 10.7* Revising analysis with minimum disturbance

prompt us simply to treat the categories 'differences' and 'stereotypes' as subcategories of 'substance'. This involves minimal disturbance as it requires the least adjustment to our previous thinking.

However, we cannot consider the question 'where should this category go?' without also considering the question 'why should it go there?'. The conceptual distinction we have drawn between stereotypes and differences may be clear enough, but its analytic significance remains obscure. This may become clearer if we recollect the other categories we previously included in our analysis of the substance of humour – 'victims' and 'values' (Figure 10.8).

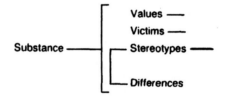

*Figure 10.8* Comparing subcategories of 'substance'

With each of our previous categories we addressed some related questions whose answers could make a significant contribution to our understanding of the substance of the humour.

| | |
|---|---|
| Victims | Who are the victims of the humour? |
| Values | What values are affirmed or subverted? |
| Stereotypes | What stereotypes are invoked? |

The question 'What differences are referred to?' hardly carries the same analytic import. Unlike victims, values and stereotypes, in substantive terms these characteristics are incidental rather than integral to the achievement of humorous effects.

It may seem that we have gone up a blind alley. In any route through our analysis there are likely to be several such cul-de-sacs. All may not be lost, however. Before we despair of integrating the category 'differences' into our analysis, we should consider whether the data it 'contains' relates to any other aspects of the analysis. There are at least two possibilities worth exploring. One would be to consider whether the differences we have noted may illuminate our questions about victims and values. For example, is Woody Allen poking fun at various artistic or professional values through his transposition of occupational characteristics? If we can answer questions like this in the affirmative, then we may still be able to learn something about the substance of his humour from our differentiation of occupational characteristics.

Another possibility – perhaps more promising – would shift our focus from substance to style. We may decide that our interest lies less in the occupational characteristics themselves than in the incongruous effects of their transposition. Instead of invoking or depending on stereotypical images, the databits assigned to the category 'difference' rely rather on the absurd results of transposing characteristics from one occupation to another. It is through the incongruity of these images that Woody Allen achieves his humorous effects.

To check out these possibilities, we can look at empirical as well as conceptual relationships between our residual category 'differences' and other categories used in the analysis. For example, we can check how often those databits assigned to 'difference' have also been assigned to 'transposing', 'empathizing' and so on. Suppose it turns out that all the 'difference' databits have also been assigned to the category 'transposing', because they involve a transposition between the characteristics we associate with artistic and dental work. For example, in the image of a dentist autographing his work the incongruity arises from a straight transposition of occupational characteristics.

From this point of view, we could perhaps consider whether the use Woody Allen makes of 'differences' illuminates some aspect of incongruity as a form of humour. The fact that these transpositions depend mainly on familiar occupational characteristics may further illuminate the manner in which Woody Allen achieves his comic effects. Comedy is culturally dependent and transposition therefore requires ready recognition of what is being transposed. If we felt this aspect was important enough, we could perhaps justify retaining 'differences' as a category in our analysis. However, we might reconceptualize this as an aspect of style, for example recategorizing these databits under the new category 'familiar' to indicate those transpositions which depend upon ready recognition of just what is being transposed. Before doing so, we could check all the databits which have been assigned to 'transposing' but not to 'differences' to see whether these might also be categorized as 'familiar' or 'unfamiliar'. Whether we introduce or retain such categories would then depend on how effectively they discriminated between different aspects of transposition.

Overall, what began with a reinterpretation of a relatively minor subcategory, 'task', has led us to make a major shift in analytic emphasis. The importance of the category 'stereotypes' has been weakened, and with it the role of 'substance' rather than 'style' in our analysis (Figure 10.9).

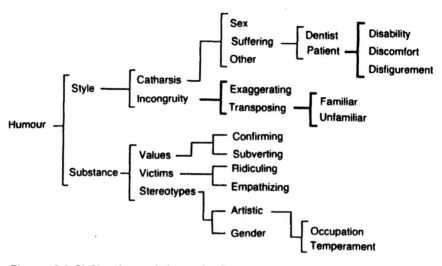

*Figure 10.9* Shifting the analytic emphasis

Attention has shifted to the role of 'incongruity' and in particular of 'transposing' in achieving humorous effects. At the same time, we have sharpened our conception of 'stereotypes' and can have more confidence in the empirical relevance of our analysis.

In splicing categories, we clarified relationships between categories, but we have not reduced the overall number of strands in our analysis. This might seem retrograde – surely in splicing categories, we want to reduce the number of separate strands? Yes, indeed. But splicing is not just a question of bringing categories together. We also have to consider the relevance and boundaries of the categories themselves. We must first identify clearly the separate strands, if we hope to weave them together effectively in our analysis.

A cynic might comment that we could have avoided all this trouble by thinking more clearly in the first place. But if we could think clearly enough in the first place, we wouldn't need to retrieve and analyse our databits at all. By categorizing the data, we provide an empirical testing ground for our conceptualizations. By comparing the databits within and between categories, we can clarify the boundaries and relationships between our concepts.

**Issues in splicing categories**
- How central are the categories analytically?
- How are they distinguished conceptually?
- How do they interrelate?
- Are they inclusive or exclusive?
- Are they of the same status or super/subordinate?
- What steps in analysis led to their emergence?
- How have category definitions evolved?
- Does evidence of retrievals support these definitions?
- How much data do the categories encompass?
- How well do they discriminate amongst databits?
- How much overlap is there between categories?
- How do categories contribute analytically?

# Chapter 11

# Linking data

Categorizing the data allows us to compare observations in terms of relations of similarity and difference. Of any two observations, X and Y, we can ask if they are similar or different. How are they the same, or how do they differ? This is powerful stuff; categories are the conceptual building blocks from which we can construct our theoretical edifices. But they also have limitations. In breaking up the data, we lose information about relationships between different parts of the data. We lose our sense of process – of how things interact or 'hang together'. To capture this information, we need to link data as well as categorize it.

To recall a distinction made earlier, linking data involves recognizing substantive rather than formal relations between things. Formal relations are concerned with how things relate in terms of similarity and difference – how far they do or do not share the same characteristics. Substantive relations are concerned with how things interact. Things which are connected through interaction need not be similar, and vice versa (Sayer 1992: 88). For example, in formal terms we can distinguish 'dentists' and 'patients' as two distinct categories, based on differences between these social roles. However, there is a substantive connection between these two roles, despite the formal differences between them. Dentists have skills and patients need treatment. Indeed, one cannot be a dentist without a patient, or a patient without a dentist. To understand these social roles, we have to recognize the substantive relation that exists between them.

Sayer (1992: 88–89) distinguishes between relations which are 'internal' or 'necessary' and relations which are 'external' or 'contingent'. The relation between dentist and patient is internal or necessary in the sense that one social role necessarily presupposes the other. An external or contingent relation is one which may exist but need not do so. For example, dentists need to make a living, but how this is financed and whether or not the patient pays for treatment at the point of service is a contingent relation between the two. A dentist cannot practise without a patient, but a dentist can practise without receiving direct payment from the patient. Where the patient has to pay at the point of service, this establishes a substantive but contingent connection between patient and dentist. Clearly, contingent relations may be as significant as necessary relations in understanding how things interrelate.

In categorizing Vincent's letters, we have explored the formal character of Woody Allen's humour – for example, his use of incongruous images created by the transposition between dentists and artists, and the element of cathartic humour in his treatment of patients. We have not examined the substantive connections between these different aspects of humour. For example, is there a connection – internal or contingent – between the two types of humour we have identified? How can we begin to answer this question?

In relation to categorizing data, the computer facilitates a traditional methodology; in relation to linking data, the computer transforms it. The 'links' we can now make electronically between one bit of data and another have only become practically possible with the advent of the computer. I shall refer to these electronic links between bits of data as 'hyperlinks'. These simply could not be achieved by paper and pen, or even xerox machine. Indeed, it is only with recent software developments, and in particular the availability of electronic card index applications with Hypertext facilities, that the tools could be created for analysing data in this way. These facilities are still not commonly available amongst the range of packages produced for analysing qualitative data.

Let us look first at what a hyperlink between two bits of data looks like. In practical terms, a hyperlink involves an electronic connection between the two bits of data, so that whenever we want to, we can go directly from one bit to the other. If we take two bits of data, X and Y, then whenever we encounter X we can go directly to Y (and vice versa). We could compare our hyperlink to a piece of string which we sellotape to two cards holding separate bits of data and stored in separate locations, perhaps even separate filing cabinets. We know from the existence of the string that there is a hyperlink between the two cards, and by following the string we can go from one directly to the other (Figure 11.1).

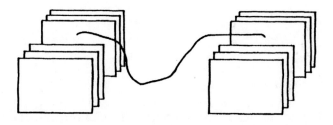

*Figure 11.1* Single hyperlink between two bits of data stored separately

This is a simplified view. In practice, we may attach many strings to each bit of data, each string attached to other bits of data held on other cards or files. There is no limit (at least in theory) to the number of strings we can attach, making a set of pathways within the data, with each pathway incorporating a chain of links between different bits of data (Figure 11.2).

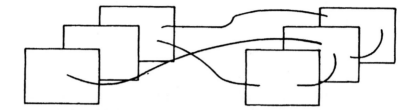

*Figure 11.2* Multiple hyperlinks between bits of data stored separately

In conceptual terms, the resulting complex of pathways may be more perplexing than illuminating, if we fail to distinguish between the different strings attaching different bits of data. Retaining the visual image, we have to colour code the strings if we are going to disentangle the different paths and not become confused by twists and turns and overlaps amongst the different strings. It is not enough just to make an electronic link: we also have to describe it.

Like categorizing, linking therefore has a conceptual as well as a mechanical aspect. We make hyperlinks between two bits of data only if we think they are linked conceptually in some way. For example, suppose we want to note the substantive relations between dentists and patients discussed earlier. We could do so using the links 'treat' and 'pay' as in Figure 11.3.

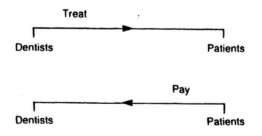

*Figure 11.3* Linking dentists and patients

In this respect, linking is akin to categorizing. For the sake of clarity and consistency we need to create a list of links which we can assign to the links we observe between bits of data. Like our category set, our link list ought to be conceptually and empirically 'grounded' – conceptually in the ideas and objectives which inform our research, empirically in the observations we make of interrelationships within the data. We can devise links in much the same way as we devise categories – by deriving them from our initial questions and interests, and/or by inferring them from the data. Again we may be influenced by theoretical concerns, substantive interests, practical policy problems, or rely mainly on generating ideas through our interaction with the data. Like our category set, we may make a list of links in advance and modify it as we go along, or we may prefer to derive it directly from the data. However we proceed, the links we devise ought to meet both our conceptual and empirical requirements. There is no point in devising a link which is fine in theory but has no practical application; nor is there any point in making links which do not relate to the overall analysis.

Like our category set, we also have to decide how long our links list should be. This again will depend upon the volume and complexity of our data and the conceptual aims of our analysis. Unlike our category set, though, our links list can be very short, confined to only a few items or perhaps even (dispensing with a list altogether) to a single item. We could not base a categorical analysis upon a single category, but we could confine our analysis of relationships to a single link, such as causality. On the other hand, if we identify too many links, we may be overwhelmed by the complexity of relationships which we can observe within the data, and lose consistency and coherence in our analysis.

Potentially, there are as many links as there are transitive verbs in the English language. A transitive verb is an archetypal link which connects a subject and an object. When we parody, satirize, lampoon, mock, or ridicule something, we establish a relation between ourselves and the (unfortunate) object of our attentions. In practice, only a subset of possible relationships is likely to be of interest to the analyst. Our link list will reflect our preoccupations – if we are mainly interested in how meaning is communicated, for example, we will focus on different links than if we want to account for social action. Amongst social scientists, one common interest is in causal relationships, where X causes Y (or Y is caused by X). But causality is only one, if the most obvious, of many possible links (Illustration 11.1). We may be interested in the intelligibility of social action, for example, and devise a range of links such as explanation, exculpation, rationalization and so on. We may look for consistency or contradictions within the data, looking for areas of mutual support or opposition. Or we may on theoretical grounds anticipate more specific connections, and observe through linking how far these are evident in the data. For example, we may ask what it is about humour which creates laughter in an audience.

*Illustration 11.1* **Possible links**

X explains Y
X exculpates Y
X rationalizes Y
X supports Y
X opposes Y
X amuses Y
X bores Y
X praises Y
X criticizes Y
etc. etc.

In creating a link list, we must obviously take account of the data. Let us take as an example the sketch 'The library' we considered earlier. Suppose we are interested in how Victoria Wood achieves her humorous effects in this conversation. In the sketch one male character after another receives rough treatment from Victoria. 'Debunking' involves exposing a reputation as false, and this fits perfectly the cynical comments with which Victoria greets each contender. 'Debunking' is an interesting link because it relates to humour as criticism – our tendency to laugh at faults and failings, to mock vanity and ridicule pretension. Suppose we use this as the link between our databits. We might observe several such links within the data (Figure 11.4).

Debunked by

| | |
|---|---|
| Rodney had white towelling socks | Which in my book makes him unreliable, untrustworthy and prone to vaseline jokes. |
| Mark the solicitor | He does a lot of conveyancing so that'll be seventeen phone calls just to meet him for a cup of coffee. |
| Simon – the gynaecologist | No – too inhibiting. You can't flirt with someone who can visualise your Fallopian tubes. |
| Malcolm – what do you think he meant by a 'lively social life' | Drink |
| He wants a breezy, uninhibited companion | To drink with |
| What do you think he meant by 'life peppered with personal tragedy' | Hangovers |

*Figure 11.4* Observing the link 'debunked by' between databits

In each case, we have an image presented which is then punctured by a debunking comment. As the images get grander, the comments become more biting. We could bring out this cumulative effect by adding further links, this time to capture the way the sketch proceeds towards a climax through a process of repetition and progression. For example, we could link the shift from Simon to Malcolm as a progression – Victoria's comments acquire more bite – while the next two comments reinforce this effect through repetition. By linking data, we can examine more effectively the process as well as the substance of humour. Since links are not exclusive, there is no implication here that this is in any way an 'exhaustive' analysis. We may observe other links within the data. It is a question of identifying links which we find interesting given our analytic inclinations.

---

**Linking data**
- Links must be labelled
- Use a links list for clarity and consistency
- Use a limited links list to reduce complexity
- Ground links conceptually and empirically

---

So far, we have proceeded as though linking data and categorizing data were two quite distinct activities. This may be a bit misleading. It is true that we can identify links without having categorized the data. In the 'debunking' example, we identified links between bits of data which we had not explicitly categorized. However, the data has to be categorized at some point if we are to understand what it is we are linking. In practice it may be convenient to undertake these tasks together. Although linking and categorizing are separate tasks, each complements the other (Figure 11.5).

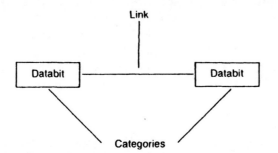

*Figure 11.5* Linking and categorizing complement each other

If categories are the building blocks of the analysis, links can provide the mortar. Or in a more fanciful image, if categories keep the analysis afloat, links can sail it along to a successful conclusion. Let us return to Vincent's letters, and see how linking data can be incorporated into our analysis.

Suppose we want to examine the connections between incongruity and cathartic humour in Vincent's letters. To do this we shall link as well as categorize the data. First of all we have to decide on what constitutes a 'bit' of data. Once again we have to choose between a more or less detailed breakdown of the data. This time, though, we are linking data as well as categorizing it. We shall therefore pay more attention to the internal dynamics of the text. In general, we can expect to identify links within as well as between sentences, reflected in the use of link words like 'because', 'but' and so forth. Conjunctions can reveal a range of links – causal, contradictory, additive and temporal (cf. Bliss 1983: 156). Take the second databit we distinguished on categorizing the data as an example.

> [Mrs Sol Schwimmer is suing me because I made her bridge as I felt it and not to fit her ridiculous mouth.]

In categorizing the data earlier, we ignored the distinction between the two parts of this statement, and treated them as one bit of data. We simply categorized the databit under 'transposing' and 'tasks' as an example of incongruous expectations of what dental work requires. Now we may want to distinguish the two parts of the statement, which Vincent differentiates into cause and effect by using the conjunction 'because':

> [Mrs Sol Schwimmer is suing me] [because] [I made her bridge as I felt it and not to fit her ridiculous mouth.]

Once we start looking for links, the distinction between making the bridge and being sued may seem more significant. Vincent's despair does not arise directly from making a bridge to suit himself rather than the patient, but rather as a result of being sued in consequence. Linking data may therefore encourage us to use a more detailed breakdown of the data, though it does not require this of us. There is no point in making distinctions just for the sake of it. It only makes sense to distinguish between Vincent's action in making the bridge as he 'felt it' and Mrs Sol Schwimmer's decision to sue if this may possibly prove pertinent to our analysis.

| | |
|---|---|
| Mrs Sol Schwimmer is suing me | because I made her bridge as I felt it and not to fit her ridiculous mouth! |

*Figure 11.6* Linking two databits

Suppose we want to characterize the hyperlink we have made between the databits in Figure 11.6. What kind of link is this? The data offers us a clue, in the use of the conjunction 'because' to connect the two parts of the statement. We could regard this as an example of action and consequence, where the 'action' refers to Vincent's bridge-building activities and the consequence is Mrs Sol Schwimmer's suing him. Causal connections refer to events 'out there' in the real world of social action. Here we have Vincent's report on those events. Does this give us enough information to justify characterizing this link as causal? We have to rely on Vincent's interpretation: he says Mrs Sol Schwimmer is suing because her bridge doesn't fit. He doesn't offer any alternative explanations, for example that Mrs Sol Schwimmer has litigious inclinations and sues every dentist she encounters – though this may be so. On the other hand, we may consider that Vincent's interpretation has a plausible ring, for we can recognize it as conforming to an established pattern, where the action (malpractice) has this result (litigation) as a possible (and perhaps even probable) consequence.

Attributing a link between databits is like assigning a category to a bit of data: it is a matter of judgement. We 'observe' links within the data; but we will not find them unless we look for them, and we have to be wary of finding what we are looking for, regardless of the data. Even though Vincent claims a causal connection between the two, we have to assess the plausibility of his claim, and weigh the evidence in its support, before we can characterize this link as a causal one with any confidence. Where there is no certainty, there is a risk of error. Here we must balance the error of failing to characterize this as a causal link (if it is one) against the error of so characterizing it (if it is not).

The closer we stay to the data, the less prone we become to error. Suppose we characterize this link as explanatory rather than causal. We can take Vincent's explanation at face value, without worrying unduly whether the causal assumptions he makes (or implies) in his explanation are in fact true. Whatever actually prompted Mrs Sol Schwimmer to sue, we can be reasonably confident that this is Vincent's explanation of it. Of course, we cannot be sure that it is his only explanation. There may be other factors Vincent simply hasn't bothered to mention. Perhaps they are recorded in other letters which we have not discovered. Nor can we be absolutely certain that Vincent isn't lying to his brother, and inventing some plausible reason why Mrs Sol Schwimmer is suing him, in order to disguise the real one. Or it may be that Vincent is sincere, but deceiving himself. Staying close to the data may reduce the possibility of error, but it does not eliminate it altogether.

In this instance, let us opt to characterize this link as explanatory rather than causal (Figure 11.7). We lack corroborative evidence for the events Vincent describes, and this should encourage a certain caution in the inferences we make. In any case, we are dealing with fictional letters rather than real documentary evidence, and can therefore concentrate on the internal characteristics of the data rather than their veracity.

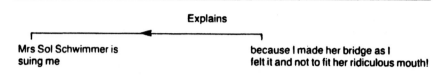

Figure 11.7 An explanatory link between two databits

Suppose we now try to categorize both parts of the statement. First we have to think about appropriate categories. The second part of the statement is no problem, for in making the bridge 'as he felt it' Vincent works as an artist rather than a dentist. We can assign this the categories 'transposing' and 'task'. What of the first part? If we take this as evidence of 'patient suffering', indicated by the decision to sue, we can see the results of our analysis in Figure 11.8.

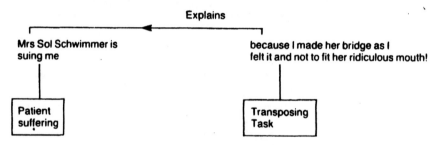

Figure 11.8 Linking and categorizing two databits

The same information is displayed in a different format in Table 11.1, where I have added a reciprocal element to the link between the two databits. This allows us to identify a direction in the relationship, though obviously this does not apply to all links (e.g. contradiction).

Table 11.1 Result of linking and categorizing two databits

| Databits | Categories | Links |
|---|---|---|
| 1. Mrs Sol Schwimmer is suing me | Patient Suffering | Explained by 2 |
| 2. because I made her bridge as I felt it and not to fit her ridiculous mouth. | Transposing Task | Explains 1 |

The link we have established between these two databits suggests there may indeed be a connection between incongruity and cathartic humour.

First we have a hint at cathartic humour, in the reference to Vincent being sued by a patient – implying that something has gone badly wrong. Then we have Vincent's explanation, which reveals his incongruous conception of what is required of a dentist. This example should therefore encourage us to look for any further evidence of connections between the two types of humour.

The link we have just made was very straightforward. Conjunctions such as 'because' make explicit reference to links within the data. Can we also reasonably infer such links even where they are not explicitly stated? For example, can we regard Vincent's despair as a result of his being sued, even though he does not make an explicit link between the two?

> [Will life never treat me decently? I am wracked by despair! My head is pounding.]
> [Mrs Sol Schwimmer . . .]

It seems plain that Vincent intends his statement about being sued to be understood as an explanation of his physical and mental suffering, even though he doesn't make this explicit (Figure 11.9). We can legitimately infer this meaning from the context, although other interpretations are possible – for example Vincent could simply be making two quite independent statements without meaning to imply any link between them. In making such inferences, therefore, we must proceed with caution, and recognize that our grounds are less secure than when a link has been referred to explicitly in the data.

Explains

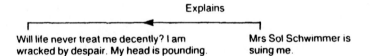

Will life never treat me decently? I am          Mrs Sol Schwimmer is
wracked by despair. My head is pounding.          suing me.

*Figure 11.9* Inferring an explanatory link between two databits

Our second databit, Mrs Sol Schwimmer's litigation, is now linked to two other databits – as an explanation of Vincent's despair, in turn explained by Vincent's artistic endeavours (Table 11.2). We can link one bit of data to as many others as we like.

There is no reason why we should confine links to bits of data which appear sequentially in the text. For example, we may decide that Vincent's despair is linked, not only to the episode with Mrs Sol Schwimmer, but also to his experience of sharing an office with Cézanne. Here again linking encourages us to pay more attention to the internal dynamics within the data, and differentiate between parts of the data we previously regarded as a whole. We might therefore also record the links noted in Table 11.3.

*Table 11.2* Multiple links between databits

| Databits | Links |
|---|---|
| 1. Will life never treat me decently? I am wracked by despair! My head is pounding. | Explained by 2 |
| 2. Mrs Sol Schwimmer is suing me | Explains 1<br>Explained by 3 |
| 3. because I made her bridge as I felt it and not to fit her ridiculous mouth. | Explains 2 |

Because Vincent precedes his account of Cézanne with another outburst – 'Theo I can't go on like this much longer' – we can be more confident in linking this episode to his opening confession. Sometimes, however, it is not at all obvious how to link data, even where the databits we want to link are in sequence. Take the statement 'I can't go on' in the middle of Vincent's letter, as an example. Does this statement conclude the previous account of bridge building, open the new one on Cézanne, or both? Or take Vincent's concluding statement 'What to do?' Does this refer to Cézanne's incompetence, to his own legal problems, to his despair, or to a culmination of all three? The fact that links may bridge separate parts of the data makes matters more complicated rather than less.

*Table 11.3* Linking non-sequential databits

| Databits | Links |
|---|---|
| 1. Will life never treat me decently? I am wracked by despair! My head is pounding. | Explained by 2<br>Explained by 13 |
| 12. I asked Cézanne if he would share an office with me but he is old and infirm and unable to hold the instruments and they must be tied to his wrists | Explains 13 |
| 13. but then he lacks accuracy and once inside a mouth, he knocks out more teeth than he saves. | Explains 1 |

As with assigning categories, we may want to spell out as far as possible the criteria we use in making a decision between these options, so that this can guide us over future judgements. For example, we may decide to restrict a link to the preceding data, unless there are empirical grounds for linking it to other databits. We may have more confidence that Vincent is referring to Cézanne's incompetence, which he has just been discussing, than to the bridge-building episode. If we use proximity as a guide, then we should include this in the criteria we use in determining whether and how to link data. On the other hand, we may be especially interested in ambiguity of meaning, and how one statement can link to other parts of the text. In that case, we may take inclusion of all potential meanings as a guide to our linking.

In any case, sometimes we may want to adopt an interpretation deliberately at odds with that of our subjects. To digress for a moment, let us look at how the episode with Mrs Sol Schwimmer could be analysed in terms of explanatory links, but looking at possible explanations in the data for her litigation. Although Vincent is apparently exasperated at her action, and finds it absurd, we can identify a number of reasons in Vincent's account why Mrs Schwimmer might resort to litigation. To do so, we must opt for inclusion rather than proximity as our rule for linking databits. For convenience I have presented these links graphically (Figure 11.10).

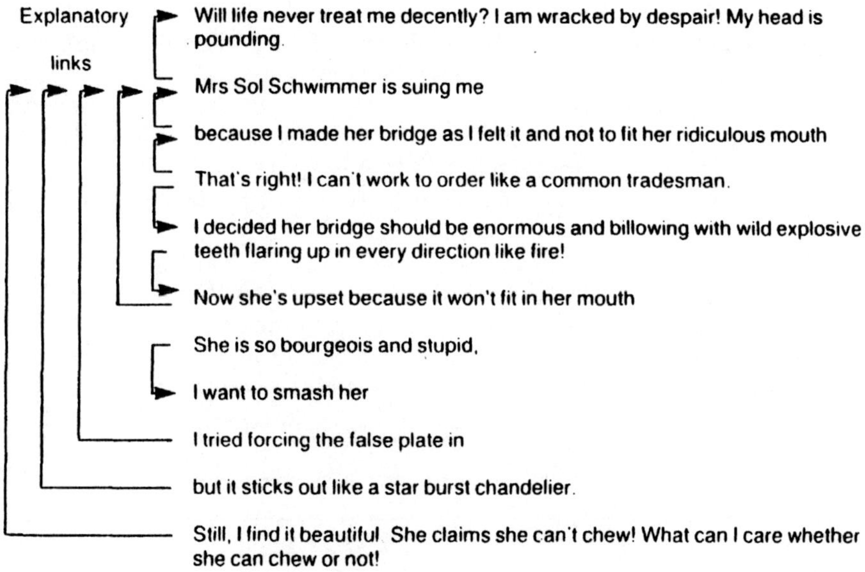

Figure 11.10 Explaining Mrs Sol Schwimmer's litigation

Exactly how the results of linking are recorded and displayed by the computer will depend on the software being used.

This analysis is governed by two decisions. First, our decision to characterize the links as explanatory rather than causal. Second, our decision to adopt an 'inclusion' rule, permitting a link to be inferred even if not referred to explicitly in the data, and regardless of whether or not the databits are sequential. Obviously different decisions could produce a very different analysis. It is therefore important to record our reasons for making decisions and not simply putting them into effect without explanation. Justice must not only be done – it must be seen to be done.

---

**Assigning links**
- Look out for link words in the data
- Only identify links pertinent to the analysis
- Stay as close as possible to the data
- Use caution in inferring links
- Specify 'rules' governing link decisions

---

The mechanics of linking data should be as straightforward as those of categorizing. Once each bit of data has been selected and a link chosen, the computer should be able to do the rest. It should be possible to link data prior to categorizing, while categorizing or after categorizing. What do we produce through linking databits? In practical terms, the computer can store for each databit any information about links we have made between it and other databits, and what those links are called. The particular format used does not matter, so long as the computer stores the relevant information in a practical way. This should allow us, on analysing our databits, to go directly from a databit to any other databit linked to it. When we come to analysing databits, therefore, we can display information not just about the categories to which they belong, or the context from which they are drawn, but also the other databits to which they relate.

Earlier we looked at an example of the information which might be held by the computer for our first databit. We can now extend this to include information about the links with other databits (Illustration 11.2). It doesn't matter how the databit is indexed – I have just taken the first three words of each databit as an index – so long as the computer can use the index to locate any linked databits. There should be no practical limit to how many links we can record for any particular databit.

*Illustration 11.2* Information held on linked databits

| Index | Mrs Sol Schwimmer |
|---|---|
| Databit | Mrs Sol Schwimmer is suing me |
| Categories | Transposing Occupation |
| Case | Letter01 |
| DataRef1 | Vincent |
| DataRef2 | Theo |
| Date | 1.4.91 |
| Analyst | Ian Dey |
| Comment | Is 'occupation' assigned correctly? |
| Links | Explains 'Will life never'<br>Explained by 'Because I made'; 'Now she's upset'; 'I tried forcing'; 'But it sticks'; 'Still I find' |

From an empirical point of view, we can weave a complex web of links between different bits of data. How does this help us conceptually? I shall consider this question in more detail in the next chapter. Meantime, let us conclude by noting two contributions which linking data can make to our analysis.

One way linking can help our analysis is in the description of singularities. By recording each link in a chain of events, we can observe chronological or causal sequences, making it easy to extract from the data a series of events and the relationships between them. Linking thereby allows us to give a dynamic account of what has happened. Let us take another of Vincent's letters as an example.

Dear Theo
I think it is a mistake to share offices with Gauguin. He is a disturbed man. He drinks Lavoris in large quantities. When I accused him, he flew into a rage and pulled my D.D.S. off the wall. In a calmer moment, I convinced him to try filling teeth outdoors and we worked in a meadow surrounded by greens and gold. He put caps on a Miss Angela Tonnato and I gave a temporary filling to Mr Louis Kaufman. There we were, working together in the open air! Rows of blinding white teeth in the sunlight! Then a wind came up and blew Mr Kaufman's toupee into the bushes. He darted for it and knocked Gauguin's instruments to the ground. Gauguin blamed me and tried to strike out but pushed Mr Kaufman by mistake, causing him to sit down on the high speed drill. Mr Kaufman rocketed past me on a fly, taking Miss Tonnato with him. The upshot, Theo, is that Rifkin, Rifkin, Rifkin and Meltzer have attached my earnings. Send whatever you can.
Vincent.

In Figure 11.11, this incident out-of-doors is presented through a number of links in a chain of events which again culminate in litigation. To elucidate this simple episode, I have used only two links, conditional and causal, but obviously more links might be required to identify relationships within a more complex sequence of events. In this way, linking can be used to establish connections between the different elements in a singularity.

Another aim in linking data is to provide an empirical basis for connecting categories. When we look for possible relationships between categories, we can do so on the basis of our observations of links between the databits. Each time we link two databits, we also connect the categories assigned to those databits. For example, in linking Vincent's bridge building and Mrs Sol Schwimmer's suing, we also connect the categories assigned to the former with the categories assigned to the latter. Returning to our interest in the connection between incongruous and cathartic humour, we can identify various examples where these two types of humour are connected through links we can observe in the data. Figure

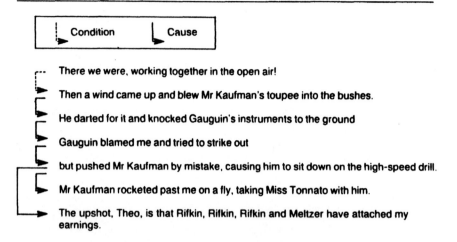

*Figure 11.11* Conditional and causal links in the tale of Kaufman and Tonnato

11.12 shows two examples from the out-doors incident we have just discussed.

Note that the two links differ, one being conditional and the other causal. You may recall that in our earlier discussion, we opted for explanatory rather than causal links between the episodes discussed by Vincent in his first letter. Each of these different links nevertheless connects the categories which we have used to explore incongruous and cathartic

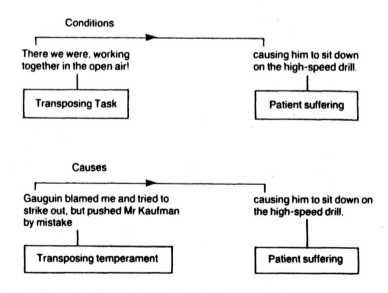

*Figure 11.12* Connecting incongruous and cathartic humour

humour. Whether incongruous actions and events condition, cause or explain cathartic humour, exemplified in the various modes of suffering inflicted on patients, we have here some further evidence that there may be a connection between the two (Figure 11.13).

Some of the links are between transpositions of task and patient suffering, while others are between transpositions of temperament and patient suffering. This underlines an important point about the open-ended relationship between linking data and connecting categories.

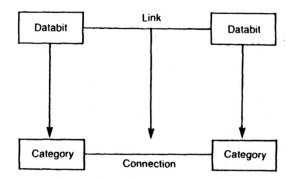

*Figure 11.13* Linking data and connecting categories

The links we observe between different bits of data establish connections between the categories we assign to that data. But as we saw earlier, our categories may be subject to continual refinement and revision through the process of analysis. Having observed links between different bits of data, it remains an open question which categories these links will connect. How we answer this question is taken up in the next chapter.

# Chapter 12

# Making connections

Imagine a snapshot of an athlete clearing a hurdle. What can we tell from our snapshot about what is happening? Although we have only a static image, we will have some idea of what has just happened, and what is going to happen. We may not understand the law of gravity, but we do have sufficient grounds for inferring that what goes up must come down. All the same, we would be happier with a succession of images which provide more direct evidence of what is going on. A videotape would do nicely. Then we would be in a much better position to answer the question 'what happens next?' Qualitative data often provides us with just this sort of direct evidence about the dynamics of what is happening.

How can we analyse these dynamics? One way involves analysing data into categories which capture the main elements of social action, and then noticing and documenting how these categories interconnect. For example, suppose we have three successive images of our athlete. In the first, the athlete is poised to jump or has just sprung into the air. In the second, the hurdle is cleared. And in the third, the athlete has landed on the other side. We could categorize these as three actions – jumping, clearing, and landing. Suppose we find these actions tend to recur together in the data, and in a regular sequence. If we find the data conforming to this pattern, we may conclude that there is a connection between them.

What is the probability, we may ask, of finding these three categories associated in a regular sequence in the data? How often is jumping succeeded by clearing the hurdle? How often is clearing the hurdle followed by landing? If these actions are connected, then the probability is high that we shall observe them in the expected sequence – unless other factors intervene. And here, of course, we must acknowledge that it is not enough just to jump – our athlete must jump high enough to clear the hurdle. We may find many – perhaps even a majority of – examples in the data, where the jump is not high enough, the hurdle is not cleared, and there is no happy landing on the other side. We must therefore introduce as a condition or intervening variable, that the jump reaches a certain height. Then we can check the data to see if our observations match our expectations.

This way of analysing dynamics infers connections from the regular association of categories in the data. This is because our categories break up the data into a succession of images or events, and then somehow we have to find a way of putting them together again. We could call our athlete David Hume, after the Scottish philosopher who wrestled with this problem of how we can connect together what we experience as separate impressions. Hume's answer – that we can infer causation from the constant conjunction of impressions – was not very different from the way of connecting categories we have just considered. This indirect procedure for connecting categories stems from fragmenting the data into a succession of discrete impressions or events in the first place.

If we link as well as categorize our data, we can offset this initial fragmentation of the data and provide more direct empirical grounds for making connections between categories. We no longer have to base our analysis on separate events, for as well as distinguishing these events we can also link them. Suppose we link our observations of 'jumping' to 'clearing the hurdle' and our observations of 'clearing the hurdle' to that of 'landing'. We could call the first link 'going up' and the second link 'coming down'. Now when we want to connect the categories 'jumping' and 'clearing the hurdle' we can find all the data where we have already linked our observations. We no longer need to infer between categories on the basis of concurrence, for we have already observed and recorded the corresponding link in the data.

This contrast between inference and observation can be overdrawn, for observation itself involves an element of inference. When we watch the videotape of our athlete ascending and descending, we make the inference that it is the athlete who is moving, and not the hurdle. This inference is, of course, entirely reasonable, but it is no less an inference for that. Think of those movies where we are supposed to think a stationary car is moving, because we see moving traffic behind the car. Special effects rely on our ability to make mistaken inferences. Anyone who has mistakenly inferred that their own (stationary) train is moving because a train alongside is pulling out of the station will know that we cannot always trust our senses in real life. We also have to make sense of the information they provide.

How we make sense of connections is rooted in reasoning based on our observation and experience of links and how they operate. We can think of links as the sort of 'connecting mechanisms' (cf. Sayer 1992) between events which we experience in everyday life – why the door bangs when we slam it; why the light comes on when we operate the switch; why eating satisfies our hunger. We connect these things because we understand the links between them. If the light does not come on, we do not revise our thinking to take account of this 'irregularity' – we change the bulb. Of course, our reasoning may be mistaken – perhaps the fuse has blown. And it may be more or less sophisticated. At a common sense level, we know what jumping is because we have had experience of it. We have also experienced and observed the effects of gravity. At a more abstract level, we know that energy is needed to counter gravity – energy provided through the act of jumping. We know that once that energy is exhausted, gravity will reassert itself – and the athlete will return to the ground. On conceptual grounds, therefore, we can make a connection between the different actions. We can show that David Hume jumped the hurdle, without relying on an inference connecting two previously unconnected events. Our explanation is couched rather in terms of what jumping involves: it is through understanding the link between energy and gravity that we can connect these events with confidence.

On the other hand, our identification of links is itself influenced by the regularity with which events are associated. If things (on earth) fell any which way, rather than in one direction, would we have discovered gravity? If people didn't laugh at jokes, would we know they were funny? Moreover, our interest in understanding links is rarely to enjoy a moment of pure intellectual satisfaction; it is related to practical tasks. We usually want to avoid mistakes and exploit opportunities, to better influence or control future events. For example, comics who fail to make their audience laugh may want to learn why their jokes fell flat. Here again, our concern is with the regular association of one thing with another, even if only to break that association and change future events.

We can contrast these different approaches pictorially as in Figure 12.1. Associating events involves identifying the events as occurring together. Linking events implies an interaction between them.

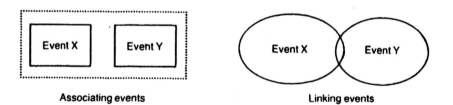

Associating events                                   Linking events

*Figure 12.1* The difference between associating and linking events

Despite the sometimes rather acrimonious debates which take place between rival epistemologists, from a pragmatic point of view neither of these approaches has a monopoly of wisdom. Just as meaning and number are different but mutually dependent, so too are association and linking as a basis for establishing connections between things. We can draw another T'ai-chi T'u diagram to symbolize this relationship (Figure 12.2).

The regular association of events provides a basis for inferring possible connections between them, but subject to conceptual confirmation through

*Figure 12.2* Association and linking as mutually related means of establishing connections

establishing some links or connecting mechanisms which operate between them. The conceptual identification of links provides a basis for identifying connections between events, but subject to empirical confirmation through regular association between them. At the extremes, as our T'ai-chi T'u suggests, we may rely almost entirely on one rather than another – but for the most part, establishing connections depends on elements of both approaches.

Let us return to our analysis of humour, and consider each of these approaches in turn, starting with inference from the association of categories.

## CONNECTING THROUGH ASSOCIATION

Suppose we suspect a relationship holds between two of our categories. Let us take 'temperament' and 'suffering' as examples. For simplicity's sake, let us question whether there is a causal relationship between these categories, such that episodes where Vincent (or another dentist) displays an artistic temperament result in 'suffering' being inflicted on the patient. We see intimations of this already in the first letter, where Vincent seems excited by his aesthetic achievement (we could argue that his language betrays his excitement) with the bridge, while his antipathy to Mrs Sol Schwimmer leads to the rather aggressive outburst 'I could smash her'. His patient, as we have seen, suffers in several ways as a result of his attentions. Can we find similar examples in the data?

Suppose we have categorized the data under the two categories:

'temperament' and 'suffering', restricting the first to dental displays of artistic temperament, and the second to the experience of suffering by dentists or patients. Once the data has been categorized, we can no longer observe directly how these categories might be connected: we have organized the data into distinctive and separate categories. However, we can compare the data assigned to the two categories, and look for evidence of a possible connection between them.

To compare the categories, we need to retrieve all the databits which have been assigned to one category, but not the other. We can also retrieve all the databits which have been assigned to both categories. This gives us a cross-tabulation in Table 12.1. One virtue of cross-tabulating the data in this way is that it obliges us to take account of all the databits which do not meet our criterion. This data which shows no concurrence between the categories is no less important than the data which does show concurrence.

Table 12.1 Concurrence between categories

| Temperament | Suffering | |
| --- | --- | --- |
| | Assigned | Not assigned |
| Assigned | Databits | Databits |
| Not assigned | Databits | No data |

In three of the 'cells' of this table we have a list of databits which fulfil the conditions of our retrievals. The first cell, for example, contains all the databits which were assigned to both 'temperament' and 'suffering'. Note though that the last cell contains no data, as there can be no retrieval for data which has not been assigned to one or other of our categories! This means that there are limits to what we can do with our cross-tabulation – for example, we cannot total the data and work out proportions for all the rows and columns.

These retrievals do let us do three things (Table 12.2). First, we can see how many databits have been assigned to either or both categories. Second, we can compare the databits within the first cell, which contains the data where the categories concur, looking for evidence of connections between those databits assigned to both categories. Third, we can compare the databits across the different cells. Is there any difference between those databits where both categories have been assigned, and those where only one category has been assigned but not the other?

In cross-tabulating databits, it may be more convenient to refer to them by an indexing title (here I have used the first words of each databit) rather

*Table 12.2* Comparing databits between the different cells

| Temperament | Suffering | |
|---|---|---|
| | *Assigned* | *Not assigned* |
| *Assigned* | Gauguin blamed me (Toulouse-Lautrec) too proud I love her | Gauguin flew into |
| *Not assigned* | Gauguin had his knee | No data |

than the whole databits, which can be listed separately (Table 12.3) or retrieved as required by the computer.

Comparing the databits within the first cell, we can see that where 'temperament' and 'suffering' have both been assigned to a databit, the data does tend to confirm a pattern whereby artistic temperament results in patient torture. By contrast, where only one category or the other is assigned, we have examples where there is no connection between the two. The first is an example of 'suffering' which doesn't result from 'temperament', and the second is an example of 'temperament' resulting in 'suffering', but experienced by Vincent himself rather than a patient. If we have categorized the data to differentiate between 'patient suffering' and 'dentist suffering', then we can incorporate this category into our cross-tabulation by further retrievals.

*Table 12.3* List of indexed databits

| Index | Databit |
|---|---|
| Gauguin blamed me | and tried to strike out but pushed Mr Kaufman by mistake, causing him to sit down on the high-speed drill. |
| (Toulouse-Lautrec) too proud | to stand on anything. Arms over his head, he gropes around their lips blindly, and yesterday, instead of putting caps on Mrs Fitelson's teeth, he capped her chin. |
| I love her. | I was looking down into her mouth today and I was like a nervous young dental student again, dropping swabs and mirrors in there. |
| Gauguin had his knee | on Mr Nat Feldman's chest with the pliers around the man's upper right molar. |
| Gauguin flew into | a frenzy! He held my head under the X-ray machine for ten straight minutes and for several hours after I could not blink my eyes in unison. |

Let us look for a moment at the character of the retrievals on which these cross-tabulations are based. We have used two different types of retrieval. First, we have used a retrieval which has asked the computer to collect all examples where the categories 'temperament' AND 'suffering' have been assigned to a databit. Note that this means BOTH categories have been assigned and it excludes those where only one OR the other has been applied. In our other retrieval we asked the computer to collect all examples where one category BUT NOT the other has been assigned to the data. Using 'X' and 'Y' for our categories, we can see that our retrievals are based on the following operations:

retrieve all 'X' AND 'Y'
retrieve all 'X' NOT 'Y'

These are often called 'boolean' operators after the nineteenth century logician, George Boole, who first distinguished them. There is another operator we may find useful as a basis for retrievals:

retrieve all 'X' OR 'Y'

This would allow us to retrieve all the data which has been assigned to either of two different categories. For example, we could retrieve all the databits assigned to 'dentist suffering' and 'patient suffering'. Notice that in ordinary language, we tend to use 'and' rather than 'or' when we refer to retrieving all the databits for each of the categories – meaning 'all X and all Y'. Confusion arises if we think about the results of the retrieval – which will include all 'X' and all 'Y' – rather than the decisions on which it is based. To avoid confusion, we need to consider how the retrieval 'operates' on each databit. It is this decision which we must be clear about: i.e. do we include this databit or not? The boolean operators provide a logical basis for deciding on inclusion or exclusion in terms of how our categories have been assigned (Table 12.4)

*Table 12.4* Boolean operators for category retrievals

| For each databit, decide whether categories are | Boolean operator |
| --- | --- |
| Both assigned | 'X' AND 'Y' |
| Only one assigned | 'X' NOT 'Y' |
| Either assigned | 'X' OR 'Y' |

Cross-tabulations based on such retrievals involve looking for connections where categories do or do not concur. The evidence these retrievals produce is embedded within each databit. The databits within each cell have no relationship to each other, other than that they have been assigned to the same category or categories. This has limitations, for what if there are relationships between databits which have been assigned to non-concurring categories? We may want to look for evidence where categories may not concur, but are nevertheless close to each other in the data. For example, we could look for categories which have been assigned to consecutive databits, or categories which have been assigned to databits which fall within a certain distance of each other in the data. This distance could be defined in terms of a number of characters, a paragraph, section or even a whole case. Using either sequence or proximity as a condition for our retrieval, we can produce a cross-tabulation of all the databits which have been assigned to one or other categories and do or do not fulfil this condition. For example, in Table 12.5 we have a cross-tabulation of categories where they have been assigned, not to the same databit, but to one falling within a specified distance. Of course, a condition of proximity includes all the databits where categories are concurrent, overlapping or consecutive within the data. We could even impose the requirement that categories should have been assigned to the data in a certain order.

*Table 12.5* Retrieval based on categories assigned to proximate bits of data

| | Suffering | |
|---|---|---|
| *Temperament* | *Proximate* | *Not proximate* |
| *Proximate* | Databits | Databits |
| *Not proximate* | Databits | No data |

So far we have made no comment on the numerical aspects of our cross-tabulation. As well as assessing the databits we have retrieved, we may also take account of the number of databits accumulated in each cell (Table 12.6). For example, if virtually all the databits are concentrated in the first cell, and display the suspected association between categories, then we will doubtless feel more confident in inferring a connection between the categories than if the converse holds true, and only a small minority of databits are located in the first cell. For each category, we can consider the proportion of databits which is associated with the other category.

*Table 12.6* Retrieval based on categories 'temperament' and 'suffering'
assigned to proximate bits of data

| Temperament | Suffering | |
|---|---|---|
| | Proximate | Not proximate |
| Proximate | 16 | 5 |
| Not proximate | 7 | No data |

From Table 12.6 we can tell that most of the databits (sixteen) assigned
to the categories 'temperament' and 'suffering' fell within a defined distance
of each other (however that was defined). These databits were 'proximate'.
However, there were seven databits assigned to 'temperament' which fell
outside this distance, as did another five assigned to 'suffering', so twelve
databits were not proximate. To consider whether this pattern constitutes
evidence of a connection between the categories, we still have to return to
the original data.

---

**Some retrieval procedures**
- Concurrence – do databits concur?
- Overlap – do databits overlap?
- Sequence – are the databits consecutive?
- Proximity – are the databits within a given distance?
- Precedence – does one databit precede another?

---

So far we have considered retrievals in relation to the data as a whole.
Depending on the nature of our data, we may also be interested in relating
our retrievals to the cases which form the basic units of our analysis. For
example, we could take each of Vincent's letters as a case, and consider
whether we can identify relationships which hold across some or all of
these cases. Perhaps we may be interested in drawing some conclusions
about the content and construction of the letters. This example may seem
rather fatuous, but in relation to interview data or observations of
different agencies, we may well want to analyse our data in terms of cases.

What information do we have about our cases? Well, for each category
we have used in our analysis, we can tell whether or not we have assigned
the category to that case. We can also tell how often we have assigned the
category to the case. Taking 'temperament' and 'suffering', for example, we
can produce a table indicating whether and how often each of these categories has been assigned to each of Vincent's letters (Table 12.7). In effect,
we treat category assignation as a case variable.

*Table 12.7* Categories analysed as case variables

| Cases | Temperament | Suffering |
|---|---|---|
| Letter 1 | 5 | 4 |
| Letter 2 | 2 | 2 |
| Letter 3 | 0 | 1 |
| Letter 4 | 0 | 1 |
| Letter 5 | 3 | 1 |
| Letter 6 | 3 | 1 |
| Letter 7 | 2 | 3 |
| Letter 8 | 3 | 2 |
| Letter 9 | 3 | 3 |
| Letter 10 | 1 | 2 |

Our categories express ideas about differences and similarities within the data as a whole, but treated as case variables, they can express values for particular cases. For example, the category 'temperament' expresses the idea that transpositions of temperament are a distinctive element in the data, and our definitions and databits contribute to elucidating and developing this idea about the data. But the category 'temperament' as a case variable tells us whether or not the category 'temperament' has been assigned to each letter. If this information is to be useful, we have to ensure that it is meaningful to treat category assignations as features of cases. Does it make sense, for example, to regard 'temperament' and 'suffering' as features of our letters rather than as concepts applied to the data as a whole?

If we proceed in this way, we can create a dataset through which we can explore regularities and variations across cases. I shall return to the use we can make of data matrices in the next chapter. Meantime, it is sufficient to note the extra dimension this approach adds to our analysis of the association between categories. We can now identify for each case which categories have been assigned to that case, separately or in combination. We can look for evidence of whether or not variables are associated. Do they covary! Table 12.8 shows how the results might look for the ten letters from Vincent to Theo.

*Table 12.8* Cross-tabulating categories as case variables: 'temperament' and 'suffering' in Vincent's letters (N = 10)

| Temperament | Suffering | |
|---|---|---|
| | *Assigned* | *Not assigned* |
| *Assigned* | 6 | 1 |
| *Not assigned* | 2 | 1 |

Notice how this cross-tabulation compares with that in Table 12.2, where we had no figure for the final cell – you may recall that when analysing the data as a whole, there can be no retrieval for data which has not been assigned to one or other of our categories. When analysing variables across cases, though, we can complete the final cell, which gives the number of cases where neither variable has been assigned to the data. Now we can complete totals and proportions for all the rows and columns in our cross-tabulation. We can compare the proportion of cases where 'temperament' and 'suffering' concur with the proportion where they are assigned separately, or are not assigned at all. If we have satisfied the conditions for statistical tests – which may require a minimum number of randomly selected cases – we may even conduct tests of the significance of any association we observe between the variables. Essentially this involves matching the observed values in cells with the values we would expect if there were no association between the variables.

In looking for associations, we may be interested in a number of different possibilities, and not just evidence of a high positive correlation between two variables. We may look for precisely the opposite – a high negative correlation, so that high values for one variable, are associated with low values for another. We may also be interested in changes in values – whether more or less of one value for a variable raises or lowers the values for another variable.

| X high   | Y high   |
| X high   | Y low    |
| X higher | Y higher |
| X higher | Y lower  |

These are only some of the associations we may be able to identify (cf. Miles and Huberman 1984: 225–6).

Our analysis need not be confined to categories regarded as variables whose values express the number of times the category has been assigned to each case. We can incorporate variables giving background characteristics of the case – often called 'facesheet' variables because such background data may be recorded on the front page of an interview or set of fieldwork notes. These variables, expressing perhaps the age and gender of a respondent, the size and location of a site, or the type and functions of an agency, may then be related to the variables emerging from the categorical analysis. The latter may also assume a more sophisticated form, if we can identify connections between categories and integrate them in terms of some underlying variable.

For example, suppose we have analysed the data in terms of three subcategories of 'suffering' – 'discomfort', 'disfigurement' and 'disability' – and we find that (contrary to the evidence of the first letter) these are rarely if ever assigned to the same case. We may want to record which of the categories have been assigned to which cases. If we are satisfied that these subcategories are conceptually distinct, then we could regard them as values of the underlying variable 'suffering' and assign these values accordingly. We could then discriminate between cases in terms of the variable 'suffering' and relate this variable to others in our analysis. Of course, the values for our variable must be exhaustive as well as exclusive, so we might include a value such as 'other' (or 'awkward' might do as well) for any cases, such as our first letter, where the categories are assigned in combination.

The identification of variables with exclusive and exhaustive categories might itself be regarded as a major achievement of categorization. From a conceptual point of view, this requires a clear distinction between the boundaries of individual categories which can be grouped under an overarching category. The categories must not only be 'exclusive'; they must also relate to and express the concept embodied in the overarching category. This is a task which I alluded to in discussing the problems of 'splicing' categories. The computer can support this conceptual task by providing quick access to category definitions and the results of assignment decisions. From an empirical point of view, we must check that one and only one value can be – or has been – assigned to each case. The computer can help by allowing us to look for and deal with 'overlaps' where more than one value which we want to regard as exclusive has been assigned to a case. For example, it could locate for us those databits from the first and any other letters where more than one of the values ('discomfort', 'disfigurement' and 'disability') has been assigned to the case for the variable 'suffering'. We can then check whether our initial assignment was reasonable, and if so assign this a residual value such as 'other'. Providing there are not too many 'others' our variable may still prove a useful way of discriminating between cases.

A simpler but less conceptually rewarding method of generating values is to note the number of times a category has been assigned to a case. In Table 12.2 we assumed our variables would have two values, either assigned or not assigned. But what if we have assigned a category to several databits for each case? For any category, we can treat the number of assignations as a value for each case, and then use this as a basis for our cross-tabulations. The computer can easily identify these values for us, and provide information about the frequencies with which categories have been assigned to cases as well as the basis for cross-tabulating variables.

Some qualitative analysts may feel very uncomfortable with some of the procedures we have just discussed. There is a strong aversion to numbers in some quarters, and a reluctance to accept that numerical considerations influence qualitative judgements. Nevertheless, it is difficult to see how, in practice, it is possible to identify associations between categories or assess the strength of relationships without recourse to a numerical evaluation. If we are looking for substantive connections between categories which are 'contingent' i.e. not true by definition, then we should be concerned to make an empirical (and numerical) assessment of our evidence. If we want to claim that transpositions of temperament result in infliction of suffering on patients, we want to know whether and how far the evidence supports this connection.

Of course, within the context of qualitative analysis, an enumeration of this kind is not the whole story by a long shot. The cells in a qualitative evaluation are never mere numbers. The numbers summarize our category decisions, and express information about databits in aggregate form. Associations between categories are suggestive not conclusive evidence of connections between categories. For one thing, the existence of an association is not sufficient evidence that such a connection exists. We need to look beyond the evidence of association, to a qualitative account of how and why the categories may be connected. Moreover, the existence of a regular association may be misleading. There are many occasions where we identify connections between events regardless of regularities (Sayer 1992: 131). For example, as I write these lines (in March 1992), the poor performance of the Conservative Party in the current election campaign is widely attributed to the 'grey' personality of the incumbent Prime Minister. In everyday life, we identify connections through analysing the capabilities and liabilities of actors, not merely nor perhaps even primarily through some regular association between events. The existence of such regularities is not irrelevant, but it is indirect and inconclusive evidence of connections between categories. For direct evidence of whether or not a connection exists between categories, therefore, we must still look closely at the data on which the numbers are based.

## CONNECTING WITH LINKED DATA

One reason qualitative analysts have relied – rather surreptitiously, perhaps – on quasi-quantitative assessments may be the lack of more direct methods of identifying connections between categories. By allowing us to make hyperlinks between different bits of data, the computer has now opened up new and more direct ways of connecting categories. Let us look at how we can use linked data to connect categories more effectively. As we are considering the most recent innovations in computer applications for qualitative analysis, it may be some time before software supporting these procedures becomes widely available.

First let us recall that linking data has a mechanical and conceptual aspect. The mechanical aspect refers to hyperlinks created between different databits. The conceptual aspect refers to the identification of the nature of the link between the databits – e.g. is it causal, explanatory or whatever. Linking allows us to treat our databits as individual points in a complex web of relationships, rather than as unrelated bits of data. What does this mean in practice? Hyperlinks allow us to do two things. First, we can follow hyperlinks through the data, going from one databit to any of the others linked to it, and so on until our links are exhausted or we reach full circle and start again. Instead of browsing through the data sequentially, or selectively through keywords, or categories, we can browse through the data using the links we have created between the databits. We can therefore focus our attention on the relationships between different parts of the data, and peruse more effectively the processes which unfold within it (Figure 12.3).

In Figure 12.3 I have presented only one pathway through the data. We can identify as many different pathways as we have identified different types of links. In Figure 12.4 I have overlaid the first pathway with another, representing a different link between the databits.

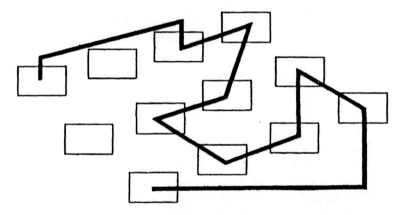

*Figure 12.3* Following a trail of links through the data

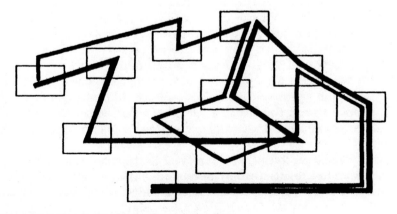

*Figure 12.4* Two trails of links through the data

In Figure 12.4 I have presumed that in browsing through databits our pathways are dictated by the type of link we are following. However, we may also browse through the databits following (or rather, constructing) a pathway composed of different types of link (Figure 12.5).

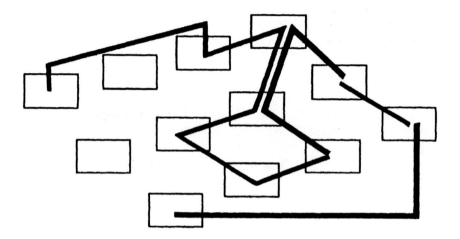

*Figure 12.5* Following a trail of different links through the data

All this looks like a frightful mess! In practice, the analyst following a trail of links will not see the entanglements which arise as his path criss-crosses the data. This is because the focus is always on the previous or the next step, so that the pathways followed through the data remain invisible unless we deliberately try to plot them.

And plot them we can, for another thing we can do with electronic links is 'retrieve' them, or rather retrieve all the databits which have been linked together in some way. We can then examine and compare all the linked databits collected together through our retrieval. For example, we can look at all the causal links we have made between databits. We can then compare these causal links, and examine more thoroughly the basis on which we have linked the data in this way. Fortunately, our retrievals can be presented in more orderly fashion. Figure 12.6 shows the causal relationships between databits as a 'chain' of links. Sometimes there are 'missing' links in the chain where there has been no link noted between the databits.

If each databit represents a unique event in the data, then we can also use this procedure to identify the main strands linking events. Our purpose is descriptive rather than conceptual. Such descriptive work may be an end in itself or it may lay the foundation for an assessment of how categories can be connected.

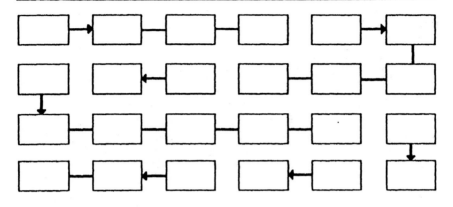

*Figure 12.6* A 'chain' of causal links in the data

Suppose for example we want to tell the story of Vincent's affair with Claire Memling, and we have linked together the bits of data which constitute the main elements in this story (Figure 12.7). We may have categorized these databits under 'Memling' so that we can retrieve only those links pertaining to this story. For simplicity's sake, let us suppose that all the links we have noted between the databits are 'chronological' in character, though other links could also be retrieved. Our retrieval produces all the relevant databits and the links between them.

These databits do not appear consecutively in the data; in fact the Claire Memling story is told over a couple of letters, with a third letter intervening between them. Nor are all the links we have noted in consecutive order. Life is not like that. We often come across explanations of some event sometime after it has appeared to puzzle us in the data. By retrieving links, we can abstract from the diversity and digressions of the data and make connections between the main elements in the story.

We can compare data we have linked one way with data we have linked in other ways. In this way, we can explore and re-examine the types of links we have observed within the data. By comparing within and between these different types of link, we can clarify our understanding of the different processes we have observed. This may be particularly useful where we can compare causal or chronological links with explanatory ones. For example, suppose we had Claire Memling's version of events in Vincent's surgery, and perhaps even an eye-witness account given by Vincent's assistant. From these various sources we can construct a chronological sequence of events. We could then compare these chronological links with Vincent's explanations of what happened, which we can also link to the same events (Figure 12.8).

So far we have used linked data to identify connections between 'singularities' in the data. We can also used linked data to identify

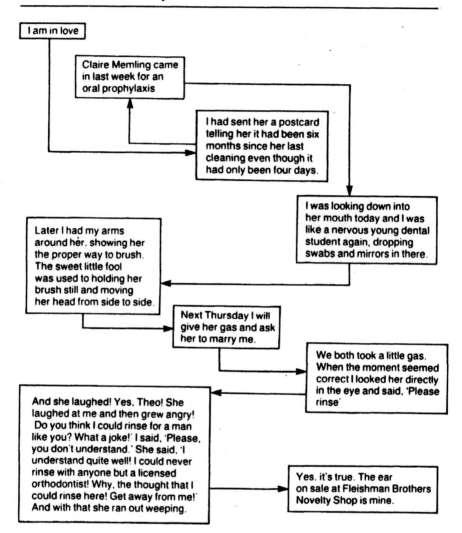

I am in love

Claire Memling came in last week for an oral prophylaxis

I had sent her a postcard telling her it had been six months since her last cleaning even though it had only been four days.

I was looking down into her mouth today and I was like a nervous young dental student again, dropping swabs and mirrors in there.

Later I had my arms around her. showing her the proper way to brush. The sweet little fool was used to holding her brush still and moving her head from side to side.

Next Thursday I will give her gas and ask her to marry me.

We both took a little gas. When the moment seemed correct I looked her directly in the eye and said, 'Please rinse'

And she laughed! Yes. Theo! She laughed at me and then grew angry! Do you think I could rinse for a man like you? What a joke!' I said, 'Please, you don't understand.' She said, 'I understand quite well! I could never rinse with anyone but a licensed orthodontist! Why, the thought that I could rinse here! Get away from me!' And with that she ran out weeping.

Yes. it's true. The ear on sale at Fleishman Brothers Novelty Shop is mine.

*Figure 12.7* Retrieving chronological links in the Claire Memling story

'patterns' by establishing connections between categories. In the Claire Memling story, Claire suffers Vincent's advances, but suppose we are interested in whether there is a pattern to the suffering experienced by patients.

We can look for connections between categories on the basis of hunches and hypotheses which have emerged from our analysis so·far. Or we can explore the databits using links, to look for evidence of possible connections. When browsing through the linked databits, we can look at how they have been categorized. Can we detect any emerging patterns in how linked

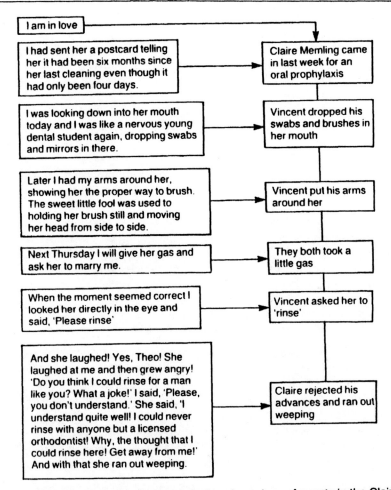

*Figure 12.8* Vincent's explanations linked to chronology of events in the Claire Memling story

databits have been categorized? For example, suppose we search causal links between databits. Do we find that most of the 'cause' databits have been assigned to a common category or categories? Do we find that most of the 'consequence' databits also share a common category or categories? Then we have evidence suggesting a possible connection between these categories.

We can also use retrieval procedures in an exploratory way to identify possible connections between categories. If we retrieve the information about which categories have been assigned to linked databits, we can use this to identify possible connections between categories. If 'Z' is our link then this involves retrieving all the databits linked by 'Z':

Retrieve all 'Z' links (and look at the variation in categories)

This approach is very exploratory, and we could also explore the data from the opposite direction by retrieving all the databits categorized under 'X' OR 'Y' (recall that this means all the 'X' and all the 'Y' databits) and then look for links between them:

Retrieve all 'X' OR 'Y' (and look at the variation in links)

This procedure may prove useful because it allows us to focus on different ways in which the categories we are interested in may be connected. A number of different links exist between the two categories, and we can compare the frequency and content of these links as another way of analysing the character of the relationship between the categories.

If we have a large volume of data assigned to a particular link, we may want to be more specific (and efficient) by specifying further conditions for our retrieval. For example, we could specify which 'X' or 'Y' categories we are interested in:

Retrieve all 'X' with a 'Z' link (and look at the variation in 'Y' categories)
Retrieve all 'Y' with a 'Z' link (and look at the variation in 'X' categories)

For example, suppose we want to explore the factors which are connected with 'suffering'. We can do this by treating 'suffering' as our 'Y' category and 'caused by' as our 'Z' link. We can then retrieve all the databits which have been assigned to category 'Y', and all the databits linked to these by link 'Z'. By examining the categories assigned to these linked databits, we may identify possible connections between categories. In Table 12.9, it is clear that most 'X' databits have been assigned to the categories 'transposing' and 'temperament'.

*Table 12.9* Identifying connections between categories for databits assigned to category 'suffering' and databits linked to these by the link 'caused by'

| 'X' categories | 'X' databits | 'Y' databits | 'Y' categories |
| --- | --- | --- | --- |
| Transposing Temperament | Gauguin blamed me and tried to strike out but pushed Mr Kaufman by mistake, | causing him to sit down on the high-speed drill. | Suffering |
| Transposing Temperament | (Toulouse-Lautrec) is too proud to stand on anything. Arms over his head, he gropes around their lips blindly, | and yesterday, instead of putting caps on Mrs Fitelson's teeth, he capped her chin. | Suffering |

| | | | |
|---|---|---|---|
| Transposing Occupation | Gauguin was in the midst of an extraction when I disturbed him | Gauguin had his knee on Mr Nat Feldman's chest with the pliers around the man's upper right molar | Suffering |
| Transposing Temperament | Gauguin flew into a frenzy! | He held my head under the X-ray machine for ten straight minutes and for several hours after I could not blink my eyes in unison. | Suffering |
| Transposing Temperament | I love her. I was looking down into her mouth today and I was like a nervous young dental student again, | dropping swabs and mirrors in there. | Suffering |

So far we have focused on retrieving links in an open-ended way, and exploring evidence of possible connections. By combining link and category retrievals, we can establish connections in a more direct way. We can ask the computer to retrieve all the data where databits assigned to category 'temperament' have been causally linked to databits assigned to category 'suffering'.

With this retrieval, we cannot compare different categories or links, but we can list and examine all the databits which have been linked in this way. We can examine the internal evidence of a connection between categories by considering the links between the databits that these categories have assigned to.

Retrieve all 'X' with a 'Z' link to 'Y' (look at internal evidence of databits)

We can use this retrieval to evaluate whether the empirical links between the databits assigned to these categories justify the inference of a conceptual connection between categories X and Y. Any such inference can be empirically grounded in the observed links between databits.

---

**Connecting categories through linked data**
- Retrieve all 'Z' links (look at variation in categories)
- Retrieve all 'X' OR 'Y' (look at variation in links)
- Retrieve all 'X' with a 'Z' link (look at variation in 'Y' categories)
- Retrieve all 'Y' with a 'Z' link (look at variation in 'X' categories)
- Retrieve all 'X' with a 'Z' link to 'Y' (look at internal evidence of databits)

Returning to the Claire Memling story, Table 12.10 presents the results of a retrieval with 'transposing' and 'temperament' as our 'X' categories, 'causes' as our link and 'suffering' as our 'Y' category.

In considering the basis for inferring a connection between the categories 'tranposing' and 'temperament' on the one hand, and 'suffering' on the other, we can now examine causal links we have observed between the databits assigned to these categories. Examining links is not just a matter of finding out how many such links there may be. We may also want to consider whether these links express the conceptual connection we are postulating between the categories.

*Table 12.10* Connecting 'X' categories 'tranposing' and 'temperament' to 'Y' category 'suffering' through causal links between the databits

| 'X' categories: Transposing Temperament | 'Y' categories: Suffering |
| --- | --- |
| I am in love | Claire Memling came in for an oral prophylaxis. |
| I was looking down into her mouth today and I was like a nervous young dental student again | dropping swabs and mirrors in there |
| As she sat in the chair, the draining hook in her mouth, my heart thundered. I tried to be romantic. I lowered the lights and tried to move the conversation to gay topics. We both took a little gas. When the moment seemed correct, I looked her directly in the eye and said 'Please rinse' | And she laughed. Yes, Theo! She laughed at me and then grew angry! 'Do you think I could rinse for a man like you? What a joke!' I said, 'Please, you don't understand.' She said, 'I understand quite well! I could never rinse with anyone but a licensed orthodontist! Why, the thought that I could rinse here! Get away from me! And with that she ran out weeping. |
| Theo! I want to die! I see my face in the mirror and I want to smash it! Smash it! | Yes, it's true. The ear on sale at Fleishman Brothers Novelty Shop is mine. I guess it was a foolish thing to do but I wanted to send Claire a birthday present last Sunday and every place was closed. |

This involves checking both the categorization of the databits and the link between them. For example, why have we categorized Vincent's premature letter to Claire as 'suffering?' Is it reasonable to infer that an early return to the dental chair will be experienced as 'suffering' by the patient? We have to check whether this inference conforms to the criteria we have used in assigning the category 'suffering'.

What about the causal links we have recorded between these databits? Have we reasonable grounds for linking these databits? In each case, we have evidence of Vincent's mood ('in love', 'nervous', 'heart thundering' 'I want to die'). But is it reasonable to infer a causal link between this mood and the corresponding event? There are some hidden premises in these links: it is the premature postcard, the dropped instruments, the request to 'please rinse', and the ghastly birthday gift which result in 'suffering' for the patient. Is it reasonable to attribute these actions to Vincent's moods? We must look for evidence in the data to confirm or contradict our assumptions. Connecting categories may therefore require a re-examination of earlier decisions. One advantage of retrieving linked data is that each link can now be reconsidered in the light of other examples.

Another way of examining the internal evidence is to look for consistency across subcategories. If we have previously subcategorized 'suffering' into 'patient' suffering and 'dentist' suffering, we can check whether the link between databits holds for each subcategory as well as for the overarching category. If it does, we may have more confidence in the connection we are inferring between the categories. If it does not, then we may have to refine our analysis and consider whether the connection exists between one or more subcategories rather than the overarching category. In examining the links between subcategories, we also have to examine the internal evidence of a connection.

For example, suppose we subcategorized the last databit, referring to Vincent's ear, as an instance of 'patient suffering' as well as 'dentist suffering'. To see it as 'patient suffering' we have to assume that Vincent did send his 'birthday present' to Claire – though we are not told how it ended up in the Novelty Shop. We also have to assume that Claire suffered as a result. These are not unreasonable assumptions, and these nuances of meaning are a vital part of the text. Nevertheless, we have to acknowledge the inferences involved in assigning categories and links to the data.

In considering the connection between categories, we also have to review the conceptual intelligibility of the relationship we are examining. If we claim a causal connection between the categories 'temperament' and 'suffering', just what are we asserting? Reviewing the evidence, we might reflect on the respective capabilities and liabilities of Vincent and his patients. We might consider that Vincent's capacity to inflict suffering is inherent in his role as a dentist, with the technical and professional power to dictate the form and course of treatment. The patients by contrast are predominantly consigned to a passive role, vulnerable to Vincent's whims and predelictions. Those who resist (Mr Greenglass and Ms Memling) do so by escaping from the dentist–patient relationship. Thus we can understand the connection between Vincent's volatile temperament and patient suffering in part as a consequence of the imbalance in power arising from their respective social roles. In this way we can try to establish and account for the causal connection between the two categories.

Finally, what of the connection between incongruity and cathartic humour? The causal mechanism connecting these two categories (via 'temperament' and 'suffering') centres on the dentist–patient relationship. However, we also have to consider whether the categories may be connected in other ways. For example, does cathartic humour which focuses on fears of the patient role depend for its effectiveness – as humour – on the creation of incongruous images and absurd behaviour? Is there a necessary connection between the two? Is there a contingent relation, such that we laugh more readily at suffering in an incongruous context, but we might laugh all the same? Do we laugh more readily at incongruity, when catharsis adds a certain spice to the proceedings? Or is there no connection between the two at all? Having established that there are some connections between transpositions of temperament and patient suffering, these are issues which we can explore through a thorough qualitative assessment of the data.

To offer one example, consider the connection between Vincent being 'like a nervous young dental student again' and his 'dropping swabs and mirrors' in Claire's mouth. Does the incongruous image of Vincent as a nervous young dental student make it easier for us to enjoy a laugh at the unfortunate result for Claire? I think it does: if this incongruous image is removed, the event is less obviously humorous. This interpretation is further reinforced by another incongruous image, for Vincent exaggerates to the point of absurdity in claiming to drop impossibly large objects into Claire's mouth. The lack of realism reassures us that this episode did not occur as narrated, and this makes it easier to find it funny. Now suppose Vincent had dropped his swabs and mirrors on the floor, rather than in Claire's mouth. Once again, we may doubt whether this would have a similarly humorous effect. The cathartic element seems important in giving a comic edge to the incident, at least as it is narrated on paper. Now imagine a film version of this event. On screen, it would be impossible (without special effects) to drop swabs and mirrors into Claire's mouth. However, the floor may do just as well, for on screen we may identify more fully with Vincent and empathise more readily with his embarrassment and clumsy gaucherie towards Claire. Here too, the effectiveness of the humour may reside in its cathartic effect in relation to our own fears of embarrassment and humiliation.

The technique we have used to explore this example is not unfamiliar – we discussed 'transposing data' as a technique to enhance the interactive reading of text. The same techniques can contribute to elucidating the existence and character of connecting mechanisms.

Each of the procedures we have considered in this chapter depends on combining evidence of empirical association between categories with a conceptual appraisal of connecting mechanisms. The difference between them lies mainly in precedence and priority. The procedure for analysing association between categories puts regularity first on the agenda, but then requires conceptual appraisal of the data to confirm whether or not connnecting mechanisms are operating. The procedure for analysing categories connected through linked data puts the conceptual appraisal of connecting mechanisms first, and then requires some assessment of the regularity with which these occur in the data. While neither approach has a monopoly of virtue, connecting categories through linking data has advantages worth noting. First of all, it allows for information about possible connections between bits of data to be observed directly during the initial analysis of the data, rather than trying to identify these *post hoc* following observed association between categories. Secondly, it allows this evidence to be recorded systematically, so that it can retrieved and analysed thoroughly and comprehensively. By comparison, to go beyond observations of associations between categories without the evidence of linked data, we may once again have to fall back on impressionistic and unsystematic procedures characteristic of more traditional analysis.

# Chapter 13

# Of maps and matrices

A novelist can take ten pages to describe a scene which a film can convey in a single image. Text is a useful vehicle for presenting information, but often pictures can perform the same task more succinctly. Moreover, pictures may correspond more closely to how we actually think (Buzan 1989). Where we are dealing with complex and voluminous data, diagrams can help us to disentangle the threads of our analysis and present results in a coherent and intelligible form. We may not want to accept the claim that 'you know what you display' (Miles and Huberman 1984: 79); but we can readily recognize the virtues of displaying what we do know in the most effective manner. Text can be a tedious and tiresome way of expressing information which could be encapsulated in a few lines and boxes. This is especially so when we are trying to convey sequentially, through text, information which is more easily grasped simultaneously through diagrams.

Diagrammatic displays are not just a way of decorating our conclusions; they also provide a way of reaching them. By contrast with the flat and linear trajectory of text, diagrams provide us with a multi-dimensional space in which to think about our data. Because this space is multi-dimensional, information can be summarized within it which would otherwise be dispersed across a long sequence of statements. In Figure 13.1, for example, we can only see one bit of the textual information, and none of the connections between the dozen different bits of information. But we can see all the information distributed spatially at a glance, and also see some of the connections between the different bits of data.

Diagrams are especially useful when we have to think through such complexities as the relationships between categories (or variables) and the ways in which processes permeate the data. By trying to construct diagrams, we can force ourselves to clarify the main points in our analysis and how these interrelate. But diagrams can also help with more mundane tasks, such as making comparisons between categories, or identifying gaps in the data. This is because they can allow us – or perhaps, oblige us – to think more systematically, more logically, and even more imaginatively about our data.

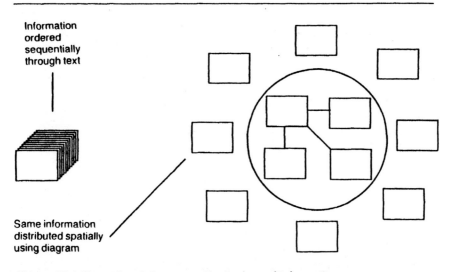

Information
ordered
sequentially
through text

Same information
distributed spatially
using diagram

*Figure 13.1* Textual and diagrammatic displays of information

Diagrams are not immune to the problems which can afflict text. Overburdened with detail, they can become cluttered. Overburdened with complexity, they can become inaccessible. In using diagrams, the watchwords 'simplicity' and 'clarity' have much to commend them. Diagrams can also be very seductive. They can tempt us to impose an order on the data, perhaps for the sake of simplicity and clarity, which is neither adequate nor accurate. We can therefore add 'relevance' and 'appropriateness' to our list of watchwords. Precisely because they are such powerful tools for condensing data and comparing categories, diagrams must be handled with care.

In this chapter I shall consider two sorts of diagrams we might use: matrices and maps. A matrix means a rectangular array of data in rows and columns, though it can also mean a womb or a place where a thing is developed (Concise Oxford Dictionary 1976: 674). Both meanings are apt; the latter tells us what we can accomplish through a matrix, namely the development of our analysis; and the former tells us how it can be accomplished, namely by systematic organization through cross-tabulation of our data. Maps are less structured representations of selected features of our analysis, which can be used both to denote significance (giving prominence by putting something 'on the map') and to relate the different elements of our analysis.

## MATRICES

We can use matrices to compare information across cases. For example, Table 13.1 shows how we can analyse information about the letters

Vincent has written to Theo. For the sake of simplicity I have confined the table to only two of the ten letters. We can see at a glance that there is no variation in the data. From a statistical standpoint, this absence of variation would be depressing. But from a qualitative perspective, sometimes 'no news is good news'. We may be as interested in identifying regularities, or singularities, as in patterns of variation in the data.

*Table 13.1* Comparing information across cases

| Cases | Writer | Recipient |
| --- | --- | --- |
| letter 1 | Vincent | Theo |
| letter 2 | Vincent | Theo |

In this instance our matrix is a testament to the futility of presenting meaningless information in a pretty way. But we can include within our matrix any background information which may seem relevant to the analysis. For example, we may want to include information about where and how we obtained the data about each case. We may want to include some of the main characteristics of each case, such as the age and gender of respondents, or the location and type of sites we have researched. By bringing together information of this kind in a matrix, we can gain a better overall grasp of the quality of our data, make a more comprehensive assessment of our sources, become more sensitive to possible strengths and weaknesses of the data, and identify any glaring gaps or inconsistencies in our data collection.

We can use a matrix to display potentially interesting information about the content of the data (Table 13.2). Some of this material may be noted in our summaries of each case. Note that we needn't assume that our 'variables' have unique or exclusive values. We can list in each cell a number of values for the variable in question. Thus we can include all relevant information about each case in the appropriate cell. In the second letter, for example, the letter refers to two male dentists (Vincent and Degas) and two female patients (Mrs Slotkin and Mrs Zardis).

*Table 13.2* Matrix with non-exclusive values

| Cases | Episodes | Dentists | Patients |
| --- | --- | --- | --- |
| letter 1 | Billowing bridge<br>Cézanne's infirmity | Vincent<br>Cézanne | Mrs Schwimmer<br>Unknown |
| letter 2 | Degas discord<br>Root-canal<br>despondency | Vincent<br>Degas | Mrs Slotkin<br>Mrs Zardis |

Notice that the matrix also includes an instance where the name of the patient is unknown. It would be easy to overlook or discount this and simply pick up only instances where the name (and gender) is given. However, we may then gain a quite different impression of the data. Neither would be unreasonable. The important point is the virtue of being as explicit as possible about the criteria we use for allocating values to the cells in our table.

By organizing the data in this way, we can produce a useful overview of the main features of each case. We can then compare cases more effectively and also look for possible singularities, regularities and variations within the data. For example, suppose we pursue the question of who are the victims of Woody Allen's humour. We would surely notice that all the dentists in these first letters are male, whereas, where the information is available, the patients are female. In fact all the dentists in these letters are male, while most but not all of the patients are female. The fact that the dentists are all male is a regularity which we might relate to issues of power and professionalism. What of the variation in the gender of female patients? If all the patients had been female, we might have been tempted to contrast their role as passive victims with the professional and overpowering role of the dentist. But some of the patients are male. Using our matrix we can explore the significance of this variation, for example by relating it to the episodes narrated in the letters (Table 13.3).

Table 13.3 Using a matrix to explore variation in the data

| Cases | Episodes | Dentists | Patients |
|---|---|---|---|
| letter 1 | Billowing bridge | Vincent | Mrs Schwimmer |
| | Cézanne's infirmity | Cézanne | Unknown |
| letter 2 | Degas discord | Vincent | Mrs Slotkin |
| | Root-canal despondency | Degas | Mrs Zardis |
| letter 5 | Gauguin disturbed | Vincent | Miss Tonnato |
| | Open-air dentistry | Gauguin | Mr Kaufman |
| letter 8 | Knee-chest extraction | Vincent | Mr Feldman |
| | Head in X-ray | Gauguin | |

I have added to the matrix two letters where male patients figure in Vincent's stories. Once we relate these to the episodes narrated in the letters, we may observe that in both stories the male patients are far from passive. The episodes themselves are only indexed in the matrix, where excessive detail may impede overall comprehension. But using the computer, we can easily retrieve the original text if required.

[In a calmer moment, I convinced (Gauguin) to try filling teeth outdoors and we worked in a meadow surrounded by greens and golds. He put caps on a Miss Angela Tonnato and I gave a temporary filling to Mr Louis Kaufman. There we were, working together in the open air! Rows of blinding white teeth in the sunlight! Then a wind came up and blew Mr Kaufman's toupee into the bushes. He darted for it and knocked Gauguin's instruments to the ground. Gauguin blamed me and tried to strike out but pushed Mr Kaufman by mistake, causing him to sit down on the high-speed drill. Mr Kaufman rocketed past me on a fly, taking Miss Tonnato with him. (Letter 5)]

Although Mr Kaufman gets the worst of it, he is far from passive and indeed it his action in darting for the toupee which leads to catastrophe. Mr Feldman is even less passive.

[(Gauguin) was in the midst of an extraction when I disturbed him. He had his knee on Mr Nat Feldman's chest with the pliers around the man's upper right molar. There was the usual struggle and I had the misfortune to enter and ask Gauguin if he had seen my felt hat. Distracted, Gauguin lost his grip on the tooth and Feldman took advantage of the lapse to bolt from the chair and race out of the office.]

Contrast this incident involving Mr Feldman with the cosy intimacy conjured up in the Claire Memling story or the passivity of Mrs Zardos waiting patiently for her dentist to return. This variation in the data is suggestive and might encourage us to look closely at different roles in which Woody Allen casts his male and female patients.

As well as identifying regularities and variations, our matrices can draw our attention to singularities in the data. One of these is the Claire Memling story, where the male–female relationship assumes its own peculiar dynamics. The associations with entrapment and vulnerability we noted earlier acquire a particular resonance when Vincent is vibrant with sexual passions. Although the Claire Memling story is a singular episode, not repeated with other patients, we may see it as encapsulating some of the themes which animate other parts of the data, and therefore worthy of particular emphasis.

So far we have used our matrices to complement the analytic work we have accomplished through categorizing the data. But we can also use a matrix to comprehend the results of our categorization. We could choose, for example, to display our databits by case and category. If we did this for our first letter, the result might look something like Table 13.4.

A problem with this approach may be immediately apparent. If we insist on preserving its full detail, our matrix is quickly overloaded with data. We may therefore prefer to summarize the data, for example by using only databit indices within the matrix (Table 13.5).

Table 13.4 Databits by case and category

| Case | Temperament | Occupation | Suffering |
|---|---|---|---|
| letter 1 | 1. Will life never treat me decently? I am wracked by despair! My head is pounding. 2. That's right! I can't work to order like a common tradesman. 3. She is so bourgeois and stupid, I want to smash her 4. Theo, I can't go on like this much longer! 5. What to do? | 1. Mrs Sol Schwimmer is suing me because I made her bridge as I felt it and not to fit her ridiculous mouth. 2. That's right! I can't work to order like a common tradesman. 3. I decided her bridge should be enormous and billowing with wild, explosive teeth flaring up in every direction like fire! 4. It sticks out like a star burst chandelier. Still, I find it beautiful. 5. (Cézanne) is old and infirm and unable to hold the instruments and they must be tied to his wrists | 1. Now she is upset because it won't fit in her mouth! 2. I tried forcing the false plate in but it sticks out like a star burst chandelier. 3. She claims she can't chew! What do I care whether she can chew or not! 4. (Cézanne) lacks accuracy and once inside a mouth, he knocks out more teeth than he saves. |
| letter 2 | etc. | etc. | etc. |

Table 13.5 Data indices by case and category

| Case | Temperament | Occupation | Suffering |
|---|---|---|---|
| letter 1 | 1. Will life never treat 2. That's right! I can't 3. She is so bourgeois 4. Theo, I can't go 5. What to do? | 1. Mrs Sol Schwimmer is 2. That's right! I can't 3. I decided her bridge 4. it sticks out like 5. (Cézanne) is old and | 1. Now she is upset 2. I tried forcing the 3. She claims she can't 4. (Cézanne) lacks accuracy and |
| letter 2 | 1. When he left, I 2. I attempted some root-canal | 1. I took some dental 2. I completed her mouth | 1. When I returned, she |
| letter 3 | | 1. Once again I am 2. I am working almost | 1. Today I pulled a |
| letter 4 | | 1. (Gauguin) is a fine 2. I filled his lower 3. someone saw it lying | 1. tried to remove it |

Now we can compress more data into our matrix, perhaps at the expense of immediate intelligibility – although on screen we can compensate for this by using the computer to retrieve data as required. We can make comparisons across rows or columns and also gain a better overall sense of the data. Contrast the use of 'temperament' in the first couple of letters with those which follow, for example. The use of transpositions of 'temperament' to create humorous effects is uneven. Compare this with the other transpositions, which are far more pervasive. And there is always some element of 'suffering' by patients in each of the letters included in our matrix.

Our matrix is still fairly cumbersome, and with many cases and categories, we may still very rapidly find ourselves 'overloaded' with data. There are limits to how much information we can absorb at any one time. Matters are eased somewhat by the computer's ability to handle many columns and rows, presenting on screen only those in which we are currently interested. But if we have a lot of material, we may opt for an even more abstract way of summarizing the data, by reducing it to numbers. For example, Table 13.5 could then be reduced to the information in Table 13.6.

*Table 13.6* The number of assignations of each category by case

| Case | Temperament | Transposing | Suffering |
| --- | --- | --- | --- |
| letter 1 | 5 | 5 | 4 |
| letter 2 | 2 | 2 | 1 |
| letter 3 | 0 | 2 | 1 |
| letter 4 | 0 | 3 | 1 |
| letter 5 | 3 | 5 | 1 |
| letter 6 | 3 | 3 | 1 |

The inferences which we drew from Table 13.4 about the use of different categories could equally be made on the basis of Table 13.6. Indeed because the detail has been eliminated and the data reduced to numbers, the points we noted earlier emerge with greater clarity.

It may seem strange, in a qualitative analysis, to introduce numbers as a means of data reduction. However, whenever we make a qualitative judgement about the data by assigning a category to the data, we also create numerical data. For we can enumerate the qualitative decisions we make and relate them to the cases we are analysing. We can count the number of times we have assigned any category to the data. Only prejudice would prevent us from using this information if it can help us to identify patterns within the data.

On the other hand, we are faced with a matrix whose meaning has been reduced to whether or not a category has been assigned to the data. The interpretation of this information depends entirely upon the decisions we have made in creating categories and assigning them to the data. We may be wary, therefore, of drawing conclusions on the basis of such limited evidence. Any inferences we can draw about regularities and variation in the data must reflect the confidence we can place in our initial conceptualizations. The matrix can be useful, but we may need to return to the original data as often as possible, for confirmation of patterns apparent within the data or to reexamine and modify our earlier judgements. With its facilities for searching and retrieving data, the computer should make it possible to do so with a minimum of fuss.

If our variables describe properties of cases, we may be able to 'recode' these values to make a more meaningful classification. Suppose, for example, that it made sense to think of the degree to which these letters rely upon stereotypes of artistic temperament. Then we might 'recode' our data to discriminate between those where Woody Allen relies heavily on artistic stereotypes and those where he doesn't use them much if at all. We might distinguish two or more values of the variable 'temperament', such as 'high' and 'low'. To recode the data in terms of these values, we would need to identify a cut-off point above which the existing values would be recoded as 'high' and below which they would be recoded as 'low'. Of course we also have to decide whether to record values which are at the cut-off point itself as 'high' or 'low'. Deciding where to make a cut-off point is a conceptual and empirical problem. Empirically, we may be influenced largely by the pattern of existing values. Is there a natural break in the data? Does some subdivision of the range of values (e.g. midway) give a useful distinction between 'high' and 'low' values? Conceptually, we have to be sure that it is meaningful to describe some values as 'high' and others as 'low'. These are of course relative terms, and we have to consider the context in which they are made. If stereotypes of artistic temperament are used five times in the space of a short letter, can this reasonably described as 'heavy' usage?

By reducing the number of values, we not only summarize the data but also render it more intelligible. We translate numbers into meaningful values. Our measurement may be less exact, but our classification is more useful. The matrix in Table 13.7 shows one possible recoding of the values in Table 13.6.

*Table 13.7* Recoding data to express more meaningful values

| Case | Transposing | Temperament | Suffering |
|------|-------------|-------------|-----------|
| letter 1 | high | high | high |
| letter 2 | low | low | low |
| letter 3 | not assigned | low | low |
| letter 4 | not assigned | moderate | low |
| letter 5 | moderate | high | low |
| letter 6 | moderate | moderate | low |

We can see at a glance the patterns of usage for some of the main categories in our analysis. On the other hand, these patterns are a product of a series of decisions we have made in interpreting the data through categorizing and recoding it. We must therefore avoid any presumption that in some sense they really exist in the data, rather than as a result of how we have observed and analysed the data for our own purposes.

As well as recoding values, another path to data reduction is through reducing the number of variables. This can also improve the intelligibility as well as the economy of our analysis. For example, we can see from Table 13.6 that most of the values assigned for 'suffering' are exclusive i.e. for most cases, only one value has been assigned to that case. The table would be more intelligible and meaningful if we could name these values. However, we can only do so if the values are exclusive. Suppose we have subcategorized 'suffering' into three subcategories, 'discomfort', 'disability', and 'disfigurement'. Because these subcategories are not exclusive (all three occur in the first letter) we cannot analyse them as separate values of the variable 'suffering'. We would have to analyse them as separate variables, as in Table 13.8.

*Table 13.8* Analysing subcategories as separate variables

| Case | Disability | Discomfort | Disfigurement |
|------|-----------|-----------|---------------|
| letter 1 | assigned | assigned | assigned |
| letter 2 | not assigned | assigned | not assigned |
| letter 3 | not assigned | assigned | not assigned |
| letter 4 | not assigned | assigned | not assigned |
| letter 5 | not assigned | assigned | not assigned |
| letter 6 | not assigned | not assigned | assigned |

This is hardly the most economical or intelligible way to present the data. As there is only one case where more than one subcategory has been assigned, we could accommodate this exception by introducing an additional subcategory, such as 'multiple'. Then we could treat each of the subcategories as values of the overarching variable 'suffering' (Table 13.9).

Table 13.9 Recategorizing variables as values of 'suffering'

| Case | Temperament | Occupation | Suffering |
| --- | --- | --- | --- |
| letter 1 | high | high | multiple |
| letter 2 | low | low | discomfort |
| letter 3 | not used | low | discomfort |
| letter 4 | not used | moderate | discomfort |
| letter 5 | moderate | high | discomfort |
| letter 6 | moderate | moderate | disfigurement |

This is not ideal, for we are assigning values in terms of more than one dimension, something all the books warn us not to do! We are distinguishing between those cases where only one aspect of 'suffering' is apparent, and those where more than one aspect is in evidence. And where only one aspect is evident, we are also distinguishing the type of 'suffering' which is inflicted on the patient. If at all possible, we should avoid such composites and analyse variables in terms of a singe dimension. Logically, we could do so in this case by adding values for all possible combinations, such as 'discomfort and disfigurement', 'disfigurement and disability' and so on. But the conceptual complexity this produces is not commensurate with the data, as only very few cases have been assigned to more than one subcategory. In short, it is not worth the conceptual effort. It is better to be forbearing, to accept the compromise of a composite variable, and use a dustbin category such as 'multiple' for the residual values which don't fit the main dimension.

The virtue of reducing values and variables is that we can increase the focus of our analysis. It is a bit like a drawing. By eliminating detail, the artist can render more effectively and dramatically the main features of his subject. The emerging image may also clarify the relationship between different elements in the picture. We can use our matrix to explore these relationships by visual inspection, but a further process of abstraction may also prove invaluable. For any variable, we can analyse the frequencies with which values occur, as in Table 13.10.

*Table 13.10* Frequencies for the variable 'suffering'

| Suffering | Count | Percentage |
|:---:|:---:|:---:|
| disability | 0 | 0 |
| discomfort | 4 | 66.7 |
| disfigurement | 1 | 16.7 |
| multiple | 1 | 16.7 |
| not assigned | 0 | 0 |

We can also cross-tabulate variables to identify possible relationships between them (Table 13.11).

*Table 13.11* Cross-tabulating 'occupation' and 'suffering'

| Suffering | Occupation | | |
|:---|:---:|:---:|:---:|
| | high | moderate | low |
| disability | | | |
| discomfort | 1 | 1 | 11 |
| disfigurement | | 1 | |
| multiple | 1 | | |

We can use frequencies and cross-tabulations of variables to identify patterns holding in the data. For example, we might be tempted to conclude from Table 13.11 that where letters rely heavily on transpositions of 'occupation' patients tend to experience various forms of 'suffering'; whereas when reliance on transposing 'occupation' is low, patients tend to experience a particular form of 'suffering', i.e. 'discomfort'. We may be tempted, but of course we would be wrong to draw any such conclusion. First, there is simply not enough data to merit any such inference. However, this is a peculiarity of my example, rather than a characteristic of qualitative analysis, where the problem is usually that we have too much rather than too little data to work with! Second, any evidence of possible relationships in the data is at best suggestive rather than conclusive. We still have to return to the data to examine evidence in detail. Nor should we forget that our cross-tabulation is an artefact of how we have analysed the data.

Each cell of the matrix results from a complex process of decision-making. This process includes the creation of memos and categories, the demarcation of databits and their assignment to categories, the splitting and splicing of categories, and the translation of categories into variables together with any subsequent recoding. For example, for the category 'temperament' we have memos recording our initial ideas about the use of stereotypes; we have our initial category definition and how that evolved over time; we have the databits which have been assigned to that category; we have the reassessment of the relationship between this category and others. If we were to include all this detail, then our matrix would quickly become more meaningful in parts but less intelligible as a whole. The computer can help us to maintain a reasonable balance between individual and overall intelligibility by allowing quick access to all the relevant decisions and data which culminate in a particular value being assigned to a particular cell.

---

**Using matrices to make comparisons**
- Analyse background information, case content and categories
- Reduce data through indices and category assignations
- Recode values and recategorize variables
- Analyse variable frequencies and cross-tabulations

---

## MAPPING

'The Admiralty sent HMS Beagle to South America with Charles Darwin on board not because it was interested in evolution but because it knew that the first step to understanding – and with luck – controlling – the world was to make a map of it.' (Jones 1991). Whether or not the Admiralty had such insight, making maps is certainly a useful way of making sense of data. Because they deal with the relationship between one point and another, maps are particularly useful in analysing the connections between the categories we have used in our analysis.

Unlike matrices, maps do not conform to any particular format. The geographer's map of an area will differ significantly from a five-year-old's map of her house, but they may both prove useful representations of reality. We can devise all sorts of ways of mapping data – we are limited only by our imagination. Drawing maps can be fun as well as illuminating, though there is a temptation to get carried away with the task and become needlessly elaborate.

For mapping, we require only two things. First, we need some way of representing the 'points' of our analysis. Second, we need some way of representing relations between these points. Let us start with a simple map with which we are already well acquainted – the diagram of a relationship between two concepts (Figure 13.2). We have represented each concept by a box, and the relationship between them is represented by a line. What could be simpler? Yet we can use such simple tools to represent quite complex relationships between the concepts used in our analysis (Figure 13.3).

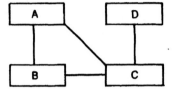

*Figure 13.2* Map of relationship between two concepts

*Figure 13.3* Map of complex relationships between four variables

In Figure 13.3 we have represented in a simple diagram quite complex relationships between four concepts. We have shown that concept A is related directly to concepts B and C, but not directly related to concept D; and that concept A is indirectly related to concept C through concept B, and to concept D through concept C and through concepts B and C. Concept B is related directly ... and so on! By mapping, we can express in a few symbols what would otherwise take many words.

As well as symbols representing points and relationships, we also have to provide the information needed to interpret our maps. Take the diagrams in Figure 13.4 for example. The diagram on the left might be taken for a rounded egg, or a slightly flattened ball; perhaps a geographer might take it as globe. Without the interpretive labels, no one (I presume) would take this as a map symbolizing the whole history of the universe through time!

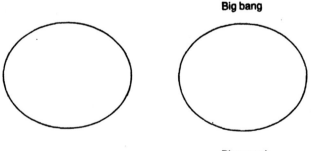

*Figure. 13.4* The history of the universe through time
*Source*: adapted from Hawking 1988: 138

Incidentally, Hawking's argument is that the universe can be both finite and without boundaries; and that the origin and end of the universe can be singularities (i.e. unique events) which nevertheless obey the laws of science. These ideas are neatly conveyed in a diagram of a finite space without edges; and although two-dimensional or three-dimensional representations of four-dimensional space-time may be inadequate in some respects, they do help to make intelligible concepts which it might otherwise be difficult if not impossible to grasp.

If the whole history and future of the universe through time can be reduced to a single ellipse, then we can certainly use simple graphic tools to express complex ideas, especially as we can also add to our toolbox in useful ways.

We can introduce a variety of shapes to represent different types of concept. For example, we can use squares to represent events, circles to represent people, ovals to represent conditions. We can also use various thicknesses of line around boundaries and use different patterns within them (Figure 13.5). The computer's graphic facilities make it easy to devise a range of symbols to represent various elements in our analysis. There is no limit to the range and variety of representational devices we can employ, other than our own imagination and the need to present a clear and intelligible picture – uncluttered by excessive variation. Figure 13.6, for example, is a map of Vincent's first letter, showing some of the key concepts and relationships. Circles have been used for people, differentiated by patterns between dentists and patients; boxes have been used for 'events' (psychological as well as social), differentiated between our main categories by vertical and horizontal lines; and ovals have been used to express consequences.

*Figure 13.5* A small selection of symbols based on computer graphics

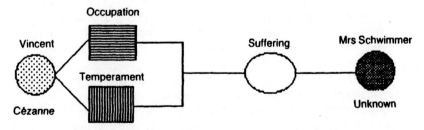

*Figure 13.6* Differentiating concepts through different shapes and patterns

This diagram shows the main features of Vincent's first letter in terms of the categories central to our analysis. The dentists involved are Vincent and Cézanne. Through the transpositions of 'occupation' and 'temperament' these dentists display, 'suffering' is inflicted on the patients. We also have something of a vicious circle here, because Mrs Sol Schwimmer reacts by suing Vincent and exacerbating his depression.

We can easily incorporate more detail in our map, for example by differentiating between subcategories as in Figure 13.7.

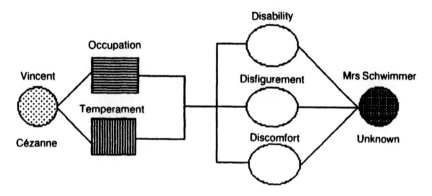

*Figure 13.7* Incorporating detail by including subcategories

Maps involve location of one point in relation to another, but they may also convey information about size as well as position. We can use the size of the shapes we use to take convey information about the scope of different categories. By scope I mean the organizing power of the category, or its applicability to the data, in terms of the number of times we have assigned the relevant category to the data. In short, how many databits have been assigned to the relevant category? This may tell us nothing of the conceptual significance of the category, but it does tell us just how much data the category has embraced. We must decide for ourselves the conceptual implications of variations in scope.

If we adjusted Figure 13.7 to take account of the scope of the categories, we might produce Figure 13.8 instead.

Now the scope of the categories is reflected in the size of the shapes which represent them. Twice as much data has been assigned to the category 'discomfort' as to the other subcategories of 'suffering', so it appears as twice their size on the map.

Issues of scope may (or may not) be trivial in relation to a single case, but if we generalize across all our cases the differences may assume a greater analytic significance. To compare the scope of different categories, we have to have some sort of standard in terms of which to make comparisons. As noted earlier, we cannot use the total number of databits as a basis

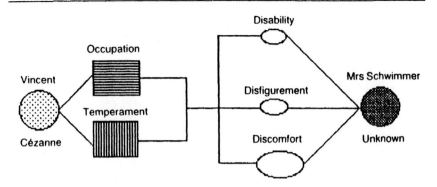

*Figure 13.8* Adjusting for the empirical scope of categories

for comparison, because this number is essentially arbitrary. Instead, we can relate the number of databits to the number of cases, which is a fixed number unaffected by the complexity or progress of our analysis. Using the computer, we can represent the scope of our categories in terms of a standard scale, such as the average number of times we have assigned a category to a case. This allows us to make graphic comparisons between the scope of the different concepts employed in the analysis (Figure 13.9).

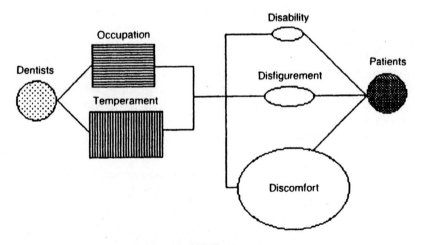

*Figure 13.9* Mapping relationships for all cases

We can see that transpositions of 'temperament' have marginally more scope than those of 'occupation'. We can also see that of our subcategories of 'suffering' most data have been assigned to the category 'discomfort', with 'disability' and 'disfigurement' figuring much less in the analysis overall than in the first of Vincent's letters.

So far we have only mapped out the broad outlines of our analysis, making no attempt to differentiate, for example, between the strength and type of different relationships. However, before we go on, let us look for a moment at other ways in which we could map out the scope of our categories. In Figure 13.10 we have aligned categories, producing a bar chart, so that differences in scope are more readily apparent.

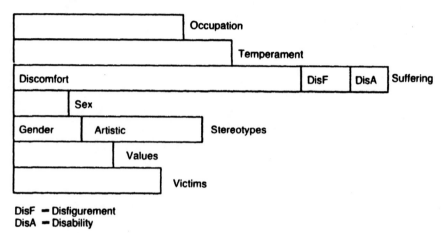

DisF ─ Disfigurement
DisA ─ Disability

*Figure 13.10* Comparing differences in scope through a bar chart

Another means of indicating scope is through overlapping shapes as in Figure 13.11. This provides a handy way of indicating differences in scale which might otherwise be less clear because of variations in the shape. Although the computer can ensure that the areas within the boundaries of a circle, oval, and rectangle (or whatever shapes are used in the analysis) are to scale, the difference in area between different shapes may be less obvious to the reader.

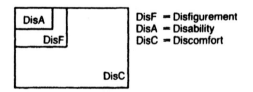

*Figure 13.11* Using overlaps to indicate scale

We can incorporate information about the scope of our categories in our representation of the different levels of classification in our analysis. In Figure 13.12, for example, we can compare the scope of the central categories in our classification of the data.

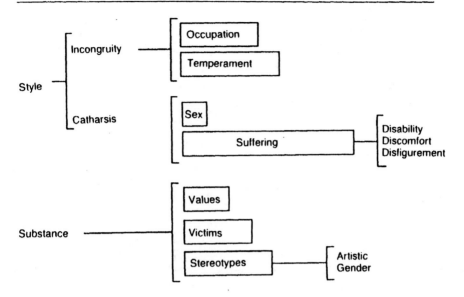

*Figure 13.12* Adjusting for scope in presenting classification scheme

This method of graphic representation could be extended to other categories as required. For example, we could also represent the scope of the subcategories of 'suffering' or 'stereotypes', or the overarching categories such as 'incongruity' or 'catharsis'. Notice though that if we indicate the scope of overarching categories, the reader cannot gain any indication of the scope of any subcategories; whereas including information on the scope of subcategories also indicates the scope of the overarching categories (Figure 13.13).

By giving the scope of the most refined categories in our map we allow the reader to assess the significance of the overarching categories. On the other hand, we may make it less easy to assess at a glance the relative scope of categories at the same level of classification. We could of course simply give the scope of all categories included in the analysis, whatever the level of classification, providing our categories are few and this does not over-complicate our presentation.

---

**Mapping categories**
- Shapes and patterns can represent different types of category
- Size can represent differences in empirical scope of categories
- Alignment can be used to compare differences in empirical scope
- Differences in scope need only be represented for the most refined categories

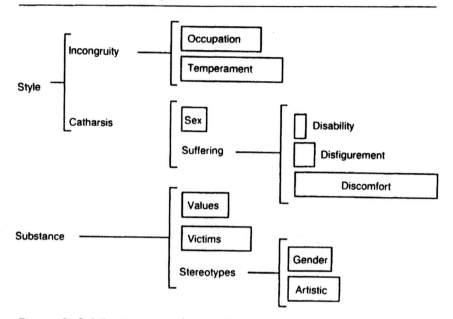

*Figure 13.13* Adjusting scope of most refined categories

So far we have concentrated on shapes, but what about the lines which connect these shapes? We can also use these lines to represent different types and strengths of relationship between categories. Some of these differences may be conceptual and some empirical. We have already discussed the logical distinction between exclusive and inclusive relationships between categories, which we represented with the annotation in Figure 13.14.

*Figure 13.14* Distinguishing exclusive and inclusive relationships

The relations of inclusion and exclusion are central to categorization, but as we have seen in discussing linked data, this may not exhaust our interest in relationships within the data. We may want to use our maps to represent other relationships, such as causal or explanatory links. Unlike relationships of order, in mapping such relationships we must also take into account questions about the direction and reciprocity.

In the diagrams (Figures 13.6 to 13.9) in which we mapped out some central relationships between categories, we failed to indicate the type of direction of the relationships being represented. If we wanted to outline a causal connection between categories, we failed to do so. These diagrams could only make sense if we made two assumptions which remained implicit. One assumption was that the reader would infer (in the absence of any other information to the contrary) that the relationships being described were causal. Another assumption was that the reader would 'read' the map from left to right, as though it were text, and therefore take the categories on the left as 'precedent', not only in our map but also in the data. To ensure a correct interpretation, our map needs to include information allowing readers (including ourselves) to understand the relationships being described (Figure 13.15).

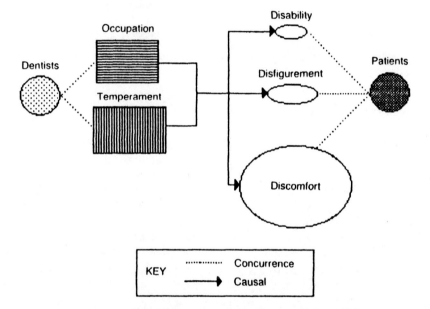

*Figure 13.15* Making relationships between categories more explicit

Figure 13.15 now spells out the different relationships between categories and also the direction of the causal relationships. We have distinguished between the types and direction of relationships between categories, but what of the strength of different relationships?

First of all, let us 'unpack' Figure 13.15 a little by distinguishing between the relationships between 'occupation' and 'temperament' as causes and 'suffering' as a consequence. Although we have presented 'occupation' and 'temperament' as interactive causes, we can distinguish between them. Is 'suffering' caused by transpositions of 'temperament', transpositions of 'occupation', or some combination of the two? Using linked retrievals, we can identify whether and how often each of three possibilities occurs in the data. The retrievals 'temperament – not occupation' and 'occupation – not temperament' would give us the separate relationships and the retrieval 'temperament – occupation' would give us the scope of the link where the two categories are combined. We can then map the results of the different retrievals as in Figure 13.16.

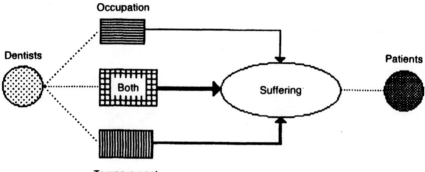

Figure 13.16 Representing strength of different causal relationships

In Figure 13.16, we can compare not just the scope of the categories, but also the scope of the causal relationships between them. Thus the strongest relationship is between 'suffering' and transpositions of 'occupation' and 'temperament' in combination, while of the separate relationships the 'occupation–suffering' connection is weaker than the 'temperament–suffering' connection.

Using the same procedure, we can map out the relationships between the categories 'occupation' and 'temperament' and each of the sub-categories of 'suffering'. In Figure 13.17 we can see that there is a stronger connection between the category 'occupation' and the category 'discomfort' than there is between 'occupation' and 'disfigurement'. The connections with 'discomfort' generally have more scope than the connection with 'disfigurement', and strongest of all is the scope of the connection between the categories 'occupation' and 'temperament' combined and 'discomfort'. In this way we map out connections between key categories and compare the scope of the connections between them. So far the mapping we have done has been quite uncomplicated, but if we put these various strands together we can handle quite complex relationships (Figure 13.18).

Now we have produced a diagram which looks as complicated as a map of the London Underground! If our computer supports it, then we too can use colour to differentiate the different connections. In the Underground, of course, trains can travel in both directions, and if need be, we might extend or amend our map to take account of reciprocal relationships or

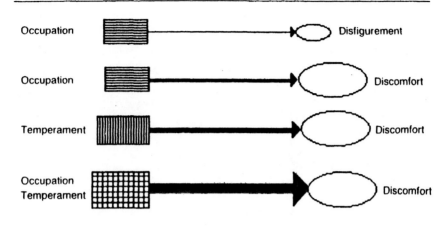

Figure 13.17 Comparing strength of relationships between categories

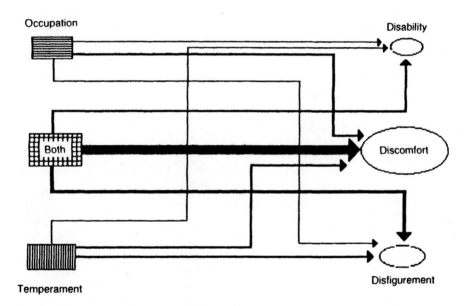

Figure 13.18 Integrating connections between categories

feedback. For example, in Figure 13.19 the connection between 'temperament' and 'suffering' is presented as reciprocal by drawing arrows pointing in each direction. This tells us that the relationship works both ways – that sometimes the 'suffering' Vincent inflicts on patients ends up exacerbating his own temperamental moods and behaviour.

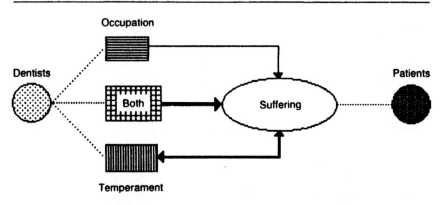

*Figure 13.19* Representing reciprocal connections between categories

If possible, though, it would be preferable to 'unpack' this reciprocal relationship, so that we can identify the strength and character of the connections involved. For example, we know that Vincent's moods resulted in part from the litigation initiated by Mrs Sol Schwimmer, and by Claire Memling's rejection of his advances. We could incorporate this as a feedback loop, as in Figure 13.20.

In identifying causal connections, we also need to take account of whether relationships are 'positive' or 'negative'. We can easily incorporate this information in our map (Figure 13.20).

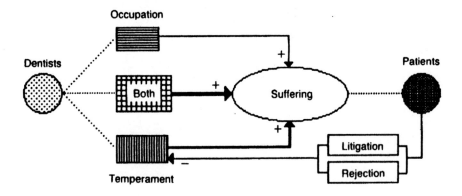

*Figure 13.20* Identifying positive and negative categories

Whereas we observe an increase in suffering as a result of transpositions of 'occupation' and/or 'temperament', the ensuing action by patients has a negative effect on Vincent's temper.

> **Using lines to represent connections between categories**
> • Length of line can represent the type of relationship
> • Arrows can represent the direction of the relationship
> • Positive and negative signs can indicate the value of the relationship
> • Line thickness can represent the empirical scope of the relationship

As well as a key to the meaning of our shapes and lines, we can provide additional information in order to interpret these maps. In order to compare the distance between two points on a map, we need to know its scale. Otherwise we may be able to tell that one distance is nearer or further than another, but we won't be able to judge what this means in terms of metres or miles. To complete the picture, therefore, we need to know what these differences in scope actually mean, for example, in terms of the average number of categorized or linked databits which have been assigned to a case. We (or rather, the computer) have to use some sort of scale in terms of which to translate a number into a shape or line of appropriate dimensions. Does a single line represent an average of one link per case, or ten links per case, or what? Whatever the scale – and we may have to adjust it according to the volume of categorized or linked data we are dealing with – if we make it explicit then the reader can interpret our map accordingly.

Although we have focused on causal connections, mapping can also be used to explore other relationships. Take the concurrence of categories, for example. Suppose we are interested in how often our two main categories, 'incongruity' and 'catharsis' concur in the data. We can map out how far the two categories concur, and how far they may have been assigned separately to the data. In Figure 13.21 I have presented two possible outcomes. In one, not much over half the examples of cathartic humour we have noted in the text concur with those of incongruity. In the other, every example of cathartic humour concurs with an example of incongruous humour. But there are elements of incongruity which don't concur with cathartic humour. From this kind of mapping we can learn something about the relationship between the two types of humour. Suppose we find that in fact all the examples of cathartic humour also involve elements of incongruity. This suggests that an element of incongruity may be an essential condition of cathartic humour. Looking back at our data, we can explore this possibility and see whether this proposition is borne out by the way the two types of humour interact.

For example, take Mr Kaufman's unfortunate accident with the high speed drill. The humour in this scene is certainly cathartic – it releases emotions connected with fear of the suffering we associate with the dentist's drill. What role does incongruity play? Well, the patient doesn't suffer in any ordinary way, and perhaps if he had – perhaps if he had sat in the dentist's chair, and suffered pain from the drill while having a filling –

*Figure 13.21* Representing concurrence between categories

we would have not found the scene amusing. But Mr Kaufman's dental work is being done out of doors, and while the drill inflicts suffering it does not do so in the usual orifice. These elements of incongruity are reassuring – this is a fantasy, not the real thing. We can laugh at another's suffering, precisely because we know that he is not really suffering. In short, without the incongruity, there might be no cathartic release.

On the other hand, we can look at the data where we have observed incongruity without catharsis. For instance, Vincent says he couldn't bring himself to sign his root-canal work he did for Mrs Zardos. Unlike his absence for several days due to depression, this does not involve any cathartic element. The humour lies only in the incongruous image of a dentist signing his work as though he were an artist. This is amusing in its own right without reliance on the release of any emotional undercurrents. We may conclude from this example that, while cathartic humour may 'fan the flames', it is not essential to ignite the spark of humour arising from disrupted expectations.

But these are only two examples. Our mapping may be suggestive of a relationship between the two categories, but in order to examine and elucidate that relationship we have to conduct a more thorough exploration of the data. Fortunately the computer through its efficient search and retrieval facilities can make this task an easy one, mechanically if not conceptually. Indeed, within an interactive environment, the computer may provide automatic access to the data which is represented by the graphic images on our map.

Another relationship we may want to map out is how categories connect over time. We may want to know how an author organizes a succession of images to achieve a comic effect; how interaction unfolds over time between different actors or agencies; or how expectations evolve and attitudes alter in the light of accumulating experiences or new information.

For questions such as these, it may be useful to map out the data from a chronological perspective.

· For example, suppose we are interested in the effects of social interaction with other 'dentists' on Vincent's feelings. This is a 'sub-plot' which figures less forcefully than the dentist–patient interactions we have already discussed, but which nevertheless contributes to the overall humour of the letters. Vincent has several dealings with Gauguin and we may decide to map out the Vincent–Gauguin interaction as it evolves over time. We tried something of the sort in presenting the Claire Memling story. However, we can map out the succession of events more effectively if in addition to lines and boxes, we utilize more explicitly an additional element in our diagrams, namely space. We can use space to represent time (amongst other things) and by doing so map out 'events' (psychological as well as social) in a more illuminating way. Figure 13.22 shows the history of Vincent's interaction with Gauguin, arranged by time and divided between the social events and Vincent's feelings at the time. This chronological sequence could be further refined and if sufficient information is available we could even differentiate between units of time.

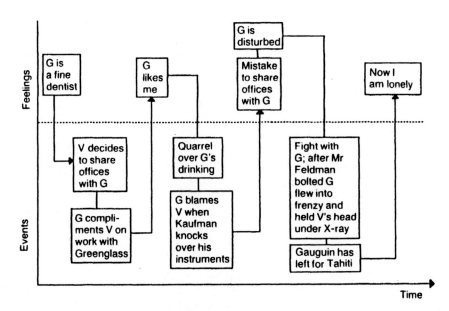

Figure 13.22 Using space to represent time

By mapping it out in this way, we can display more clearly the succession of events which makes up the Vincent–Gauguin story. We can also see more clearly the way Vincent's feelings unfold as various incidents follow his decision to share offices with Gauguin. To do so we have presented a series of databits in chronological sequence – and not necessarily, incidentally, in the sequence in which they appear in the text. We could use the same procedure with categories as with databits, to set out chronologically the relationship between different elements in our analysis just as we have set out the different elements in the Vincent–Gauguin story.

The computer can aid mapping by providing a set of graphic tools ideally suited for the task. We have also used the computer to map to scale the scope of the categories we have used in our analysis. There are other ways in which the computer may also be able to assist us in mapping. I have emphasized the role of mapping in making inferences from data, but mapping can also lead us back to the data as we draw out (literally) relationships which we have not yet observed. Mapping contributes to conceptual clarification which can encourage us to think about the data in new ways. One important function of the computer is to facilitate a close interaction between concepts and data.

# Chapter 14

# Corroborating evidence

'Inquiry is rooted not in abstraction, deduction, and formalism but rather in the dynamics and demands of judgement, argument and lived conduct'

(Giarelli 1988)

In 1952, two young men, one of them armed, were cornered by the police on the roof of a confectionary warehouse in Croydon which they were trying to rob. One of the young men, Derek Bentley, gave himself up immediately. When Detective Constable Fairfax asked the other, Chris Craig, to give up his gun, Derek Bentley allegedly shouted to his friend 'Let him have it, Chris'. Chris Craig then shot and killed PC Sidney Miles before being overpowered. In the subsequent trial, the words 'let him have it' were interpreted as an incitement to murder, and although Derek Bentley did not fire the shot, he was hanged for the crime. Ironically, the 16-year-old Craig was too young to receive a similar sentence, and served ten years in prison instead.

The case became a scandal, not least because the 19-year-old Bentley had a mental age of 11, and the jury's strong plea for mercy was ignored. Much of the subsequent controversy turned on whether or not Bentley had actually said the fatal words, and whether, if he did, they were incriminating. Craig always maintained that no such words were spoken, a claim supported later – twenty years later – by one of the policemen on the roof that night. The same words had been shouted by an accomplice (also hanged) in a similar incident only twelve years earlier. Did the police and prosecutors fabricate evidence in the light of their knowledge of the earlier case? And even if Bentley said the phrase attributed to him, how should it be interpreted? As an incitement to kill, or as a plea to pass over the gun? In the haste to secure a guilty verdict (the trial lasted only two days) Bentley's mental state was never considered. The authorities were concerned to repress early signs of a post-war youth rebellion, while the murder of a 'bobby' in those days was an outrageous crime. Did the pressure for punishment persuade them to override the requirements of justice? (Empire Magazine 1991, Trow 1992).

What happened? What was said? What was meant? These are the same questions we have to address in weighing the evidence produced through qualitative analysis. If the sociologist or the biographer is like a detective, and collecting data is like detection, then analysing data is akin to the culminating stages of the criminal justice process. It has the same potential for abuse, and therefore requires similar safeguards. Unfortunately, whereas in criminal justice the adversarial roles of prosecution and defence can be allocated to different people, in qualitative analysis the analyst often has to play both roles.

To pursue our analogy, let us consider the potential for abuse in qualitative analysis, and then consider some of the safeguards we can build into the process. We can identify several potential abuses in our account of the Derek Bentley case. These are:

• Fabricating evidence
• Discounting evidence
• Misinterpreting evidence

Let us consider each in turn.

Fabricating evidence is not a fault which we normally associate with qualitative analysis. We tend to proceed on the presumption that we can rely on the good faith and honourable conduct of those responsible. However, a similar presumption until recently pervaded public attitudes in Britain to the police and the criminal justice system, only to take a fearful battering following a series of cases of corruption and miscarriages of justice. We might be more inclined to give the benefit of the doubt to scientists rather than policemen, but in the scientific world, unfortunately, the falsification of evidence is also not unknown.

The reason is that the supposedly 'neutral' and 'objective' observer is a myth. Scientists, like policemen and public prosecutors, have their own agendas and their own interests to consider. They have careers to foster, prejudices to protect, deadlines to meet, prestigious prizes to pursue. Fame and fortune for one scientist can mean tragic failure for another, sometimes even with fatal consequences. For example, Max Theiler won the Nobel Prize for medicine for developing a vaccine against yellow fever; his rival, the eminent scientist Hideyo Noguchi, died of the disease in his attempt to prove Theiler wrong. Noguchi did not fabricate evidence, but some suspected him of committing a micro-biologists's equivalent of hara-kiri when he could not find the evidence he needed to support his own views (Dixon 1991). With so much at stake, to some scientists a little falsification may seem a small price to pay for ensuring a more satisfactory outcome!

There is no reason to suppose that social researchers are somehow immune from pressures such as these. Perhaps their careers are less illustrious and their prizes are less tempting! On the other hand, perhaps their opportunities to fabricate or falsify evidence are even greater. There are two main checks on the fabrication or falsification of evidence. One is the normative assumptions and ethical code of the research community. The other is the fear of being found out. While the former may be as strong amongst social researchers as amongst any other research community, the latter is undoubtedly weaker. To be 'found out' requires replication, and in qualitative analysis this is notoriously difficult to achieve. Unlike the physicists, who could try to replicate the research of colleagues claiming to have produced cold nuclear fusion in a test tube (and show that the supposed scientific breakthrough was a laboratory error) the results of most qualitative analysis mostly have to be taken on trust. Replication is often not a practical proposition. Aside from the pervasive preference amongst socials scientists for doing 'original' research rather than replicating the work of others, replication of most qualitative studies would require an impractical commitment of resources and effort.

The rare efforts that have been made to replicate earlier research are not exactly encouraging. Bryman (1988: 74–6) notes two cases in which the results of classic anthropological studies (by Lewis and Mead) were later hotly contested upon subsequent 'replication' by other researchers. These replications were themselves controversial, since though they produced quite contradictory results, in practice they could not replicate the original studies in terms of both time and place. Indeed, in so far as qualitative studies aim to be sensitive to factors embedded in a specific time and place, it is difficult to see how such replication could be achieved.

In place of 'external' replication by other research, then, the qualitative analyst must perforce rely on 'internal' replication of his or her own research. By 'internal' replication I mean that colleagues can inspect the procedures through which evidence has been produced – at least in principle – and check whether using similar procedures they achieve similar results with the data. There may be no direct parallel for the recent checks on whether proper procedures have been followed in the production of criminal evidence (e.g. testing to see whether notes ostensibly written during interviews have been added to afterwards). For one thing, qualitative research is noted for its lack of established procedures and agreed canons governing the conduct of enquiry. But the principle of ensuring that such procedures as are followed can stand up to scrutiny can be applied. The computer makes this more possible than previously, because it facilitates recording of successive stages in the transformation of data and easy access to the data in its original form.

I noted earlier that the qualitative analyst may have to play all the roles in the analytic drama. Ideally, internal replication involves making the research open to outside scrutiny. Of course, other researchers may be too preoccupied with their own work to bother with checking over the work of someone else. Physicists may work on nuclear fusion, but the results of qualitative research are rarely of such outstanding theoretical or practical importance as to attract such critical attentions. In any case, many qualitative studies are presented with insufficient discussion of methods to allow for replication should anyone be interested. Perhaps in this respect the student undertaking qualitative research for an examined thesis is in the 'privileged' position of having an audience as interested in the methods used as in the results produced.

At least where colleagues are collaborating on a research project, it can involve one analyst 'replicating' the results of another. Often, though, the qualitative analyst is a solitary figure, condemned to replicate his or her own findings. This is less of a paradox than it seems, if the replication in question involves new or additional data against which to judge the value of an initial result. Obviously one way of ensuring this is to obtain fresh data. This is not unreasonable in qualitative research, where data analysis may begin as soon as the first data is collected, rather than after data collection has been completed. An alternative procedure is to split the data, so that the results of a preliminary analysis with part of the data can then be replicated with the remainder. For example, the results from half the cases can be checked against the results of the other half. At least this goes some way towards testing whether one can replicate the original results.

An explanation of variations in results more acceptable than fabrication or falsification of evidence can be found in different interpretations of data. Here we shift from deliberate suppression of uncongenial evidence to unwitting neglect or misinterpretation of the data. In other words, we shift from the sins of commission to the sins of omission, which if morally more comfortable may still have equally damaging consequences for the analysis. The trouble is, of course, that we tend to see what we want to see, and hear what we want to hear. It is easy to be unduly influenced by the presumptions and prejudices with which we begin our analysis. As Miles and Huberman (1984) comment, rather cynically, 'most people are rotten scientists, relying heavily on pre-existing beliefs, and making bias-ridden judgements'. We tend to make more of the evidence that confirms our beliefs, and pay less attention to any evidence that contradicts them. This is a particular problem in qualitative analysis, because of the volume and complexity of the data. Because the data are voluminous, we have to be selective – and we can select out the data that doesn't suit. Because the data are complex, we have to rely more on imagination, insight and intuition – and we can quickly leap to the wrong conclusions.

As we search for illuminating singularities, we can easily become fixed on some striking but misleading images in the data. The most superficial impressions may carry conviction so long as they provide a plausible account of the data. And the more vivid the impression, the more plausible it may seem. Miles and Huberman describe 'plausibility' as the 'opiate' of the intellectual – perhaps rather unfairly, since anyone can fall for a plausible account. But 'plausibility' can be a seductive prize, the pursuit of which distorts our analysis. Fact is stranger than fiction, precisely because fiction has to seem plausible to the reader – with none of the messy conflicts, contradictions, and irritating 'anomalies' of real life. For example, the script writers for the film 'Let Him Have It' based on the Bentley case changed certain facts to produce a more plausible account. Bentley's father was a university graduate, but in the film becomes a cockney. Bentley hardly knew Craig, but in the film they become buddies. Awkward facts become plausible fictions. Seduced by the allure of providing a plausible account, we may ourselves produce fictions which conveniently ignore the more awkward and less easily accommodated facts in our data.

There are several ways in which we can reduce the errors associated with neglecting data. Of these, probably the most important is to look for corroborating evidence. Just how much evidence does support our impressions? I think of this as the 'name three' gambit, because when my children claim that 'everyone has one', a favourite and effective response is to say 'name three.' The salience of some parts of the data may be out of all proportion to the evidence overall. If we can assess the weight of evidence underpinning our analysis, then we can at least make a critical assessment of the empirical scope of our insights and intuitions.

As we have seen, the computer can provide procedures for enumerating the degree of empirical support for the categories and connections we have identified in our analysis. This is playing the numbers game, but it would be foolish to discount such evidence as irrelevant simply because it is not properly 'qualitative'. Numbers can be a useful corrective to initial impressions; the point is not to discount them, but to recognize that they may not tell the whole story. Suppose, for example, that we have hit upon stereotyping as an illuminating aspect of humour, largely influenced perhaps by the preeminence of stereotypes in our initial encounter with the data. Does the evidence warrant the significance we may be inclined to attach to this category as a result of its dramatic impact in the early phases of our analysis? If the category turns out to have only marginal significance in the rest of the data, then this will emerge through an enumeration of the relevant databits. We may be able to assess the weight of evidence case by case, or in the data as a whole. The frequency with which we have assigned the category will indicate its empirical scope. If we do find that the scope of the category is surprisingly slight, then we may wish to reassess its significance for our analysis overall.

Lest this seem an unduly mechanical approach, I should add that we need to take account of the quality of the evidence, and of its conceptual significance, as well as its empirical scope. One reputable witness may be worth a dozen unreliable ones. The police testimony against Derek Bentley had greater weight than Craig's testimony, not just because there were more of them, but also because they were regarded, perhaps mistakenly, as more reliable witnesses. From a more dispassionate standpoint, we might argue that Craig had less to gain in supporting Bentley than the police had to gain in accusing him. We might also note a bias towards accepting the voice of authority, the solidarity and collaboration of the police in presenting the case, and the formal and public setting in which evidence was given – all factors which may encourage greater scepticism about the reliability of the police evidence. With the benefit of hindsight, we could also note other occasions in which police perjury has been instrumental in securing convictions. All these considerations reflect upon the 'quality' of the police evidence. Finally, we may want to accord greater weight to the testimony of the policeman who twenty years later admitted that Bentley had not spoken that night. Here we have an example where a lone voice may have more credibility than all the rest put together.

In corroborating evidence, therefore, we need to think critically about the quality of the data (cf. Becker and Geer 1982). Did we observe an event at first hand, or hear about it second hand? Did we obtain the data unprompted, or in response to a question? I noted earlier the problems of relying on Vincent's account of events in his surgery. But much of the data we analyse is just what people have told us. Here are some of the questions we might ask of any observation.

Qualitative data is typically of uneven quality – and hence the importance of taking quality into account. If we have made all our observations ourselves, and made them repeatedly; and had the same observations confirmed by other, disinterested and unbiased and trustworthy observers, in neutral circumstances – we are probably not doing qualitative research.

---

**Checking the quality of data**
- Is it a product of our own observation, or a result of hearsay?
- Have any other people made or reported the same observation?
- In what circumstances was the observation made or reported?
- How reliable are those making or reporting the observation?
- What motivations may have influenced how the observation was reported?
- What biases may have influenced how the observation was made or reported?

---

Suppose we were interested in Vincent's letters, not as an example of Woody Allen's humour, but as an account of his relationships with patients and other dentists. The evidence of these letters may give us some insight into Vincent's view of these relationships, but we would hesitate before accepting this as an accurate account. The letters themselves suggest that Vincent, a volatile, self-centred person given to sudden moods of elation or depression, may be a most unreliable witness. We would surely look for corroboration, perhaps in other letters written by Vincent himself, or in recollections of the patients and dentists he mentions, or in the accounts of other observers, before we drew any firm conclusions about the events which Vincent describes.

In assessing quality, we have to beware of our own biases. Do we tend to accept uncritically the word of authority – or are we perpetual sceptics who can never accept an explanation if it is proferred by the powers that be? Do we tend to pay more heed to our own sex, race, nationality or whatever, and suspect the word and motives of others? Are we making rational or emotional judgements? In criminal justice, the art of prosecuting or defending may turn more on swaying prejudices than confirming or disconfirming facts. For example, take the description of Bentley as 'an epileptic nineteen-year-old', a point given prominence in reviews of the case. Why include the information that Bentley was an epileptic? This is presumably intended to colour our judgement of the case, regardless of any relevance Bentley's epilepsy may or may not have for the facts at issue. In assessing quality, we must be careful to give due weight to evidence, and discount information which may influence our judgement even though it is not relevant to the case.

Apart from assessing the 'integrity' of the data, we can also check on whether and how far an observation has been supported by other observations. The support offered by other observations may be more persuasive if these are genuinely independent and there is no possibility of 'collaboration' between sources. Of course, we may be lucky to find such independent sources, though by building independent measures into our research design, we can improve our prospects of doing so considerably.

As well as the quality of our data, we may also want to take account of its conceptual significance. We can justify giving extra salience to part of the data in conceptual terms even if this is out of proportion to its empirical scope. There may be turning points in our analysis, provoked perhaps by a stray remark or a sudden revelation, which alter our whole conception of what is going on. When Vincent cuts off his ear, we don't start to search the data for similar examples! Yet this is an incident which casts all the preceding events in a very different light. The same may be true of an apparently happy marriage in which one of the partners suddenly leaves for another lover. The whole relationship may be reinterpreted in the light of a single event whose significance stretches backwards as well as forwards in time. Some events do merit more weight than others in our interpretations. However, like Liza Cody's detective, Anna Lee, we must be careful not to decide too soon in an investigation just what information will turn out to be important (Cody 1991).

Few would dispute that the allegation that Derek Bentley uttered the phrase 'Let him have it, Chris' was a point of key significance at his trial. While we may doubt the quality of the data, it would seem foolish to doubt its import. If Bentley spoke these words with the intent to incite, the case against him was cast iron. By comparison, other evidence seems to pale into insignificance. On the other hand, rather than simply accepting the obvious, we have to justify assigning conceptual significance to some parts of the data and not others. Take the fact – uncontested – that Bentley gave himself up as soon as the would-be thiefs were cornered by the police. Perhaps the drama of the alleged statement eclipsed a point of equal if not greater significance. 'Actions speak louder than words' is an aphorism curiously neglected in this case. If Bentley had resisted arrest, the allegation that he incited violent resistance by Craig would be more convincing. But Bentley immediately gave himself up, an action at odds with then encouraging Craig to resist. We could make a case that the unambiguous and uncontested evidence that Bentley surrendered was more significant than the ambiguous and contested (but more dramatic) evidence about what he said after doing so.

This suggests another tack which we can pursue in seeking corroborative evidence. As well as examining the weight, quality and significance of the evidence in support, we can also look for inconsistent or conflicting evidence. The evidence that Bentley gave himself up is not consistent with and perhaps even contradicts the evidence that he encouraged Craig to resist. This is just the kind of innocuous data that we are inclined to overlook in the heat of the moment – the excitement of the chase and the thrill of the kill! Carried away by our inventions – or perhaps just relieved to have made some sense of the data – the last thing we want to do is undermine our own convictions. That's why defence is rarely entrusted to the prosecution! However, the hapless analyst who can only rely on his or her own resources, must make the best of it and accept the self-discipline required to do both jobs.

The computer can help a bit by making it easy to look for counter evidence. Instead of retrieving only those databits which support our analysis, we can also retrieve those which are inconsistent with or contradict it. We can produce negative evidence as easily as positive evidence. Suppose for example that we have mapped out the concurrence between incongruity and catharsis, and having collected some additional data our result now looks like the diagram in Figure 14.1.

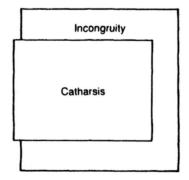

*Figure 14.1* Concurrence between categories

Some of the data no longer fits our previous argument that incongruity is an indispensable element in cathartic humour. We can retrieve the databits using a boolean search of the form 'X NOT Y' ('Catharsis NOT incongruity') to pick up these counter examples and examine them. We may have to modify our earlier argument in the light of this data. Or we may find that without the catalytic ingredient supplied by incongruity, cathartic humour falls flat, thereby providing some further indirect support for our initial view. Exceptions do sometimes prove rules. At any rate, by focusing on exceptions, extremes, or negative examples, we can counter the inclination to look only for evidence that confirms our views.

The computer can also help us to confront data more effectively, by making it easy to analyse the data in different ways. We can do this by randomizing cases – where appropriate – so that we no longer allow an arbitrary order to dictate our path through the data. If we always start in the same place, our initial impressions will always be the same and as a result some observations will loom larger than others. We can reduce this bias by starting at random points or following selective rather than sequential paths through the data. Both these procedures can help offset the tendency to concentrate attention on some parts of the data at the expense of others.

---

**Encouraging confrontation with the data**
- Enumerate the amount of data
- Evaluate the quality of the evidence
- Assess the conceptual significance of the data
- Look for exceptions, extreme or negative examples
- Follow different pathways through the data

---

The procedures we can follow to militate against neglecting data are relatively straightforward. All this really requires is a certain amount of self-discipline. The computer makes it easy to handle the mechanical aspects. By contrast, the problem of misinterpreting our data is much harder to deal with.

Even if we have confronted all the evidence, we may still 'misinterpret' our data. We can see the words 'let him have it' as either an encouragement to pass over the gun, or as an incitement to use it. If one of these interpretations is correct, the other is wrong. Supposing Bentley spoke those words, what did he mean by them? Even if Bentley said he meant Craig to hand over the gun, can we believe him? We cannot know for sure, because this interpretation was clearly so much more in his own interest than the other. We would expect Bentley to lie if necessary to protect himself from the gallows.

In interpreting this case, we are liable to make one of two errors. If we believe Bentley told the truth, we may make an error in accepting his explanation. If we believe Bentley lied, we may make an error in rejecting his explanation. Whichever interpretation we choose, we run the risk of error. Suppose we decide to reduce the risk of error by assuming that Bentley would lie to protect his own interest, though not otherwise. In trying to reduce the probability of error in one direction, we merely increase it in another. Once we suspect that Bentley might lie to protect himself, we increase the risk that we will mistakenly reject his account.

If the interpretation we choose is at odds with what actually happened, we 'misinterpret' the data. When does an interpretation become a 'misinterpretation'? There may be some reluctance to admit the possibility of 'misinterpreting' data, on the grounds that there is no such thing as an 'objective' account – we'll never know what really happened. All we have are different interpretations, and these are inevitably subjective. This assumes that each interpretation may have its own merits, but none can claim superiority over the rest – one interpretation is as good as another. The problem with this approach is that it eliminates the possibility of error, and therefore of making and learning from our mistakes. It eliminates progress and reduces social research to a useless exercise in story telling. While we do want to 'tell a story' about our data, it is not just any story, but one which we can claim is valid. My dictionary defines 'valid' as 'sound', 'defensible', and 'well-grounded' and despite the more technical interpretations of validity in social science, this is as good a definition as any. A valid account is one which can be defended as sound because it is well-grounded conceptually and empirically. If it doesn't make sense, then it cannot be valid. If it fails to account for the data, then it cannot be valid.

To produce a valid account, we need to be objective. This refers to a process, of which a valid interpretation is the product. Being objective does not mean being omniscient – it doesn't mean we can know 'what really happened.' It means accepting the canons which govern rational inquiry as a basis for realizing conclusions which are reasonable. It means taking account of evidence without forcing it to conform to one's own wishes and prejudices, and accepting the possibility of error. Errors in analysis matter, even if their consequences may be less dramatic than errors in the criminal justice.

How does the criminal justice process deal with the possibility of error? One way is to ensure that where there is doubt, different interpretations of the data are considered. Hence the role of the prosecution and the defence. A second is to suspend judgement as long as possible, and at least until each of these interpretations has been fully considered. A third way is to accept one interpretation – 'guilty' – in preference to another – 'innocent' – only if it is beyond reasonable doubt.

These are three related ways in which we can minimize the risk of error and misinterpretation of the evidence. One is to entertain rival interpretations of the data. Another is to suspend judgement as long as possible. A third is to refrain from judging between rival interpretations until we can chose one 'beyond reasonable doubt'. And in line with the presumption of innocence in criminal justice, the test of being 'beyond reasonable doubt' should be more stringent for those interpretations with the most significant theoretical or practical consequences.

Entertaining different explanations is a way of keeping an open mind. As I said earlier, an open mind is not an empty head. Some analysts recommend an approach which seems to come dangerously close to fitting the latter description. It is suggested that the best approach to evidence is to avoid developing ideas 'prematurely', until one is thoroughly familiar with all the evidence. This *tabula rasa* approach is dangerous because it leaves the analyst prone to all manner of prejudices and preconceptions, which are no less powerful for remaining subliminal. It is better to make ideas and values explicit rather than leaving them implicit and pretending that they are not there. The effort to devise alternative accounts is a more effective safeguard against preconceptions than trying to maintain a conceptual vacuum, which one's prevailing prejudices may rapidly fill.

The *tabula rasa* approach reminds me of the story of a detective who was following a suspect along a street at night, and the suspect dropped something in the gutter at a dark point in the road. Finding this action suspicious and suspecting that some vital evidence had been dispensed with, the detective decided to look for it. However, it was too dark to see anything at that point, so he moved further down the road to where there was a street-lamp, and looked for the evidence there! The detective is like an analyst who insists on using preconceived ideas to analyse his data. He will never find what he is looking for. It would be far better to get down on his hands and knees and feel around in the dark. Indeed, it might even be better to have no light at all, so that his eyes can adjust to the darkness, rather than be blinded by an adjacent light which prevents him from developing a 'night vision'.

In other words, if we rely on preconceived ideas, we may look for our evidence in the wrong place. One can feel the force of this story, but before we decide to abandon light (i.e. ideas) altogether, there is another option to consider, in which the detective takes out a torch and immediately finds the evidence he is looking for! The problem here is not the light, but the fact that it is fixed, and fixed in the wrong place. The detective grubbing around in the dark has a better chance of finding the evidence, but all the same his chances are not that high. The most effective way of finding what we are looking for, is not to dispense with light, but to make sure we can use our light flexibility and direct it where it is most useful. And that means using rather than dispensing with ideas.

Our first task, then, is to ensure that we consider alternative interpretations. We need, therefore, to devise alternative accounts. How successfully we can do this depends on our imagination. In assessing the Bentley case, we have so far considered only two interpretations – either Bentley denied any intention to incite, and he told the truth; or Bentley denied any intention to incite, but was lying. Let us look at some alternative interpretations.

Suppose Bentley wanted to play the hero, but lost his nerve at the last moment. He gave himself up, and told Craig to hand over the gun. But afterwards, he wanted to claim his part in the murder of the policeman. In this case, he might lie and claim his words were an incitement to violence, when they were nothing of the sort. We might be more inclined to doubt him if he claimed he was inciting Craig than if he denied it.

Now suppose Bentley was torn between giving himself up and fighting it out. Suppose part of him wanted to resist arrest, but another part of him wanted to give in. These inner contradictions found expression in a form of words which expressed both Bentley's conflicting wishes simultaneously. Neither at the time, nor in retrospect, could Bentley decide clearly what he meant by them. The ambiguity was the thing.

Now suppose Bentley, with a mental age of 11, was incapable of knowing one way or another what the words meant. Perhaps he just parrotted a phrase which was part of a 'make-believe' game he was playing, without distinguishing fact from fantasy and recognizing the potentially serious consequences of what he was doing – or saying.

Finally, suppose the police invented these words, in order to nail Bentley for the crime. They chose an exhortation which was deliberately ambiguous, because morally this was more comfortable than attributing to Bentley something unambiguous, such as 'Shoot!' The words 'let him have it' let the police off the hook (a little) because it was the interpretation by the court which condemned Bentley, rather than the words themselves.

We have developed – invented – a number of different interpretations, and by no means exhausted all the possibilities. Conspiracy theorists have suggested, for example, that there was a third person on the roof, who shouted the fatal phrase; or that the police shot their own colleague, and tried to cover up by shifting the blame. Even if these interpretations seem fanciful, we still have to consider the evidence before we can dismiss them. For example, evidence that Craig's gun was fired, and that the bullet from that gun killed PC Miles, might rule out the possibility of the police covering up for their own mistake. In fact the bullet from Craig's gun was never found. Therefore we cannot rule out this interpretation entirely.

While we may entertain some interpretations only to immediately discount them, we should beware of dismissing out of hand alternative interpretations which are reasonable (rather than fanciful) and consistent with the evidence. In Bentley's case, the defence was accorded only twenty seconds in the judge's summing up for the jury. In the interest of fair play, we would expect as much time to be devoted to the defence's case as to the prosecution's. Once again, the analyst has another role to don, this time to emulate the judge in summing up the evidence on either side. This summing up cannot be done if a single interpretation of the evidence has already been preselected.

Identifying different interpretations of the data may seem a daunting task, but in fact it is an integral part of the process of analysis. In annotating the data, we pinpoint various possibilities for analysis. In categorizing the data, we make judgements between different ways of classifying the data. In linking data, we make judgements about how different bits of data are related. In splitting and splicing categories, we make judgements about how categories can be related or refined. In connecting categories, and in using maps and matrices, we explore alternative ways in which the data can be integrated. Throughout our analysis, we are playing around with ideas, trying out possibilities, making judgements. The analysis can be presented as a route through a series of options to arrive at a particular conclusion or set of conclusions.

Figure 14.2 shows two different possible routes through the analysis, each arriving at different conclusions. We could think of these two routes as two cycles through the data.

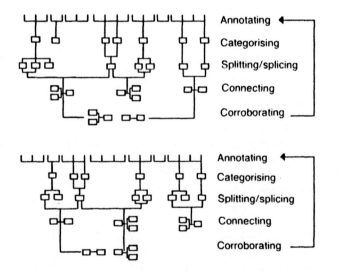

Figure 14.2 Two routes through the data, arriving at different results

Qualitative analysis is essentially an iterative process, involving repeated returns to earlier phases of the analysis as evidence becomes more organized and ideas are clarified. It is not a 'one shot' affair where by some lucky chance we can expect hit bull's eye on our first attempt. We need to fire several arrows, and see which if any land nearest to our target. In effect, we try out alternative accounts, and consider which of these accounts comes closest to describing or explaining our data. Corroborating evidence is the 'final' stage of this process, but to corroborate evidence we have to retrace our route through the previous stages.

We shall consider in a moment the kind of criteria which may influence us in weeding out weaker interpretations and narrowing our choice to those which make most sense of our data.

Just as the criminal justice process culminates in a decision about guilt or innocence, analysis is supposed to result in some conclusions. In both cases, we do not require these conclusions to be certain. It is enough that they should be 'beyond reasonable doubt'. We cannot 'verify' facts or explanations in the way that we can verify the outcome of an arithmetic sum. We are dealing with probabilities rather than certainties – no matter how certain we feel that we are right. No fact or explanation is incontrovertible. The most we can hope for is to present the best possible account of our data. Even this may not account for all the facts. We may have to settle for an explanation which accounts for most of them.

In statistics, we can measure 'reasonable doubt' in terms of some agreed standard of probability. We may decide that if the probability of making an observation by chance is less than 1 in 100 or 1 in 1,000, then it is reasonable to assume that the observation is not simply random. But what standards can we employ in analysing qualitative data? There is no obvious answer to this question, though there may be some pointers we can note.

The more complex our interpretation, the less convincing it may seem. We tend to prefer simple explanations over more complex ones – not just because they are easier to grasp, but also because they are more powerful. A complex explanation is more likely to be case-specific, and less likely to apply to other data. A complex explanation is also less likely to fit readily into other ideas and theories we may have. As well as being more powerful, a simple explanation is less likely to go wrong. Like machinery, the fewer the moving parts, the less likely it is that our explanation will break down. Also it is less likely to require constant maintenance. Simplicity can be seductive for all these reasons, though we should be wary lest we fall too readily for its appeal

A related point concerns credibility. Complex explanations can suffer a 'credibility gap' as we are required to accept more and more parts in order to justify the whole. On the other hand, when a simple explanation stretches our credulity too far, we may opt for a more complex account. Take the business of Craig's bullet, for example. Suppose the bullet could easily have been lost in the labyrinth structures of the warehouse roof. Then the simple explanation that the bullet was lost may be more credible than the complex explanation, that Craig never fired the bullet at all and there was a police cover-up. On the other hand, suppose it is almost impossible to believe that the bullet could have been lost. Then we may be inclined to a more complex account, because the simple explanation that the bullet was lost strains our credulity too far.

Another consideration is the internal coherence of our explanations. Does the machinery actually work? Are our explanations internally consistent? Do they make sense overall? How many conflicts and contradictions do they accommodate or resolve? And how much mess do they make as a by-product? We are all familiar with the 'explanation' which raises more questions than it answers. Despite claims to the contrary, we usually prefer explanations which reduce rather than increase the number of issues which remain unresolved. At any rate, we expect some improvement in our ability to handle old problems, even if in resolving these we pose a set of fresh questions.

We have considered earlier the problems of neglecting evidence. Another factor influencing our choice may be the empirical scope and completeness of different explanations. How well do they account for the evidence at our disposal? How many loose ends do they tie up? Is our explanation sufficiently wide in scope to include most of the data? As we have seen, empirical scope need not be a decisive issue for any one part of our analysis. But overall, our explanations will be more convincing if they include the bulk of our data.

In choosing between rival explanations, we may also be influenced by their conceptual significance for current ideas and contemporary theories. Here again, our prejudices may incline us in one direction rather than another. The arch-critic may find irresistible the exciting prospect of debunking established theory. The arch-conformist may look for comfortable explanations which can fit into established concepts and explanations.

Another factor which may influence our judgement is the practical significance of our explanations. In social science, the ultimate test of any explanation is practical, and any explanation which has practical also has moral implications (Giarelli 1988). If one explanation promises to have a more acceptable practical import than another, then other things being equal we may be more inclined to adopt it. Practical import cannot be separated, of course, from value judgements, since we have to consider who will benefit (or suffer) and why. In the Bentley case, the 'incitement' explanation suited the authorities who were keen to punish the murder of a policeman, but could not hang Craig because he was too young. The practical significance for the authorities was the deterrence through exemplary punishment of violent crime. For the defendant, the practical significance of the 'incitement' explanation was death. This conflict of interests is recognized in the criminal justice process, which attempts to afford through the initial presumption of innocence a measure of protection for the defendant. Though perhaps honoured in the breach in Bentley's case, the presumption of innocence is a way of protecting individuals from potential injustice. The equivalent in research terms is to advance a 'null hypothesis' that no relationship exists, unless we show otherwise 'beyond reasonable doubt'. Research results can also harm individuals. Where this is the case, we may also apply a more stringent requirement about the level of reasonable doubt we can tolerate. Practical concerns may therefore make us insist on a higher rather than a lower level of confidence in our conclusions.

---

**Choosing between rival explanations**
- Which explanation is simpler?
- Which explanation is more credible?
- Which explanation is more internally coherent?
- Which explanation has greater empirical scope?
- Which explanation has the greater conceptual import?
- Which explanation has the more acceptable practical import?

---

Naturally, the answers to these questions may not be clear or consistent, and the analyst – like the jurist – may be left to choose in terms of a balance of conflicting probabilities. While we may never be certain that our judgement is correct, at least we can reduce the chances of error.

Fortunately, in this task of arbitrating between alternative explanations, our lonely analyst can finally appeal to others for assistance. Pursuing our analogy with the process of criminal justice, we have cast our analyst in the role of prosecuting and defending lawyers, and even of the judge in summing up. But there is no need for the analyst to play the part of the jury. The jury provides an audience before whom the whole courtroom drama is performed, and it has the responsibility for finally judging between the conflicting accounts. For the qualitative analyst, the equivalent of the jurors may be colleagues, supervisors, academic rivals, external examiners, research contractors, policymakers or even the subjects themselves. Any research has to address a variety of audiences which will ultimately determine the value of the analysis.

Since the analysis ultimately has to convince others, there may be some virtue in involving others in the analysis. Here we depart from the formal procedures of the courtroom, where the jury is condemned to silence until delivering a final verdict. In qualitative analysis we may want to involve our 'jury' in earlier stages of the analysis, and not simply leave it to evaluate the final product. Our subjects may be able to comment on the authenticity of our accounts. Our colleagues may be able to suggest different interpretations. Supervisors may suggest inadequacies in the coherence of our explanations. Research contractors may refocus our attention on the issues of greatest theoretical import. Policy-makers may emphasize the practical significance of under-developed aspects of the analysis.

This traffic is never one-way, and it may pose problems as well as giving guidance to the analyst. Different constituencies have different interests, and are likely to give guidance accordingly. By trying to please everyone, we can end up pleasing no one. Ultimately, we have to remain responsible for the analysis – within any constraints imposed by academic requirements or contractual arrangements – and treat advice sought from other sources as precisely that: only advice.

Suppose we sought advice from the 'subjects' of our research, Victoria Wood or Woody Allen, about our analysis of humour. No doubt if they could spare us the time, we would learn a great deal from what they have to say. It would be interesting to learn whether they would acknowledge the role of incongruity and catharsis in humour, for example. There may be aspects of their humour which we have missed altogether. Their own accounts of their work may be very illuminating. However, suppose that they are also very critical of our analysis. As creative people, this is not how they think of humour at all. In fact, they may argue that to analyse humour in this way may impede creativity. It is therefore a useless and pointless exercise. Such an unsympathetic response from the subjects of our research would be quite reasonable. Our analysis is not geared to their interests and experience as creative writers.

While we can learn from the subjects of our research, and modify our analysis accordingly, we cannot allow them to become its final arbiters. Even if our account makes no sense to the subjects of our research, even if they fail to recognize the relevance of our interpretations, even if they reject the value of our explanations, we are entitled to persevere with our analysis. The validity of our account does not depend on acceptance by those who are subject of it. Indeed, a critical account which reinterprets social processes and events may be deliberately set against the current preconceptions of those who are subject to the research. Take gender stereotyping for example. The social scientist concerned to identify gender stereotypes in humour cannot allow subjects the final say over whether and how they utilize stereotypes. The 'emancipatory' role of research indeed requires the social scientists to say things which the subjects of the research may reject. There is no 'emancipation' involved in telling people what they already know, or confirming what they already believe.

I have emphasized the 'critical' role of the analyst, because it is sometimes suggested that a good test of an analysis is whether or not it is credible to the subjects of the research. This may be true, but it is not the whole truth. In so far as qualitative analysis aims only to describe the experiences and perspectives of subjects of the research, this is a fair point. For example, if we want to describe how Woody Allen sees his own work, then we should have to do so in terms which Woody Allen can recognize. If Woody Allen rejects our description, then we have no alternative than to revise it in the light of his criticisms. However, in so far as our qualitative analysis goes beyond description, to provide an explanation of Woody Allen's humour, it need no longer rely on describing humour in his terms.

While the analyst remains responsible for 'summing up' the analysis, and in the process may weigh the evidence, outline alternative interpretations and suggest certain conclusions can be drawn, it is the 'jury' which ultimately assesses the value and credibility of the analysis. In the policy-making context, many a research report reputedly lies on the bottom of a dusty shelf, its contents, no matter how apparently worthwhile to the researchers, happily ignored by those who commissioned the research. Nor is publication any guarantee of attention. Our jury may be composed of a variety of different audiences, and it is a sad but inescapable fact of life that their response to our analysis may be dictated as much by its style as its substance. We may be reluctant to ape the lawyer who 'plays to the gallery' to win his case. But it would be equally unreasonable to refuse to present our case as persuasively as possible. The problems of presenting our analysis form the subject of next chapter.

# Chapter 15

# Producing an account

'The novel is the most effective instrument for a criticism of society and social arrangements that we possess'

(Allan Massie 1991)

What you cannot explain to others, you do not understand yourself. Producing an account of our analysis is not just something we do for an audience. It is also something we do for ourselves. Producing an account is not just a question of reporting results; it is also another method of producing these results. Through the challenge of explaining ourselves to others, we can help to clarify and integrate the concepts and relationships we have identified in our analysis. The techniques of producing an account – drawing diagrams, tabulating tables and writing text – are similar to those we have used already in analysing the data. To produce an account, we have to incorporate these disparate elements into a coherent whole. In doing so, we can reassess the shape and significance of the separate parts. When we write, for example, the discipline of producing an account which is ordered, sequential and detailed can stimulate our thinking in fresh and original ways.

Producing an account is therefore another tool in our analytic tool-kit. As the ultimate product of the analytic process, it provides the overall framework for our analysis. We can also produce 'interim' accounts at various stages in the process. Its value lies in the obligation it imposes upon us to produce an accessible and acceptable report of our analysis. For an account to be accessible, it has to be clear and coherent, unencumbered by needless digressions, convoluted arguments and distracting detail. For an account to be acceptable, it has to be convincingly grounded conceptually and empirically, so that it both makes sense in itself and makes sense of the data.

We have already indicated some of the features of such an account in the previous chapter on corroborating evidence. An account is the equivalent of 'summing up' in a trial before the jury reaches its verdict. We have to confront all the evidence, not just the bits that fit our analysis. We have to consider alternative interpretations, not just select the one that suits us best. But we cannot simply reproduce the evidence and arguments in all their detail; we have to select and summarize. Nor can we give all the evidence equal weight; we have to stress some points at the expense of others. And we cannot review the evidence and arguments in the disjointed and haphazard way in which they may have come to our attention; we have to present the salient elements of our story in an orderly and systematic manner.

Any social researcher worth his or her salt will be stung by Alan Massie's celebration of the novel as the most effective instrument of social criticism. For where does that leave social research? It would be hard to deny that research reports rarely make easy reading. This may be a feature of the obligations they entail with regard to presenting evidence. On the other hand, some researchers may feel that the substance of their report is more important than its style. They may feel their job is to complete the research; what happens to the results is someone else's problem. One can sympathize with this view, while noting its dangers. The price of virtue may be too high, if it creates barriers to the fertile exchange of information. If the results of research are worthwhile, why make them inaccessible?

In making our account accessible to others, we may take a leaf from Massie's book and employ some of the techniques involved in 'telling a story'. Story-telling is an art form, usually with three basic ingredients: a setting, characters and a plot. All these ingredients are likely to figure in any account produced through qualitative analysis. We have a 'setting' in which we have collected our data, whether in the general social context of our interviews and observations, or the particular site(s) where we have undertaken our fieldwork. We have 'characters' in the shape of 'actors' who may be our informants or respondents, or the individuals or agencies we have observed. And we have a 'plot' in the shape of the 'social action' in which they are involved, which may be their individual life histories, or their interaction in various social or institutional contexts. How can we describe our settings, develop our characters and present our plot in ways which engage our audience?

Consider how each of these different ingredients can contribute to the creation of a good story. One contribution is through vivid and convincing description of the setting. This provides an authentic context in which characters and plot can unfold. Another is the ability to empathize with one or more of the characters. The story then engages our attention by making us care what happens to the characters. A third is the evolution of the plot towards some sort of climax or resolution. The story becomes a 'drama' which grips our attention through uncertainty about the outcome. Dramatization need not involve exaggeration; it depends on our sympathy with the characters and their situation, and our uncertainty about how this will finally be resolved.

An analysis is ultimately concerned with human situations and social processes. Each of these ingredients in story-telling (and no doubt there are others) can be used to make our analysis more accessible, perhaps as much to ourselves as to an outside audience. This is not just a matter of making our analysis accessible in the sense of an 'easy read'; it is also about engaging the moral attention and interest of the reader, and hence enhancing the human value and impact of our analysis. It is a way of returning our analysis to its roots in a world of practical human and social – and not merely abstract academic – concerns.

Appropriately, enhancing an account through story-telling techniques is more a question of improving quality than adding quantity. To describe a setting vividly and convincingly need not take endless pages of detailed description. Consider the classic beginning of a fairy-tale: 'Once upon a time'. This short phrase, resonant with magical and mystical associations of a world long passed, sets the context of the story in a time 'other than our own'; as Bettelheim (1991) suggests, it immediately sets the story in 'psychic space' rather than in the real everyday world. To stimulate sympathy for characters, it is necessary only to recognize them as human beings, rather than dehumanized 'actors' embodying some abstract set of psychological or social characteristics. In practical terms, we may, for example, use real or fictional names instead of case numbers. We may write our story in an active rather than passive mode, with real subjects taking action, not just being acted upon. To create a concern for outcomes, we need only pay heed to the uncertainties of the story as it unfolds, and avoid foreclosing through the benefit of hindsight choices and dilemmas inherent in social action. This may mean, for example, using incidents and anecdotes to reveal themes, before identifying and commenting upon them, rather than the reverse.

A good story is like a journey, in which we travel with the characters through the intricacies of the plot, to arrive at a conclusion. The evolution of the plot is as integral to the story as the final resolution. Indeed, in many respects it is the journey that counts, rather than the destination. In this respect, also, we may learn from story-telling in reporting on our analysis. Analysis is also like a journey, and its conclusion can be reached and understood only by travelling on it. This does not mean that we must reconstruct every step of the way. The original journey was, no doubt, full of the usual blind alleys, switch-backs, short-cuts which proved to be long cuts, and so on. But having finally discovered the right path to our conclusion, we need to mark that path for those that we would have follow and arrive at the same destination.

To trace our journey, or at least the main routes we have followed, and the major choices we have made, we need to have kept an 'audit' of our account. That means we have to keep track of the decisions we have taken at various points in our analysis. We have been making such decisions from our initial search for a conceptual focus right through to our final efforts to produce an integrated account. This includes our first creative encounters with the data when reading and annotating, our efforts to conceptualize the data through categorizing and linking, our attempts to identify relationships between concepts through matrices and mapping, and our 'testing' of ideas and evidence when searching for corroboration. If we have noted our decisions at each stage in the process, we should have a wealth of material to draw upon in auditing our account.

For example, take the evolution of categories which we have used in the analysis. By keeping a 'dictionary' of category definitions, we not only increase the efficiency and reliability with which we can assign categories during the analysis. We also provide an interesting record of how that category has evolved during the analysis. As we encounter new data and add new criteria to govern their assignation, the boundaries of the category become less permeable and the concept it expresses becomes more transparent. Or perhaps we find that we cannot develop a set of criteria, sufficiently distinctive and internally coherent to justify the continued use of the category, and amend (or discard) it accordingly. This conceptual evolution involves a succession of 'close encounters' with the data and it is the reasoning provoked by these encounters which shapes the final outcome of our analysis. In other words, the product – a particular conceptualization – is embedded in the process we have followed; and we cannot account for the product without also explaining the process.

Stories are also accessible because the separate elements of the story blend together into a satisfying whole which is more than the sum of the individual parts (Figure 15.1).

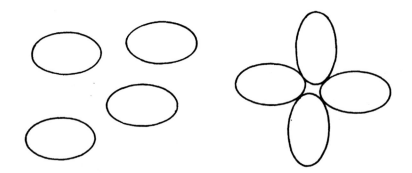

*Figure 15.1* The whole is greater than the sum of the parts – 1

The story is not just a juxtaposition of individual parts, for these have to be organized in a way which makes it in some sense holistic and indivisible. The story moves us in its entirety. This requires an integration of the various elements, so that the story acquires an intelligible shape, just as – to ressurect an earlier analogy – the bricks and mortar are brought together to form a building (Figure 15.2). The plan of the building has its parallel in the plan of the story. The story line has to follow this plan in unfolding the tale in a logical way, so that shifts from one element of the story to another are strategically related to realization of the overall plan.

*Figure 15.2* The whole is greater than the sum of the parts – 2

In producing our account, we may also benefit from developing a plan. Just like most buildings, most plans may follow a standard format. Our design may include an introductory hallway, some public rooms where most activity is concentrated, one or more bedrooms we can relax in or sleep in, and perhaps even a bathroom or two for cleaning up or waste disposal! There is nothing wrong with a standard design, and it still leaves plenty of leeway for interesting layouts and distinctive features. But designs should be adapted to the functions of the building and the materials and resources available for its construction.

With regard to functions, we have to adapt our design to suit the nature of the audience, and in particular the time, resources and attention which we can reasonably expect them to devote to our report. This may vary widely, depending on whether we are addressing the subjects of the research, an academic audience, funders, policy-makers or perhaps even a wider public. Our purpose in addressing each of these audiences may vary from giving a general overview of selected aspects to giving a full and detailed account of the analysis, and the character of our account may vary accordingly.

There is no point in constructing an elaborate edifice if our guests can only be expected to stick their heads through the front door. This may be the most we can expect in some cases. For example, if we are reporting our conclusions to policy-makers who have very full agendas, and can only spare a very limited amount of time on our report, then we can hardly insist that they bury themselves in the intricacies and detail of our analysis. The most we can expect is that they will take the time to consider a clear and concise summary of the main points. Of course, even if they have no time to inspect it themselves, our busy guests will still want to know that the whole construction has been completed.

Even in a clear and concise summary of the main points of our analysis, we may want to avoid reducing our report to a set of apparently firm conclusions. Once research 'findings' become public, they can be used for a variety of purposes over which we as analysts have little if any control. We may therefore be wary of pressures to produce 'results' which can be used without due qualification, heedless of their tentative and contingent character. Like the phrase 'data collection', the term 'findings' is really grossly misleading, with its implication that we have only 'found' what was already in the data simply waiting to be discovered. If this was the case, qualitative analysis would be as straightforward as collecting rubbish. And if we were to adopt this approach, rubbish is all we might be able to produce! As I have emphasized throughout this book, the results of our analysis are shaped by the conceptual tools we create and adapt for use in examining the data. Our 'facts' are produced through our conceptualizations. As Bohm (1983) has noted, the root of the word 'fact' is 'that which has been made' as in manufacture – our 'facts' therefore depend on how our perceptions are shaped by our thinking. Even in summarizing briefly the main points of our analysis, we should be wary of simply reporting a series of conclusions as 'facts' and thereby investing our results with a spurious value they do not merit.

As well as function, we need to consider the materials at our disposal. Most likely these will be far in excess of the space we have available, even in a very full report of our analysis. Sigmund Freud may have written twenty-four volumes, but most of us have to be somewhat more modest in our ambitions, and confine ourselves to a single – and reasonably slim – volume. The shorter the report, the more disciplined we have to be in producing it. Basically, we have to be ruthless in retaining our focus on the key elements in our story. This does not mean that all embellishments and elaborations must be excised, for they may contribute significantly to our portrayal of setting, character or plot. We have to strike a balance between depth and detail on the one hand, and breadth on the other. Better to tell one story well, than to attempt several tales, and end up telling them all badly. We not only have to focus on the key elements in our story; we also have to ensure we have sufficient space to do justice to our narration.

Research is essentially an exercise in selection. If we still harbour any lingering illusions on this point, the discipline of producing an account of our analysis should dispell them. Interesting themes, colourful incidents, and intriguing anecdotes may have to be excised, simply because they are not sufficiently important and central to merit inclusion in our account. It may be very difficult to contemplate leaving things out. But as Patton (1980: 429) notes, if we spare ourselves the agony of selection we simply impose upon our audience the agony of having to plough through all the things that were not omitted and should have been.

Perhaps the easiest way to facilitate this process of selection is to consider our analysis as a tree-shaped diagram. The main thrust of the analysis forms the trunk of the tree, with subsidiary themes forming the branches and the so on until we clothe the tree with leaves which provide the necessary colour and detail. We can create our tree graphically, but we can give substance to our representation by summarizing the main and subsidiary themes of our analysis in writing, until we have reached a sufficient level of detail to allow decisions to be made about the direction ‚and emphasis we want to develop.

Once again our design must take account of the materials to hand. Take our analysis of style and substance in Woody Allen's humour. We could construct several different trees, depending on the way our analysis has unfolded and the varying emphasis we may have placed on different themes. Suppose in our analysis we found the distinction between style and substance was of comparatively minor importance; this could be represented by our first tree in Figure 15.3. If our analysis divided sharply and evenly between these two aspects, this could be represented by the second tree. In contrast, our third tree represents an emphasis on one aspect and a relatively minor role for the other.

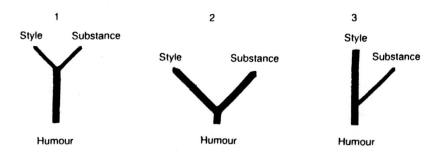

*Figure 15.3* Tree diagrams representing different analytic emphases

By outlining the shape of our analysis in this way, we can see at a glance the trade-off involved in including or excluding different aspects of the analysis. We would place far more emphasis on the style–substance distinction in the second case than in the first. We might even dispense with the distinction altogether in the third case, and concentrate our attention on issues of style which occupy the bulk of our analysis. But before taking any drastic steps, we may want to elaborate on our diagram by drawing in subsidiary aspects of the analysis.

Suppose the third tree comes closest to representing the shape our analysis has actually taken. Again the way our tree develops will reflect the varying emphases in the way our thinking may have developed. In Figure 15.4 we can contrast the first tree, where the main subsidiary branch is relatively undeveloped, with the second tree, where despite being less significant it still bears a considerable weight. We may be more inclined to prune the 'style' branch in the first instance than in the second.

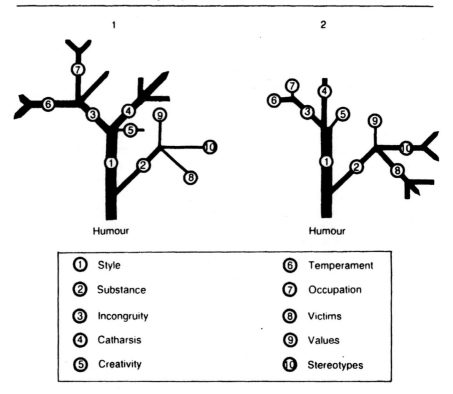

*Figure 15.4* Tree diagrams indicating different analytic emphases

We can develop these tree diagrams to whatever level of detail is required to summarize the main strands of our analysis. We can also focus on particular branches and review the concepts and relationships stemming from them in much the same way.

We may be able to base our diagrams on work we have already done in mapping our data. Indeed, as we have seen, the computer allows us to draw to scale the empirical scope of categories used in the analysis, so that our assessment of the analytic importance of any 'branch' of our analysis can be based on weighing its empirical as well as conceptual significance.

These diagrams can aid us in organizing our analysis as well as selecting its main lines and deciding where pruning may be required. Another approach to selecting and organizing the main lines of analysis is through progressive summarizing. Again we can start by summarizing the main theme of our story, and progress from there through summaries of subsidiary themes. Trying to give a very brief summary of a theme is a useful method of focusing on and explicating what is crucial to our account. It is another method of assessing significance by identifying and isolating critical features, though in words rather than pictures. This may also help to integrate our analysis by indicating possible ways of connecting the various strands in our thinking. Although summarizing along these lines may be less direct and logical than using diagrams, language can also be richer in resonance and associations, and lead us to make (or stumble upon) connections in ways we might not otherwise have anticipated.

This brings us to another aspect of story-telling, the use of language. This can be one of the most engaging aspects of a story. The overall style of a story may be inappropriate to an analytic report, though as I suggested earlier we can use some elements of story-telling to improve our presentation. But we can certainly learn from the language of story-telling. One feature of story-telling language which we can borrow is its directness. To be successful, the author has to 'make a connection' with his or her reader. To make that connection, the author must communicate effectively, with language unencumbered by needlessly technical terms and unnecessarily obtuse expressions. Plain and simple, crisp and to the point. It is well known that it is hardest of all to write stories for children. This is because the clearest and most economical language is also the most difficult to achieve. This is partly because when we write, we are often trying to do more than just communicate effectively with our audience. We may want to dazzle them! Or perhaps we want to cloak our lack of self-confidence in language, hiding the suspected poverty of our ideas and the vagueness of our thinking behind an impenetrable barrier of obscure terminology! Language can serve social as well as psychological ends, and in an academic context, this can encourage the use of needless jargon, as a way of establishing one's credentials as a member of an exclusive club. The Oxford Dictionary (1976: 578) defines jargon as follows:

> 'jargon n. Unintelligible words, gibberish, barbarous or debased language; mode of speech familiar only to a group or profession; (arch.) twittering of birds'

Perhaps the irony is unintended, but one suspects the author meant to imply that debased language is a particular prerogative of the professions!

By focusing above all on telling our story, we may be able to keep such abuses in check. Using simple and direct language is one way of establishing clear communication. Another aspect of story-telling language is the use of metaphor. We are in the middle of a metaphor at this moment, in which I am applying one idea – 'telling a story' – to another – 'producing an account' – to which it is not literally applicable. Using metaphors can enrich an account by conveying connotations which elaborate on and illuminate our basic meaning. To 'tell a story' has connotations – some of which I have already tried to indicate – which are not conveyed by the expression 'producing an account'. To 'tell a story' is to do something vital and interesting, perhaps even exciting. By comparison, 'producing an account' sounds far more pragmatic and pedestrian, even pedantic. The one is an activity we associate with novelists, the other we associate with accountants. The story-telling metaphor is an apt one (I hope), in so far as we want to stress the human and social aspects of our analysis, which may get lost in an unduly dry and abstract 'account'.

Because they invoke such associations, metaphors can take on a life of their own, not only adding a vibrant touch to our account, but also opening up new connections between concepts and suggesting novel ways of integrating our analysis. Because it can convey multiple connotations, a metaphor may be able to pull together various disparate analytic strands in a succinct and accessible way, vivid and yet concise.

All the same, we have to be careful in our use of metaphors, and not just to avoid mixing them! Qualitative data analysis is concerned with conceptual clarification and the careful specification of meaning. If we are using metaphors, we should do so consciously, paying attention to their conceptual implications. Unlike analogies or similes, where our reasoning must be made explicit, a metaphor invites concealment of the basis of comparison. But metaphors can raise inappropriate as well as appropriate connotations, and so contribute to confusion rather than clarity. For example, there are aspects of 'telling a story' which cannot be applied to the task of 'producing an account'. For one thing, stories can be fictional with all the freedom and licence that this implies. If the metaphor is applied inappropriately, the consequences could be quite unacceptable. We must therefore beware misleading connotations, and only use a metaphor within explicit and clearly defined limits. In this instance, the application of our story-telling metaphor is restricted to a concern with making our account more accessible. To apply it to the other half of our agenda, producing accounts which are acceptable, would be quite inappropriate, for the grounds for assessing the acceptability of stories and analytic accounts are very different.

While some of the techniques of 'telling a story' can make an account more accessible, in other respects they can make it more obscure. A story is not an analysis. It aims to describe, perhaps to enlighten – but not to analyse or explain. For example, the fairy story engages the child's interest and empathy, and through dramatization of external events can give the child an intuitive, subconscious understanding of how to deal with inner experiences in order to develop. But as Bettelheim says, 'one must never "explain" to the child the meanings of fairy tales' (1991: 155). Spelling out the moral of the tale destroys its magic. The purpose of the story is to enrich experience, not to dissect or analyse it.

Because stories are forms of art or entertainment, they are not an appropriate medium for analysing social action. Stories tend to gloss over characters and events, which are introduced primarily to serve a dramatic purpose. We do not question where the fairy godmother comes from in Cinderella – her function in the drama is clear enough. The drama itself is presented as a linear sequence of events, without worrying unduly about the connections between them. Why does the shoe fit only Cinderella's foot? Because that is what fits the story line. The story works as an art form, not as an explanation of events (cf. Burgess 1982).

In producing an account, therefore, we have to treat as problematic what in stories only serve as props. Because we are dealing with human beings with particular biographies, and social processes which are historically specific, we can learn from the techniques of story-telling. However, we must also take care to avoid its pitfalls, for otherwise our account may obscure more than it reveals. Story-telling techniques can be used to enhance analysis, but not as a substitute for it. Our choice of techniques must be guided by the object of our research and our purpose in presenting an account (Sayer 1992: 262). Our overriding concern must be to produce an account which is adequate as well as accessible.

> - Engage interest through description and dramatization
> - Trace the evolution of our account
> - Develop overall coherence
> - Select key themes
> - Use simple language
> - Make concepts and connections explicit

Before we leave the issue of accessibility, I must recommend a book by Becker (1986) on writing for social scientists for a fuller discussion of issues (including the use of metaphors) which I can only touch on here. As well as noting some of the qualities of good writing, such as the avoidance of abstract nouns, passive constructions and the like, Becker emphasizes the importance of reviewing and editing what you have written. Why use twenty words when two will do? We may use twenty words in our first draft, as we struggle to express some bashful idea through a process akin to free association or brain storming. But there is no excuse for retaining those twenty words, once the idea has been brought to light and we have had an opportunity to revise our thinking (and writing) to render it more precise (and concise). Unless you are one of those rare geniuses like Mozart whose compositions come original and complete in every detail, redrafting is essential to eliminate the needless repetition and unnecessary clutter associated with creative writing.

If editing – and re-editing – offers the key to using clear and direct language, the computer offers the key to editing. As Becker suggests, the computer can change the way we think and write. This is because the editing facilities it provides are so powerful. Because the 'on-screen' text can be amended instantly and with ease, the computer encourages a freer and more spontaneous flow of ideas. Becker also points out that the computer privatizes the production of a draft, making it a less public exercise, and therefore less subject to the kind of anxiety familiar in 'writer's block' and similar psychological afflictions which can impede the writing process.

On the computer, the first draft we produce 'on-screen' loses its permanent and immutable character, and we can therefore feel free to experiment with ideas and language, knowing that later we can tidy up the good stuff and cut out the rubbish. Later may only be moments later, for the computer allows us to write and edit in one process. The text no longer has the fixed character it acquires when 'stored' physically rather than electronically, so redrafting need no longer await the completion of an initial draft. Insertions and deletions can be made in the on-screen text which automatically adjusts to accommodate any alterations.

For example, I carried out many editing operations in writing the previous paragraph. Sometimes I struggled to find ways of completing a sentence, and tried out several alternatives before deleting those I liked least. Several times I reduced the length of a sentence because once completed I could see how to express the idea more succinctly. I also reordered the sequence of sentences in the paragraph to improve the continuity of the text and the logical flow from one idea to the next. I have incorporated these editing operations into my writing so that they have now become second nature. This is not how I used to write at all. Far from impeding the creative flow, this frees me from the inhibitions which arise when technological constraints condemn us to live with what we have just written without the possibility of instant revision.

What applies within a sentence or paragraph applies to the text as a whole. Text can be edited and reordered with ease across the whole document. We can carry on writing as ideas occur, confident that we can reassess later their appropriate position in the text. As well as encouraging creativity, some computer software also supports a more logical and organized approach to producing our account. For example, the package I am using offers an 'outlining' facility which allows me to organize the whole document in terms of a series of headings and subheadings. This shows at a glance the underlying logical structure of the document, and allows me to amend it with ease. I can shift the position of sentences, paragraphs, sections and even whole chapters with no more than a couple of quick commands – simply selecting the relevant heading, and moving it to the desired position. This facility supports a blend of styles which reflect the full complexity of our thinking process. Instead of writing an account in sequence from start to finish, we can create an overall structure and then 'fill in' the detail in any order we prefer. Instead of committing ourselves to an overall structure at the outset, which then imposes constraints upon the writing process, we can continually adapt the structure of our account in response to ideas which emerge through writing. The computer supports a genuine dialectic between the sequential reasoning of sentence construction and the holistic logic of structuring the document overall.

In Figure 15.5 I try to convey the difference between this and an orthodox writing strategy for a document with four sections. In practice, the computer does not require us to adopt one particular strategy but lets us shift backwards and forwards between them.

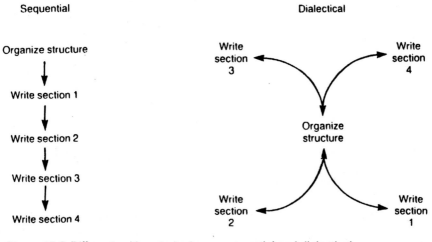

*Figure 15.5* Different writing strategies – sequential and dialectical

Finally, the computer can also aid our writing in more pragmatic ways. Providing we invest in learning the necessary skills, the keyboard is much quicker than pen and paper. Depending on our software, it may also support a range of facilities for checking spelling, numbering sections and pages, creating tables, inserting graphics, indexing and the like which all improve the efficiency and effectiveness with which we can produce an account of our analysis. The computer saves us time, though this may not mean we spend less time at the computer. Its facilities allow us to do things we otherwise would not contemplate. But if we spend as much time producing our account as before, that time is likely to be spent much more productively.

## PRODUCING AN ACCEPTABLE ACCOUNT

We have to produce an account which is acceptable as well as accessible. What is acceptable will depend on the purpose of our account and the nature of the audience. The requirements of a doctoral thesis differ from those of an academic journal, or a research report for a policy-making agency. The first step in producing an acceptable account is to clarify these requirements and ensure that the style, structure and substance of our account meet them successfully (Dixon *et al.* 10987: 216). While the length, format and substance of our account will vary according to whether we are producing a three page summary for policy-makers or a three hundred page thesis, there are some general criteria we have to address irrespective of how we report the results of our analysis.

What criteria does an 'acceptable' account have to meet? We can employ the three standard criteria for any analytic work. Is it reliable? Is it valid? And how representative is it? These criteria are really quite simple, as we can see if we take the example of telling the time. If my watch is reliable, it will be consistent, going neither fast nor slow. If my watch is valid, it will tell the right time. If my watch is representative, I'll know that other people (in a particular population) share the same time. An acceptable account has to convince its audience that it can meet each of these criteria. Let us consider each in turn.

The essence of reliability is consistency through repetition. Suppose my watch is wrong. It may be unreliable, or simply set at the wrong time (i.e. invalid). If I want to know whether my watch is reliable, I need to make repeated observations of the time. If I set it accurately and then, after an interval of say fifteen minutes, it is no longer accurate, then I know it is unreliable. If it is accurate, can I infer that it is reliable? In practice, I might – but not if my life depended on it! The interval may be too short to show up error. Or it could be that my watch is very erratic, sometimes going too fast and sometimes too slow, and by pure chance was again telling the right time. If I can obtain consistent results over repeated observations, at wider intervals, then this will give me more confidence that my watch is reliable. Notice how much harder it is to be positive than negative. It may take many repeated observations to acquire confidence in the watch's reliability, but only one negative observation to undermine it.

If our research is reliable, then others using the same procedures should be able to produce the same result. The trouble arises because analytic procedures are typically ill-defined, and replication by others is in any case a difficult if not impossible task. I suggested earlier that in corroborating evidence, we have to undertake 'internal replication' to test the reliability of our analysis (cf. Shimahara 1988). We may obtain some assurance in this way that we at least can reproduce the same results by using the same procedures on other parts of our data. But how do we assure others of the reliability of our analysis?

Suppose I want to vouch for the reliability of my watch, but cannot let others use it to make repeated measures. Not surprisingly, they are liable to become suspicious of its reliability. How could I convince them otherwise? My only option is to explain to them how the watch works, and convince them that every precaution has been taken to ensure that it works as expected. In other words, I would have to explain the principles of the measurement I am making, and what steps if any I have taken to eliminate or reduce potential sources of error. Depending on how my watch (or clock) operates, I may have to explain the mechanics of a pendulum or the vibrations of a quartz crystal. Reliability is not primarily an empirical issue at all, but a conceptual one. It has to be rooted in a conceptual framework which explains why in principle we can expect a measuring instrument to produce reliable results. The empirical aspect comes later, when we check repeatedly to see whether in practice these results are achieved. Here, in the absence of repeated observations, all we can do is check that our 'apparatus' is in good working order.

If we cannot expect others to replicate our account, the best we can do is explain how we arrived at our results. This gives our audience the chance to scrutinise our procedures and to decide whether, at least in principle, the results ought to be reliable. The crucial procedures will be those we have followed in categorizing or linking data, but we may also explain the procedures we have followed in summarizing data, splitting and splicing categories, making connections and using our maps and matrices. It may be useful to lay these out in algorithmic form (Figure 15.6).

Figure 15.7 shows how this can be done for the overall decision-making process we have followed throughout our analysis. Using a similar approach, we can also detail the substantive decision-making which has governed our conceptualizations of the data, and the connections we have made between concepts. We can improve internal reliability by ensuring our conceptualizations relate closely to our data, by testing them against a variety of data sources.

As well as outlining our procedures, we can try to identify possible sources of error. For example, what about 'mistakes' in categorization? As the assignment of categories involves judging in terms of a range of criteria, which may be vaguely articulated and which may also change over time, the opportunity for error is obvious. Some data which should be assigned to a particular category may have been overlooked. Other data have been assigned inappropriately. We could call these the sins of commission and ommission. Similar sources of error can be found in linking data and looking at connections between categories. There are procedures for reducing such errors, for example, through repeating the process of categorizing the data. The computer through its search facilities can help to locate data which may have been overlooked in our initial categorization. The converse error, of assigning a category (or a link) mistakenly to the data, can be identified through critical assessment of the results of category retrievals.

· We may correct such errors, but if time does not permit a full-blooded reassessment, we may settle for an estimate of the degree of error, by taking a sample of categories or databits and checking the accuracy with which categories have been assigned.

In assessing the potential for error, we can also call upon the procedures for corroborating evidence which are relevant in identifying sources of error. In looking at the quality, distribution and weight of evidence under-

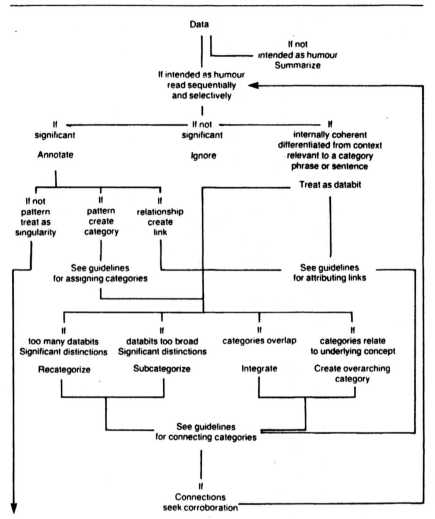

*Figure 15.6* Decision-making laid out in algorithmic form

pinning our categorizations, we can observe the weaknesses as well as the strengths of our evidence. By presenting the degree of empirical support for our categories, our audience can judge for themselves the strength of our evidence and the potential for error. The computer can help us to do this by cross-tabulating category variables or mapping out the empirical scope of our concepts and the connections between them.

Qualitative analysts have been notoriously reluctant to spell out even in the vaguest terms the decision-making processes involved in their analysis. They have been reluctant to admit of the possibility of error, preferring to

*Incongruity*

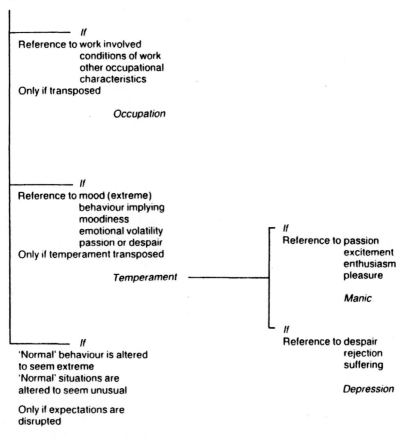

*Figure 15.7* Procedures for assigning categories in algorithmic form

present only such evidence as supports rather than contradicts their analysis. They have tended to rely instead (perhaps unwisely, given our discussion of fabricating evidence!) on the audience's trust in the integrity of the analyst. This makes even the most cursory scrutiny of the reliability of their procedures impossible. But the time spent on laying out our decision-making processes is not wasted if it gives our audience an insight into our analytic procedures and enhances their confidence in our results.

Turning now to validity, I defined a valid account as one 'which can be defended as sound because it is well-grounded conceptually and empirically'. There is a paradox here, of course, for how do we know that an analysis is well-grounded empirically, if our only access to that data is through the analysis? We have no 'independent' access to data other than through the concepts used in our analysis. The observations we have made have been informed throughout by our conceptualizations. No more than in any other form of research can qualitative analysis provide some kind of 'privileged' access to 'how things really are' independently of our ways of thinking about them.

Before we despair, however, or abandon ourselves to an unalloyed subjectivity (which for a social scientist is much the same thing), let us take heart from our example of time. We can accept without qualms the idea that my watch is 'valid' if it tells the right time. And how do we tell the 'right' time? To check the validity of my watch, I rely on other measurements of time. In my case, I watch the six o'clock news, or I phone the speaking clock. If the time on my watch is consistent with the time as measured by other 'instruments' like the speaking clock, I am happy to accept it as a valid measure. This is so, incidentally, even though I have no idea of what time 'really' is. The common sense view of time is that an interval between two events would be the same for all observers. This does not fit with my psychological experience of time (I find the hour in which I give a lecture tends to pass very quickly, but the hour in which I listen to a lecture passes very slowly!). Nor does it fit with the modern physicist's view, where time is not separate from space, each observer has his own measure of time, and identical clocks carried by different observers won't necessarily agree (Hawking 1988: 18–22).

This process of checking the validity of my watch is more complex than it might at first appear. Let us consider it more closely. Suppose I have a digital watch with a range of functions. To check the time, I look at my watch and read off a set of numbers. What have these numbers got to do with what time it is? The answer may be – nothing. I could be looking at the date, or the time that I have set the alarm to wake me up tomorrow morning. The first thing I have to be sure of is that the numbers I'm looking at are about what time it is, and not about something completely different. If my watch only has one function, then of course I can be pretty sure. But even so, this assumes that I have at some point set the watch so that it will tell the time. If my niece has in the meantime got hold of my watch, and treated it as an interesting toy rather than a measuring instrument, I may be misled. If the reading I make doesn't 'fit' with the reading I'd expect if my watch was telling the time, I may begin to doubt its validity as a measure of time. This fit (or lack of it) between our observations (the numbers) and our concept ('telling the time') is aptly called the 'face' validity of a measure. We have to decide whether 'on the face of it' the observation is consistent with the concept. In the case of the watch, this may be so straightforward that we take it for granted. But in qualitative analysis, the fit between observations and concepts may be far less obvious.

Once I'm satisfied that my watch is telling the time, I want to know if it's the 'right' time, and I check it against the time given by the speaking clock. In making this comparison, I am implicitly assuming that telling the time with my watch is consistent with telling the time by the speaking clock. We are both referring to a common-sense view of time, not one which might be relevant psychologically or in astrophysics. Incidentally, if I was navigating at sea and dependent on satellite signals to determine time, I would be better relying on astrophysics than on the common sense view (Hawking 1988: 33). I am also assuming a common frame of reference, such as British Summer Time. In other words, in checking validity I have to consider whether my concept of time is consistent with that employed by other measures. If my concept proves inconsistent – for example, if I have forgotten to switch to British Summer Time – then I may again doubt the validity of my measuring instrument. Of course, I could instead doubt the validity of British Summer Time, but such immodesty would be unbecoming. We have to accept the authority of established concepts unless we have very good reasons to do otherwise. This fit (or lack of it) between the concepts we are using and previously established and authoritative concepts is called 'construct' validity.

Finally, I can check that the two measurements are consistent. If my measurement does prove consistent with the measurements obtained from other indicators, then I can be confident that my own instrument is a valid measure. This fit (or lack of it) between measures provided by different indicators is called 'criterion' validity. In the case of the speaking clock, I have such confidence in its efficacy as a measure of time that I would not seek any further confirmation from other sources. The situation in social science is usually less clear-cut, because we cannot obtain established indicators through a simple phone call, and where indicators do exist they are often less authoritative. Think only of the problems in measuring class, intelligence, power, status or job satisfaction. Nevertheless, where we can find a reasonable fit between our own measurements and those derived from established indicators, we can have more confidence that we have devised a valid measure of the concept we are interested in.

In qualitative analysis, where we are often trying to break new ground and create new tools of analysis, we are more likely to be interested in the 'face' and 'construct' validity of our account. In the absence of satisfactory 'measures' achieving confidence through consistency in measurement is a less likely prospect. The 'face' validity of our account turns on the fit between our observations and our concepts, and this is something we can be more confident about. The whole thrust of qualitative analysis is to ground our account empirically in the data. By annotating, categorizing and linking data, we can provide a sound empirical base for identifying concepts and the connections between them. Other interpretations and explanations of the data may be possible, but at least we can be confident that the concepts and connections we have used are rooted in the data we have analysed. But how can we create a similar degree of confidence in others?

We can do this by demonstrating how the concepts and connections we have identified are grounded in the data. This involves more than throwing in a few anecdotes and illustrations to exemplify the meaning of a concept or a connection. This is not irrelevant, for we do have to show how our account applies to the data. But it is not enough. We need to be more systematic in considering the fit between our ideas and our data. We can do this by comparing the criteria we have employed in categorizing and linking with the data, noting and discussing borderline, extreme and negative as well as straightforward or typical examples. If the data is at all voluminous, then we cannot consider every bit of data in detail; but by considering notable exceptions as well as examples we can provide a more thorough review. As well as how our ideas apply to the data, we have to consider how far they apply. To do this, we have to consider frequency as well as content. Have we found one example, or many? Are examples concentrated in a single case, or spread evenly across cases? The computer can help us to answer such questions by making it easy to summarize information about the volume and distribution of our data. While the assumptions required for statistical analysis may not be satisfied by the way the data has been collected and analysed, it is still possible to obtain a useful descriptive overview in summary form.

These comments apply most especially where we claim to identify 'patterns' within the data. Where we are dealing with 'singularities', frequencies are irrelevant. However, we can at least improve confidence in the validity of our account by considering carefully the quality of our sources, and also by cross-referencing our observations from a range of sources. Otherwise we become unduly dependent on limited data of doubtful validity, such as Vincent's account of his relations with Gauguin or Claire Memling. Here again, our case will be strengthened if we remain open to different interpretations of the data (e.g. that Vincent has a lively imagination and a tendency to blame others for his problems) than if we simply exclude them from consideration.

Let us look at an example. Suppose we want to argue that women tend to be presented as passive patients, in contrast to the male patients and of course to the dentists themselves. Is this a valid account? First we can explicate our concept of passivity by looking at how we have defined the relevant category and some examples of how we have categorized the relevant data. Then we can look at a borderline example, and also some negative examples. Finally, we can consider how far the data supports our analysis.

Woody Allen exploits the vulnerability we feel when 'trapped' in the dentist's chair. Does he do so in a gender-neutral way, or does his humour betray some implicit sexual stereotypes? We can examine this question by considering the way he depicts patient responses to the rather bizarre dental practices which they encounter. Here we find some striking images, such as that of Mrs Zardis sitting passively in the dental chair for several days waiting for Vincent to return from his blackout by the seashore, or Mr Feldman taking advantage of Gauguin's distraction to bolt from his chair and race out of the office. The contrast between these portrayals could be taken as evidence of sexual stereotyping. To examine this issue, we categorized patient responses according to whether they seemed 'active' or 'passive'. We took passive responses to refer to lack of action by patients in situations which could be regarded in some way as provocative. This lack of action implied a submissiveness on the part of patients, either in the sense of a lack of assertiveness concerning their own interests, or in the sense of a lack of any opposition to the indignities they suffered. By contrast, an active response involved an overt response to direct or indirect provocation, either implying assertiveness concerning the patient's own interests or some resistance to the impositions they experienced. Using these criteria, databits were assigned to these categories as in Table 15.1.

Most of these examples could be assigned to either category with reasonable confidence. The patients either accept treatment which is provocative, or they resist it in some way. Sometimes responses were

Table 15.1 Databits assigned to categories 'active' and 'passive'

| Passive | Active |
|---|---|
| Mrs Schwimmer lets Vincent make her bridge as he felt like it. | Mrs Schwimmer sues Vincent. |
| Mrs Zardis remains in her chair while Vincent is absent for several days. | Mr Greenglass refuses to let Vincent remove tooth. |
| Vincent reads Dreiser to anesthetize a male patient. | Mr Greenglass sues Vincent. |
| Mrs Fitelman lets Toulouse-Lautrec cap her chin. | Mr Feldman takes advantage of Gauguin's distraction to bolt from his chair and race out of the office. |
| Claire lets Vincent bring her back early. | Claire Menling finally resists Vincent's advances and runs out weeping. |
| Claire lets Vincent drop swabs and mirrors in her mouth. | [Mr Kaufman darts for his toupee when it is blown off by the wind during open-air surgery.] |
| Claire lets Vincent put his arms round her to show her how to brush. | |

divided into more than one element, as with Mrs Schwimmer and Mr Greenglass, allowing us to recognize where a patient both accepts and resists treatment as distinct responses.

A borderline case is that involving Mr Kaufman, where although the patient is 'active' in retrieving his toupee, this is indicative of assertiveness on his part rather than any overt resistance to provocative action. However, the situation – open-air dentistry – could be regarded as provocative and Mr Kaufman if not resisting this at least actively looks after his own interests. As our criteria included assertiveness as well as opposition, on balance we decided to assign the category 'active' to this databit.

Another borderline case arises when Vincent gives Claire Memling gas before asking her 'to rinse'. Is this another example of passivity in the face of Vincent's advances? Possibly. We may hesitate to categorize it in this way, though, since this may have been a legitimate part of Claire's treatment, and what was unusual was that Vincent joined her – as he says, 'We both took a little gas'. Because the action refers primarily to Vincent, on balance, we decided to exclude this from our categorization.

We have summarized the relationship between patient gender and 'active' and 'passive' responses in Table 15.2. We can see that 'passive' responses are found predominantly amongst female patients, while 'active' responses are found predominantly amongst male patients. The vast majority of the males are 'active' while the vast majority of the females are 'passive'. Unfortunately, the number of examples is too low for this cross-tabulation to be more than suggestive.

Table 15.2 'Passive' and 'active' responses by gender

| Gender | Passive | Active |
|--------|---------|--------|
| Male   | 1       | 4      |
| Female | 6       | 2      |

(N = 13)

Of the thirteen examples, three are exceptions to the gender stereotyping pattern. It is worth considering these exceptions in more detail. Of the two women responding actively, one is Claire Memling who is finally provoked into rejecting Vincent's advances and 'runs out weeping'. Compare this with the response of Mr Feldman, who takes advantage of a lapse to break free and 'races out' – without weeping. The other is Mrs Schwimmer, who sues Vincent over the 'billowing bridge', but only after treatment is completed. Compare this with the example of Mr Greenglass,

who also sued but only after refusing treatment – he was 'adamant' that
Vincent could not remove his tooth. Finally, the gender of the 'passive'
male is mentioned almost incidentally – 'I had to anesthetise the patient by
reading him Dreiser' – receiving so little emphasis that we might have
overlooked this example had we not been looking for it in the data.
Overall, these exceptions are fairly weak and do not create a strong
'counter-impression' to the main pattern.

How strong is that pattern? If we look at the frequency and distribution
of these examples, we find a reasonable spread across the data, with no
concentration in particular cases (Table 15.3). 'Active' and 'passive'
responses are woven through the letters, with only the final letter making
no reference to patient response at all.

While this suggests a gender-stereotyping pattern is woven through the
letters, if we look at the data in terms of patients rather than responses, we
find the picture is not quite so clear. For example, three of the six examples
of 'passive' responses amongst women relate to one patient, Claire
Memling. We also find that in the case of two patients, Claire Memling and
Mrs Schwimmer, initial passivity eventually turns into an 'active' response.
That leaves only two examples, Mrs Zardis and Mrs Fetelman, where
female patients (and not just their response) are unambiguously 'passive'.

Table 15.3 Distribution of responses by case

| Letters | 'Active' | 'Passive' |
| --- | --- | --- |
| 1 | 1 | 1 |
| 2 | 0 | 1 |
| 3 | 0 | 1 |
| 4 | 2 | 0 |
| 5 | 1 | 0 |
| 6 | 0 | 1 |
| 7 | 0 | 2 |
| 8 | 1 | 0 |
| 9 | 0 | 1 |
| 10 | 0 | 0 |

Nevertheless, the balance of evidence does suggest a gender-stereotyping pattern of responses. The most clear-cut and dramatic examples in
the data all tend to confirm this pattern, while as we have seen the negative
evidence is less clear-cut and dramatic. Overall, we may reasonably
conclude that Woody Allen has portrayed a gender-stereotyped view in his
depiction of patient responses.

Although this example refers to very little data, the principles involved can easily be applied to more extensive data, without unduly extending the length of the analysis. Obviously the more data is involved, however, the more we may have to select and summarize the data, while still providing sufficient information to validate our interpretations. Unfortunately, the technological limitations of traditional forms of publication impose constraints which mean we cannot reproduce the interactive environment of a computer-based account. Ideally, we should be able to link summaries to databits, and databits to context, so that at any time readers can check for themselves the validity of our interpretations by accessing the original data in context. If accounts were stored on disk, the reader could have full access to all the data on which our analysis is based. By electronically linking our summaries and interpretations to the relevant data, our audience could then check for themselves any doubtful (or especially interesting) points in our analysis. So long as producing an account depends only on traditional forms of publication, we have to accept limitations which in principle may be overcome following the advent of desktop computing. However, this vision of a future in which the research community exchanges disks as well as papers, and accounts can be validated in a fully interactive medium, cannot be realized without the development and standardization of the relevant software.

Meantime let us return to our present problems of validation, and consider the issues posed by 'construct' validity. These refer to the fit (or lack of fit) between the concepts used in our account and those already established in the relevant field. If we have used concepts which are congruent with those employed successfully in other analyses, our audience may have greater confidence in the validity of our account. If we have spurned the conceptual tools currently available in favour of inventing our own, we can expect a more sceptical response. Even the scientific community likes to keep originality on a lead – unless its problems have become so pressing that a complete shift in paradigm is required. Before we dedicate ourselves to revolutionizing current paradigms, however, we ought to recognize the circumstances in which such changes can occur. Einstein's relativity theory explained empirical discrepancies which were inexplicable within the framework of Newtonian physics, and made some fresh predictions which could be tested against evidence. Theories in social science do not have such explanatory and predictive power. Often in place of explanation and prediction, we have to make do with insight and speculation. To our audience, these qualities, valuable though they may be, will rarely constitute an overwhelming case for changing the way they think. There is much to be said, therefore, for working with established rather than original concepts. The task of testing and honing these concepts through empirical enquiry is no less valuable than that of creating new conceptual tools.

In practice, qualitative analysis may well involve a mix of these two tasks, depending on the fit between our data and the concepts we employ at the outset. To validate new concepts, we can still consider their congruence with established thinking. If our concepts are inconsistent with established thinking, we have to accept a sterner test of their validity, if not in terms of their explanatory and predictive power, then at least in terms of the significant insights and understanding they afford. Much the same point applies to 'criterion' validity. If our observations are inconsistent with the results produced through other measures, then we have to be particularly careful to ensure that our confidence in them is not misplaced.

Qualitative analysis is often castigated as being too subjective, and as Patton comments:

> To be subjective means to be biased, unreliable and irrational. Subjective data imply opinion rather than fact, intuition rather than logic, impression rather than confirmation (Patton 1980: 336)

Those taking this view tend to equate objectivity with achieving distance from the data through formal measurement and quantification, but as Patton goes on to remark 'distance does not guarantee objectivity, it merely guarantees distance'. The problems of objectivity lie mainly in how we conceptualize data, and as I suggested earlier, this issue arises at all levels of measurement. To quote Patton again: 'numbers do not protect against bias, they merely disguise it'. This overstates the case, however, as numbers can help reduce bias, though they are not a sufficient protection against it, just as reliable measures may not be valid ones. As Shimahara (1988) comments, validity and reliability of research are crucial to all social research regardless of disciplines and the methods employed.

Finally, let us turn to the problems of representation. Even if my watch gives a valid reading, this result can be generalized only to a particular population. The 'right' time in Edinburgh is not the same as the 'right' time in New York. In telling the time, we take for granted the population to which we are referring – those that live within the same time zone. But in producing an account, we need to consider carefully to whom our account refers.

It is helpful to distinguish two aspects of 'generalizatioh' which are sometimes confused. The first involves the process of induction, whereby we infer a general proposition on the basis of our empirical observations. Generalization in this sense refers to the theoretical process of developing concepts and connections. The second involves the process of applying our theory to a wider population. This refers to ascertaining the empirical circumstances in which our theory may hold true. In both cases, we 'generalize' on the basis of the available evidence; but in the first sense, we infer a general statement about the data, and in the second, we apply that statement beyond the data on which it is based (Figure 15.8).

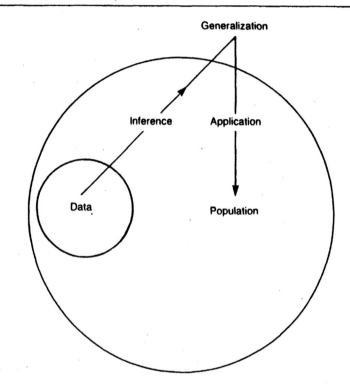

*Figure 15.8* The two aspects of generalization

To contrast these two aspects of generalization, compare problems of generalizing about artistic stereotyping in Vincent's letters and in Woody Allen's humour. In our analysis of Vincent's letters, we used the evidence of Vincent's moodiness and volatile behaviour to infer a generalization about the use of artistic stereotypes. This was generalization about the data, and to consider whether or not it is justified, we have to examine the data on which it is based. For example, we might wonder whether it is Vincent himself, as a specific historical individual, whose temperament is being ridiculed, rather than that of artists in general. On the other hand, the letters do refer to other artists, like Gauguin, Seurat and so on, who seem to behave in a similar vein. On this basis, we may justify our generalization about artistic stereotyping. The problems of generalizing about artistic stereotyping in Woody Allen's humour, though, are quite different. We can say next to nothing about artistic stereotyping in Woody Allen's humour, because we have only analysed one example of it. It may be that this is a unique case. Unless we can claim that our data is somehow representative of Woody Allen's humour, we cannot generalize about it.

Qualitative analysis often provides a better basis for inferring generalizations than for applying them. This is because qualitative data usually refers to a limited number of cases, or perhaps even a single case. Focusing in this way gives the researcher an opportunity to do a thorough analysis, thereby providing a solid basis for inference. However, it does not provide a good basis for applying these inferences to a wider population. The cases may be insufficient in number to justify such generalization. They may also have been selected on a non-random basis, precluding the use of sampling techniques to justify generalization beyond the confines of the original sample.

Some analysts see this weakness as laudable, doubting the ability of social research to produce generalizations which can apply in any circumstance regardless of context (Patton 1980: 279). This seems suspiciously like making a virtue out of necessity. Nevertheless, there may be some saving grace in the ability of qualitative analysts to identify the context in which their inferences are made. This can provide a key to elucidating the conditions under which a generalization can be expected to hold.

For example, it is hardly surprising to find artistic stereotyping in an article titled 'If the Impressionists Had Been Dentists'. However, we also found evidence of gender stereotyping, and as this is less 'context-specific' it is more likely to be located in other areas of Woody Allen's humour. The use of transpositions of occupation and temperament are likewise 'context-specific', but the underlying use of incongruity may be less so. The same is true of the relationship we observed between incongruity and cathartic humour, which we might also expect to hold in other contexts. Indeed, we could formulate this as a hypothesis which we could test through further research. For example, we could suggest as a hypothesis that incongruity is a necessary (but not sufficient) condition of cathartic humour. Or, less ambitiously, we could confine ourselves to the hypothesis that cathartic humour is often associated with an element of incongruity.

In producing an account, it is important to acknowledge the conditions under which our generalizations may hold true. As a basis for generalizing beyond our data, qualitative analysis is more likely to be suggestive than conclusive. On the other hand, in so far as our inferences are well grounded in our analysis of the data, at least we can be more confident that our suggestions are worth pursuing.

# Chapter 16

# Conclusion

I have presented qualitative data analysis as a logical sequence of steps, from our first encounters with the data through to the problems of producing an account (Figure 16.1). This sequence reflects the logical relationship between different phases in the analytic process. We cannot categorize or link data unless we have first read and annotated it; we cannot connect categories unless we have first categorized and linked the data; we cannot produce an account without first categorizing and linking the data.

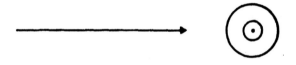

*Figure 16.1* Linear representation of analysis

However, although qualitative analysis is sequential in this sense, in practice we rarely proceed in a direct line from our first encounters with the data to our conclusions. This representation implies that we have a clear sense of direction from the outset, and this determines a straightforward path from our data to our results. It is more realistic to imagine qualitative data analysis as a series of spirals as we loop back and forth through various phases within the broader progress of the analysis (Figure 16.2).

*Figure 16.2* Loop representation of analysis

This representation emphasizes the interdependence of procedures used in the analysis. In reading and annotating data, for example, we anticipate the tasks of categorizing and linking the data. While making connections between categories, we review our initial links and categories. At any particular phase in our analysis, we may return to re-reading the data or look forward to producing our account. Thus qualitative data analysis tends to be an iterative process (Figure 16.3).

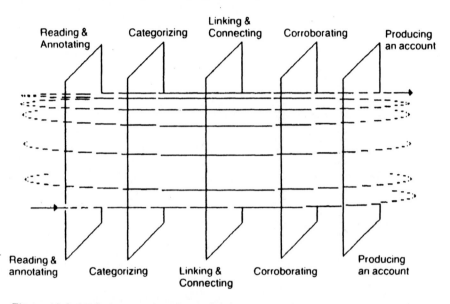

*Figure 16.3* Analysis as an iterative process

The various 'stages' of research which we have presented in logical sequence may be better thought of as recurrent 'phases' through which the analysis passes. Analysis is therefore akin to a spiral which turns through successive cycles, each (hopefully) at a higher level as more evidence is accumulated and concepts and connections become clearer.

Why present analysis as sequential if in practice it is iterative? One reason is that my account of analysis has been constrained by the medium through which I have presented it. The use of text imposes a linear and sequential mode of explanation which is not always appropriate to what is being explicated. As I suggested in Chapter 13, maps and matrices can help offset this uni-dimensional character of text, creating a multi-dimensional space in terms of which to present the multiple facets of social action. But we still depend on text to add the necessary depth and density to what we have to say.

The use of different tools and procedures may create inconsistencies in our account, but the tension between them can be useful. As Winston

Churchill said, 'consistency is a virtue of small minds'. In qualitative data analysis, we have to come to terms with a series of paradoxes. Thus we want to use existing ideas, but not prejudge the data. We want to break the data up into bits, but also to analyse it as a whole. We want to consider data in context, but also to make comparisons. We want to divide data into categories, but also to consider how these relate. We want to be comprehensive, but also selective. We want to analyse singularities, but also to generalize. We want our accounts to be accessible, but also acceptable. We want to be rigorous, but also creative.

In response to these paradoxes, researchers have tended to emphasize one approach at the expense of another, producing rigidities which can only impede the creative process. Thus qualitative data is opposed to quantitative data, qualitative analysis to quantitative analysis, thick description to thin description, grounded theories to deductive theories, analysing data in context to comparison, analysing correlations to identifying connections, narrative accounts to analytic ones, and so on and on. Researchers opt for one side or the other of these dichotomies, and then engage in a critical demolition of the alternative approach. Often this is accompanied by a token acknowledgement of the latter, as though finally reluctant to dispose of 'the enemy' which provides a foil for the favoured approach.

Where such paradoxes abound, it is not surprising to find researchers taking up positions and converting methodology into an ideological battlefield:

> ... it is well known that, while reason embraces a cold mediocrity, our passions hurry us with rapid violence over the space which lies between the most opposite extremes.

> (Gibbon 1960: 164)

While the heat generated by such ideological disputes may be warming in its way, it does not aid a cool and dispassionate appraisal of methodological options.

To clear away the debris associated with these ideological clashes is beyond the scope of this introduction. In any case, I believe such one-sided ideologies bear little relation to what researchers do in practice. It is not practically possible, for example, to adopt a *tabula rasa* approach to data analysis. It is not practically possible to proceed as though meanings can be understood in context, without also making comparisons – or vice versa. And even the most resolutely qualitative approach cannot entirely ignore the quantitative aspects of analysis.

Throughout this book, I have preferred to stress the interdependence and mutual enhancement of apparently opposing approaches. Numbers can be useful in analysing meanings. Categorizing can contribute to identifying meaning-in-context. Patterns can help to isolate and understand singularities. Linking and associating can both contribute to analysing connections. Accounts can incorporate both narrative and analytic elements. It makes little sense, in my view, to emphasize one approach at the expense of the other. For example, an emphasis on grounding theory in an empirical analysis of the data tends to discount the conceptual significance of the ideas we bring to the analysis, and the wider ideas we have to relate it to.

This view is based in part on a practical orientation to analysis. If we think in terms of an analytic toolkit, it makes more sense to consider all the available tools and not leave one half of the toolbox locked. It is only fair to add that this approach may seem heretical in some quarters, where purity of procedure takes precedence over a more pragmatic perspective. My own view is that epistemological and ontological arguments are more useful if they examine knowledge as a practical accomplishment – how research works in practice – than if they indulge in prescriptive wrangles about how we really ought to proceed. Bryman (1988: 124) likewise questions 'the role of programmatic statements in relation to the pursuit of good social research'. He suggests that research methods are probably much more autonomous and adaptable than some epistemologists would like to believe.

The computer itself may fall foul of such prescriptive perspectives on what qualitative data analysis 'ought' to be. The advent of the computer has produced partisan responses, with some regarding it as a panacea for all ills and others castigating it as a dehumanizing threat to 'all that is warm and cuddly in human nature' (Pfaffenberger 1988: 10). These responses feed off each other, as claims that the computer can do everything encourage scepticism amongst those who think it can do nothing – or at least, nothing worthwhile. Neither view is appropriate in the context of qualitative analysis. The more extravagant claims for the computer relate to its ability to replace human enquiry and analysis with artificial intelligence. The advent of 'expert systems' has given a new lease of life to these ambitions, as has research on neuron networks. However, expert systems depend upon the existence of stable knowledge systems governed by identifiable rules – two characteristics notably lacking in relation to qualitative data analysis (Pfaffenberger 1988: 64-77). Research on neuron networks looks more promising as a means of emulating human pattern recognition, but it may be some years (or decades) before its potential is realized, and even then it remains doubtful whether computers based on neuron networks can emulate the insights and intuitions characteristic of consciousness and judgement (Penrose 1990: 507-514).

Meantime, the current generation of software provides a set of procedures which can replace or facilitate the mechanical tasks involved in analysing data, but not the creative and conceptual tasks that this requires. In this respect, the concerns of those analysts wary of the quantitative and mechanical character of the computer seem somewhat misplaced. The ability to handle these aspects of analysis more efficiently and effectively can only enhance qualitative analysis. Traditional methods of handling data created a yawning gap between ideals and practice, simply because the procedures involved were so cumbersome, tedious and time-consuming. The advent of fast, efficient and eminently manageable techniques for handling data facilitates the achievement of traditional ideals. For example, it is now more feasible to reach a 'saturation' point, where all the relevant data have been incorporated into the analysis. To assess the strength of data supporting any particular conceptualization is now a much more straightforward matter. Auditing the analysis has become a much more manageable task. The computer supports a more complex and comprehensive analysis than was previously possible.

The real issue is not so much whether the computer will replace thinking, but how it may shape it. Here, the new technology offers real advances, most obviously in its powerful search facilities, and in the ability to create Hypertext links between different bits of data. Neither may be an unmitigated blessing, as text retrieval systems may encourage misplaced confidence in the computer's ability to identify relevant data (Pfaffenberger 1988: 52–6), while Hypertext procedures may encourage excessive complexity in the analysis (Cordingley 1991). However, both these facilities can support ways of thinking about data which were difficult if not impossible using traditional methods. Search facilities support a more rigorous and theoretically driven process of 'interrogating' data, exploring and testing for connections between concepts through more or less sophisticated forms of data retrieval. Hypertext facilities provide ways of overcoming the fragmentation of data, mitigating if not eliminating some of the dualisms characteristic of qualitative analysis, such as the tension between analysing data in context and through comparison. Of these dualisms, perhaps the most significant is the fragmentation of data into bits which we nevertheless want to interrelate. Through electronic linking, we can at least partially overcome this fragmentation. We can observe, record and store links between bits of data, which can then be retrieved as a means of examining substantive connections between categories. Here again, the computer offers a significant advance in flexibility and rigour by comparison with what was possible using traditional methods.

Of course, what the computer offers, and what we do with it, may be two different things. It may be that, in our enthusiasm for handling large volumes of data, or our fascination with the technology, we let the tool define the task, rather than allowing the task to dictate our use of the tool. As John Seidel puts it, we should be aware of what the computer can do to us, as well as for us (1991: 116). But problems arise when the analyst is mechanical, not the computer. The computer cannot think for us, and not much good will come of it if we entertain unreasonable expectations of what it can do. If the computer is to be used rather than abused, it must be understood in the context of the analytic tasks required of us, the analysts.

# Appendix 1

## 'If the Impressionists had been Dentists'
## (Woody Allen 1978)

Dear Theo

Will life never treat me decently? I am wracked by despair! My head is pounding. Mrs Sol Schwimmer is suing me because I made her bridge as I felt it and not to fit her ridiculous mouth. That's right! I can't work to order like a common tradesman. I decided her bridge should be enormous and billowing with wild, explosive teeth flaring up in every direction like fire! Now she is upset because it won't fit in her mouth! She is so bourgeois and stupid, I want to smash her. I tried forcing the false plate in but it sticks out like a star burst chandelier. Still, I find it beautiful. She claims she can't chew! What do I care whether she can chew or not! Theo, I can't go on like this much longer! I asked Cézanne if he would share an office with me but he is old and infirm and unable to hold the instruments and they must be tied to his wrists but then he lacks accuracy and once inside a mouth, he knocks out more teeth than he saves. What to do?
Vincent.

Dear Theo

I took some dental X-rays this week that I thought were good. Degas saw them and was critical. He said the composition was bad. All the cavities were bunched in the lower left corner. I explained to him that that's how Mrs Stotkin's mouth looks, but he wouldn't listen. He said he hated the frames and mahogony was too heavy. When he left, I tore them to shreds! As if that was not enough, I attempted some root-canal work on Mrs Wilma Zardis, but half-way through I became despondent. I realised suddenly that root-canal work is not what I want to do! I grew flushed and dizzy. I ran from the office into the air where I could breathe! I blacked out for several days and woke up at the seashore. When I returned, she was still in the chair. I completed her mouth out of obligation but I couldn't bring myself to sign it.
Vincent.

Dear Theo

Once again I am in need of funds. I know what a burden I must be to you, but who can I turn to? I need money for materials! I am working almost exclusively with dental floss now, improvising as I go along, and the results are exciting. God! I have not even a penny left for Novocaine! Today I pulled a tooth and had to anesthetize the patient by reading him some Dreiser. Help.

Vincent.

Dear Theo

Have decided to share office with Gauguin. He is a fine dentist who specialises in bridgework, and he seems to like me. He was very complimentary about my work on Mr Jay Greenglass. If you recall, I filled his lower seven, then despised the filling and tried to remove it. Greenglass was adamant and we went to court. There was a legal question of ownership, and on my lawyer's advice, I cleverly sued for the whole tooth and settled for the filling. Well, someone saw it lying in the corner of my office and he wants to put it in a show! They are already talking about a retrospective!

Vincent.

Dear Theo

I think it is a mistake to share offices with Gauguin. He is a disturbed man. He drinks Lavoris in large quantities. When I accused him, he flew into a rage and pulled my D.D.S. off the wall. In a calmer moment, I convinced him to try filling teeth outdoors and we worked in a meadow surrounded by greens and gold. He put caps on a Miss Angela Tonnato and I gave a temporary filling to Mr Louis Kaufman. There we were, working together in the open air! Rows of blinding white teeth in the sunlight! Then a wind came up and blew Mr Kaufman's toupee into the bushes. He darted for it and knocked Gauguin's instruments to the ground. Gauguin blamed me and tried to strike out but pushed Mr Kaufman by mistake, causing him to sit down on the high speed drill. Mr Kaufman rocketed past me on a fly, taking Miss Tonnato with him. The upshot, Theo, is that Rifkin, Rifkin, Rifkin and Meltzer have attached my earnings. Send whatever you can.

Vincent.

Dear Theo

Toulouse-Lautrec is the saddest man in the world. He longs more than anything to be a great dentist, and he has real talent, but he's too short to reach his patients' mouths and too proud to stand on anything. Arms over his head, he gropes around their lips blindly, and yesterday, instead of putting caps on Mrs Fitelson's teeth, he capped her chin. Meanwhile, my

old friend Monet refuses to work on anything but very, very large mouths and Seurat, who is quite moody, has developed a method of cleaning one tooth at a time until he builds up what he calls 'a full, fresh mouth'. It has an architectural solidity to it, but is it dental work?
Vincent.

Dear Theo
I am in love. Claire Memling came in last week for an oral prophylaxis. (I had sent her a postcard telling her it had been six months since her last cleaning even though it had been only four days.) Theo, she drives me mad! Wild with desire! Her bite! I've never seen such a bite! Her teeth come together perfectly! Not like Mrs Itkin's, whose lower teeth are forward of her uppers by an inch, giving her an underbite that resembles that of a werewolf! No! Claire's teeth close and meet! When this happens you know there is a God! And yet she's not too perfect. Not so flawless as to be uninteresting. She has a space between lower nine and eleven. Ten was lost during her adolescence. Suddenly and without warning it developed a cavity. It was removed rather easily (actually it fell out while she was talking) and never replaced. 'Nothing could replace lower ten' she told me. 'It was more than a tooth, it had been my life to that point.' The tooth was rarely discussed as she got older and I think she was only willing to speak of it to me because she trusts me. Oh, Theo, I love her. I was looking down into her mouth today and I was like a nervous young dental student again, dropping swabs and mirrors in there. Later I had my arms around her, showing her the proper way to brush. The sweet little fool was used to holding the brush still and moving her head from side to side. Next Thursday I will give her gas and ask her to marry me.
Vincent.

Dear Theo
Gauguin and I had another fight and he has left for Tahiti! He was in the midst of an extraction when I disturbed him. He had his knee on Mr Nat Feldman's chest with the pliers around the man's upper right molar. There was the usual struggle and I had the misfortune to enter and ask Gauguin if he had seen my felt hat. Distracted, Gauguin lost his grip on the tooth and Feldman took advantage of the lapse to bolt from the chair and race out of the office. Gauguin flew into a frenzy. He held my head under the X-ray machine for ten straight minutes and for several hours after I could not blink my eyes in unison. Now I am lonely.
Vincent.

Dear Theo
All is lost! Today being the day I planned to ask Claire to marry me, I was a bit tense. She was magnificent in her white organdy dress, straw hat, and

receding gums. As she sat in the chair, the draining hook in her mouth, my heart thundered. I tried to be romantic. I lowered the lights and tried to move the conversation to gay topics. We both took a little gas. When the moment seemed correct, I looked her directly in the eye and said, 'Please rinse'. And she laughed! Yes, Theo! She laughed at me and then grew angry! 'do you think I could rinse for a man like you!? What a joke!' I said, 'Please, you don't understand'. She said, 'I understand quite well! I could never rinse with anyone but a licensed orthodontist! Why, the thought I would rinse here! Get away from me!' And with that she ran out weeping. Theo! I want to die! I see my face in the mirror and I want to smash it! Smash it! Hope you are well.
Vincent.

Dear Theo
Yes, it's true. The ear on sale at Fleishman Brothers Novelty Shop is mine. I guess it was a foolish thing to do but I wanted to send Claire a birthday present last Sunday and every place was closed. Oh, Well. Sometimes I wish I had listened to father and become a painter. It's not exciting but the life is regular.

# Appendix 2
## Software

The reader looking for a review of software for analysing qualitative data should consult the book on this subject by Renata Tesch (1990). For a very brief summary of the main packages available, see also Fielding and Lee (1991).

**Hypersoft**, a software package developed by the author, is based on Hypercard and requires Hypercard 1.2 or 2.0 and Macintosh (system 6.05 or later). Many of the procedures discussed in the text are supported by Hypersoft.

*Managing data*: Hypersoft uses a card-based environment, with linked indexes and facilities for referencing cases, recording facesheet variable values and references within the data (e.g. to questions/sources).

*Reading and annotating*: Hypersoft supports procedures for linking memos and summary synopses to data. Keyword and key-word-in-context searches include extraction of sentences or paragraphs, and extraction of data between two user-defined delimiters e.g. all the answers to a particular question. The package does not support sophisticated searches (e.g. using synonyms, wild card characters etc.).

*Categorizing*: Hypersoft provides a simple procedure for categorizing data, automatically filing relevant contextual information (case, data references etc.). Databits are filed on separate cards, with facilities for browsing, recategorizing, subcategorizing and annotating. A 'dictionary' is provided for accessing and auditing conceptual definitions of the categories used in the analysis.

*Linking*: Bits of data can be linked before, during or after categorizing, using a simple procedure for linking any two bits of data.

*Connecting* : The retrieval procedures in Hypersoft are the basic boolean operators: X AND Y; X OR Y; X NOT Y. More sophisticated procedures (e.g. proximity, precedence) are not available. Conditions can be imposed on category retrievals, by case and data references or facesheet values. In addition, the package supports an X LINK Y retrieval, where X = data assigned to an X category or categories; LINK = a specified link, e.g. 'causes'; and Y = data assigned to a Y category or categories. Other forms of linked retrieval are not available in this version.

*Mapping*: Hypersoft supports mapping of retrievals to scale, including linked retrievals, with areas proportionate to the average assignment per case. Drawing facilities allow rectangles, circles and ellipses to be drawn to an adjustable scale. The full range of Hypercard graphic tools is also available. The card-based environment limits mapping to screen size.

*Corroborating*: Values for facesheet variables and for category assignations can be recorded in a dataset, for further analysis or export to a statistical package. Hypersoft can produce frequencies and simple cross-tabulations.

*Producing an account*: The package does not provide word-processing facilities. Fields are provided for notes, comments etc., but it is assumed that research reports will be produced using a word processing package. Procedures are included for exporting data, tables, and diagrams to text-only files.

---

Many of the packages currently available (April 1992) are distributed by Renata Tesch. For up-to-date information, contact:

Renata Tesch
Qualitative Research
Management
73425 Hilltop Road
Desert Hot Springs
CA 92240, USA
Tel (619) 329-7026

For further information about Hypersoft, contact:

Ian Dey
Department of Social Policy and
Social Work
AFB, George Square
University of Edinburgh
Edinburgh EH8 9LL
Scotland

# Glossary

| | |
|---|---|
| *Associating categories* | the process of identifying correlations between categories as a basis for inferring substantive connections. |
| *Bit of data* | a part of the data which is regarded as a separate 'unit of meaning' for the purpose of the analysis. |
| *Categorizing data* | the process of assigning categories to bits of data. |
| *Category* | a concept unifying a number of observations (or bits of data) having some characteristics in common. |
| *Category definition* | a set of criteria governing the assignation of a category to a bit of data. |
| *Classification* | a process of organizing data into categories or classes and identifying formal connections between them. |
| *Code* | an abbreviation of a category name. |
| *Coding* | the process of identifying codes for category names. |
| *Concept* | a general idea which stands for a class of objects. |
| *Connecting categories* | the process of identifying substantive connections by associating categories or linking data. |
| *Databit* | a bit of data which is copied and filed along with similar bits of data, for the purposes of comparison. |
| *Formal connection* | a relationship of similarity or difference between things e.g. X and Y belong to the same category. |
| *Hyperlink* | an electronic link between two bits of data. |
| *Index* | a list identifying a series of items (such as cases or databits). |
| *Link* | a substantive connection between two bits of data – the conceptual interpretation of a hyperlink. |

| | |
|---|---|
| *Linking data* | the process of identifying substantive connections between bits of data as a basis for identifying substantive connections between categories. |
| *Map* | a diagram representing the shape and scope of concepts and connections in the analysis. |
| *Mapping data* | the process of translating the results of retrievals into a graphic format. |
| *Matrix* | a rectangular array of rows and columns for organizing and presenting data systematically. |
| *Measurement* | defining the boundaries or limits to a phenomenon. |
| *Pattern* | observations or relationships which occur frequently in the data. |
| *Qualitative data* | data which deals with meanings rather than numbers |
| *Quantitative data* | data which deals with numbers rather than meanings. |
| *Retrieval* | a process of compiling all the data under some category or combination of categories, for purpose of comparison. |
| *Singularity* | a single constellation of observations which constitute the history of a unique event (or sequence of events.) |
| *Splitting* | the process of identifying subcategories and subcategorizing data. |
| *Splicing* | the process of identifying formal connections between categories. |
| *Substantive connection* | an interactive relationship between things e.g. X causes Y. |
| *Theory* | a system of ideas which conceptualizes some aspect of experience. |
| *Variable* | a concept which varies by kind or amount. |

# References

Allen, Woody (1978) 'If the Impressionists had been Dentists' in *Without Feathers*, London: Sphere.

Baxandall, Michael (1974) *Painting's Experience in 15th Century Italy*, Oxford: Oxford University Press.

Becker, Howard and Geer, Blanche (1982) 'Participant Observation: The Analysis of Qualitative Field Data' in Burgess, Robert (ed.) *Field Research: A Sourcebook and Field Manual*, London: Allen & Unwin.

Becker, Howard (1986) *Writing for Social Scientists: How to Start and Finish Your Thesis, Book or Article*, Chicago: University of Chicago Press.

Bettelheim, Bruno (1991) *The Uses of Enchantment: The Meaning and Importance of Fairy Tales*, London: Penguin.

Blalock, Hubert M. (1960) *Social Statistics*, London: McGraw-Hill.

Bliss, Joan *et al.* (1983) *Qualitative Data Analysis: A Guide to Uses of Systematic Networks*, London: Croom Helm.

Bogdan, Robert C. and Biklen, Sari Knopp (1982) *Qualitative Research for Education: An Introduction to Theory and Methods*, Boston and London: Allyn & Bacon Inc.

Bohm, David (1983) *Wholeness and the Implicate Order*, London and New York: Ark.

Brooks, C. and Warren, W.P. (1967) *Understanding Poetry*, New York: Holt, RineHart and Wilson, third edition.

Brown, Andrew (1991) 'How do you tell an Essex Girl from a West Coast blonde?' *The Independent*, 5th November.

Bryman, Alan (1988) *Quantity and Quality in Social Research*, London: Unwin Hyman Ltd.

Burgess, Robert (ed.) (1982) *Field Research: A Sourcebook and Field Manual*, London: Allen & Unwin.

Buzan, Tony (1989) *Use Your Head*, London: BBC Books.

Capra, Fritjof (1983) *The Tao of Physics: An Exploration of the Parallels Between Modern Physics and Eastern Mysticism*, London: Fontana Paperbacks.

Cody, Liza (1991) *Back Hand*, London: Chatto & Windus.

Cordingley, Elizabeth S. (1991) 'The Upside and Downside of Hypertext Tools: The KANT Example' in Fielding, Nigel G. and Lee, Raymond M. (eds) *Using Computers in Qualitative Research*, London: Sage.

Coveney, Peter and Highfield, Roger (1991) *The Arrow of Time*, Great Britain: Flamingo.

Denzin, K. (1978) *The Research Act*, New York: McGraw-Hill.

Dixon, Beverly *et al.* (1987) *A Handbook of Social Science Research: A*

*Comprehensive and Practical Guide for Students*, Oxford: Oxford University Press.

Dixon, Bernard (1991) 'The Man who Shot Down the Mosquito', *The Independent*, 11th November.

Edson, C.H. (1988) 'Our Past and Present: Historical Inquiry in Education' in Sherman, Robert R. and Webb, Rodman B., (eds) *Qualitative Research for Education: Focus and Methods*, London: The Falmer Press.

Fielding, Nigel and Fielding, Jane (1986) *Linking Data*, London: Sage.

Fielding, Nigel G. and Lee, Raymond M. (eds) (1991) *Using Computers in Qualitative Research*, London: Sage.

Galtung, Johan (1967) *Theory and Methods of Social Research*, London: Allen & Unwin.

Geerz, C. (1973) *The Interpretation of Cultures*, New York: Basic Books.

Giarelli, James M. (1988) 'Qualitative Inquiry in Philosophy and Education: Notes on the Pragmatic Tradition' in Sherman, Robert R. and Webb, Rodman B. (eds) *Qualitative Research for Education: Focus and Methods*, London: The Falmer Press.

Gibbon, Edward (1960) *The Decline and Fall of the Roman Empire*, London: Chatto & Windus.

Hawking, Stephen W. (1988) *A Brief History of Time*, London: Transworld.

Jones, Sue (1985) 'The Analysis of Depth Interviews' in Walker, Robert (ed.) *Applied Qualitative Research*, London: Gower.

Jones, Steve 1991 'A Message from our Ancestors' (Reith Lecture), *The Independent*, 14th November.

Marsh, Catherine (1982) *The Survey Method: The Contribution of Surveys to Sociological Explanation*, London: Allen & Unwin.

Maxwell, A. E. (1961) *Analysing Qualitative Data*, London: Methuen.

Merrill Lisa (1988) 'Feminist Humour: Affirmation and Rebellion' in Barreca Regina (ed.) *Last Laughs: Perspectives on Women and Comedy*, London: Gordon & Breach.

Miles M. and Huberman M. (1984) *Qualitative Data Analysis*, Beverly Hills CA: Sage.

Monk, Ray (1992) 'The Philosopher's New Mind', *The Independent*, 3rd April.

O'Hanlon, Redmond (1988) *In Trouble Again*, London: Hamish Hamilton.

Patton, Michael Quinn (1980) *Qualitative Evaluation Methods*, London: Sage.

Penrose, Roger (1990) *The Emperor's New Mind: Concerning Computers, Minds, and the Laws of Physics*, London: Vintage.

Peter, Laurence (1982) *Quotations for our Time*, London: Methuen.

Pfaffenberger, Bryan (1988) *Microcomputer Applications in Qualitative Research*, London: Sage.

Praverand, Pierre (1984) 'Tomorrow is already Today: Development Education and the New 21st Century Paradigm' in Garrett, Roger (ed.) *Education and Development*, Beckenham, Kent: Croom Helm.

Richards, Lyn and Richards, Tom (1991) 'The Transformation of Qualitative Method' in Fielding, Nigel G. and Lee, Raymond M. (eds) *Using Computers in Qualitative Research*, London: Sage.

Riley, Judith (1990) *Getting the Most From Your Data: A Handbook of Practical Ideas on How to Analyse Qualitative Data*, Bristol: Technical and Educational Services Ltd.

Sabatier, P. A. (1986) 'Top-down and Bottom-up Approaches to Implementation Research: A Critical Analysis and Suggested Synthesis', *Journal of Public Policy* 6, 21–48.

Sayer, Andrew (1992) *Method in Social Science: A Realist Approach*, London and New York: Routledge.

Seidel, John (1991) 'Method and Madness in the Application of Computer Technology to Qualitative Data Analysis' in Fielding, Nigel G. and Lee, Raymond M. (eds) *Using Computers in Qualitative Research*, London: Sage.

Shimahara, Nobuo (1988) 'Anthroethnography: A Methodological Consideration' in Sherman, Robert R. and Webb, Rodman B. (eds) *Qualitative Research for Education: Focus and Methods*, London: The Falmer Press.

Sperber, Dan and Wilson, Deirdre (1986) *Relevance, Communication and Cognition*, Harvard University Press.

Strauss, Anselm L. (1987) *Qualitative Analysis for Social Scientists*, Cambridge: Cambridge University Press.

Strauss, Anselm L. and Corbin, Juliet (1990) *Basics of Qualitative Research Grounded Theory Procedures and Techniques*, London: Sage.

Tesch, Renata (1990) *Qualitative Research: Analysis Types and Software Tools*, London and Philadelphia: Falmer Press.

Tesch, Renata (1991) 'Software for Qualitative Researchers: Analysis Needs and Programme Capabilities' in Fielding, Nigel G. and Lee, Raymond M. (eds) *Using Computers in Qualitative Research*, London: Sage.

Thomas, Philip (1991) 'Let Him Have It' in *Empire The Monthly Guide to the Movies*, November, pp. 82–86.

Trow, M. J. (1992) *'Let Him Have it Chris': The Murder of Derek Bentley*, Great Britain: Grafton.

Varley, Helen (1983) *Colour*, London: Marshall Editions.

Wilson, John Dover (1936) *Hamlet*, Cambridge: Cambridge University Press.

Winter, Henry (1991) 'Liverpool Require a New Forward Plan', *The Independent*, 25th November.

Wood, Victoria (1985) *Up to You, Porky: The Victoria Wood Sketch Book*, London: Methuen.

Wood, Victoria (1990) *Mens Sana in Thingummy Doodah*, London: Methuen.

# Index

abstracting data 94, 110, 128; *see also* categories; classification
academic literature *see* literature
account, producing 83, 237–63, 265–6, 267; acceptability 249–63; developing a plan 241; function 241–2, 249–50; Hypersoft and 274; language 245–6, 247; materials and their selection 242–5; as objective of analysis 47, 52; reliability 250–3, 261; representativeness 261–3; traditional forms of publication 260; validity 250, 253–61; writing strategies 247–9; *see also* text
advertising 34, 49
algorithms 251, 252, 253
Allen, Woody: humour used as example for analysis *see individual processes*; text of 'If the Impressionists had been Dentists' 269–72
annotating data *see* memos
association between categories and variables 27, 47–50, 170–80, 191
audio material: computer and 56; transcription of 74
auditing analysis 239–40; use of computer for 60, 268

Baxandall, M. 12
bar charts 208
Becker, H. 7, 8, 28, 52, 104, 224, 247
Bettelheim, B. 33, 34, 239, 246
bias 63, 87, 120, 224, 225, 227, 229, 233, 261; *see also* objectivity; subjectivity
bits of data 17–18; classification *see* classification; coding *see* coding data; and connecting categories *see* connections between categories; and creation of categories *see under* categories; generation of 115–18, 120–1, 202, 203; and grounded theory 103; labelling 96, 121; and linking *see* linking; mapping used to indicate databits in chronological sequence 217–18; and recontextualization *see* categories, splitting and splicing; subdividing 138–9

Blalock, H. M. 10
Bliss, J. 5, 7, 52, 137, 158
Bogdan, R. C. 84
Bohm, D. 17, 18, 30, 242
boolean operators 144, 174, 227, 273
Brooks, C. 94
Brown, Andrew 71
Bryman, A. 5, 17, 221, 267
Burgess, R. 5, 39, 247
Burke, Edmund 83
Buzan, T. 83, 88, 192

Capra, F. 28, 63, 94
case studies 14, 50, 75
cases 76–7, 87, 176–9; use of matrices to compare *see* matrices
categories: connections between *see* connections; creating 94–112 *see also* category sets; definitions 102–3, 122–3, 126, 179, 203, 240, 273; inclusive/exclusive 20–1, 43, 46, 107–8, 140, 144, 179, 210; mapping *see* mapping; overlapping 20, 111
categories, assigning 27, 113–28, 189, 240, 253; breaking up data into bits 115–18, 120–1; mechanics of 113–15, 119, 120, 124, 273;